W9-AMY-239

SKY HIGH

STORIES OF SURVIVAL FROM AIR AND SPACE

SKY HIGH
STORIES OF SURVIVAL FROM AIR AND SPACE

EDITED BY CLINT WILLIS

Thunder's Mouth Press
New York

SKY HIGH: STORIES OF SURVIVAL FROM AIR AND SPACE

Compilation copyright © 2003 by Clint Willis
Introductions copyright © 2003 by Clint Willis

Adrenaline® and the Adrenaline® logo are trademarks of
Avalon Publishing Group Incorporated, New York, NY.

An Adrenaline Book®

Published by
Thunder's Mouth Press
An Imprint of Avalon Publishing Group Incorporated
161 William Street, 16th floor
New York, NY 10038

Book design: Sue Canavan

frontispiece photo: Dogfight over the Western Front. Copyright © Bettmann/
Corbis.

All rights reserved. No part of this book may be reproduced in any form
without prior written permission from the publishers and the copyright owner,
except by reviewers who wish to quote brief passages.

Library of Congress Cataloging-in-Publication Data is available.

ISBN 1-56025-459-9

Printed in the United States of America

Distributed by Publishers Group West

For Eric "Wings" Schurenberg

contents

introduction

J ack Turner, a writer and mountain guide, once saw from the summit of the Grand Teton a flock of 17 white pelicans. He estimated that the pelicans were flying at an altitude of at least 19,000 feet—and wondered what the birds were *doing* up there.

The pilots whose stories you'll read in this book have their own motives for going high. They fly in part for a variety of more or less practical reasons: to make war, to make a living, to fulfill an ambition. But they also carry deeper reasons—the kind that are best expressed in stories.

The best of their stories take us flying so that we can begin to fathom a pilot's motivation. Often, the flights are bumpy—even terrifying. World War II ace Bud Anderson pulls his Mustang into a steep climb to evade a Messerschmitt on his tail; the German pilot follows, trying to get his plane's nose up and bring the Mustang into his sights. Decades later, Anderson cannot forget the moment:

> . . .I am extremely busy up here, hanging onto my propeller going almost straight up, full emergency power, which a Mustang could do for only so long before losing speed,

shuddering, stalling, and falling back down; and I am thinking that if the Mustang stalls before the Messerschmitt stalls, I have had it.

Chuck Yeager remembers his first flight in the experimental X-1, a rocket-powered aircraft, on August 29, 1947—what he calls "the kind of moment a test pilot lives for":

> You can't watch yourself fly. But you know when you're in sync with the machine, so plugged into its instruments that your mind and your hand become the heart of its operating system. You can make that airplane talk, and like a good horse, the machine knows when it's in competent hands. You know what you can get away with. And you can be wrong only once.

Yeager was known as a guy who liked to take chances—so do all the great pilots. The risk summons up what's best in them, or at least what makes them happy: competence, awareness, concentration. It's as if they take chances to remind themselves how much they have to lose. In the process, the great pilots create lives that carry an epic quality. They become heroes of sorts. David Roberts in his brief memoir of the late Alaskan bush pilot Don Sheldon notes the phenomenon: "During the years I knew Don, he went from being my hero to becoming my friend, yet he never entirely shed that quality of having stepped out of the pages of some latter-day *Odyssey.*"

Like Odysseus, pilots are voyagers. They sail into danger—often into the unknown. Many—unlike the wily Odysseus—never return. Most professional pilots have lost comrades to their line of work. Matthew Klam visits his friend Doug Hamilton, a pilot on the aircraft carrier U.S.S. *Dwight D. Eisenhower:*

> I mentioned that I'd read that Naval aviation was safer now. 'Safer than what?' Doug asked. 'I personally know ten

guys—these are guys I flew in the same airplane with, students and instructors—who died in crashes in my 12 years in the Navy . . . My roommate on my first cruise, a guy named 'Wild Bill,' was killed because of a mechanical problem in an F-14. They fixed that problem after it killed him. My T-2 instructor, Victor, had a bird strike a few years after he taught me, and the bird came through the canopy and killed him. Randy didn't fuel his plane properly, and it rolled over on him on takeoff. . . .'

And so on. Meanwhile pilots go to war or get hired by airlines or end up astronauts. They go up there with the pelicans, and keep going. Some have been as far as the moon. And many do come back, bringing with them the kind of stories that adventurers bring home from adventures: stories at once astonishing and familiar.

—CLINT WILLIS
SERIES EDITOR, ADRENALINE BOOKS

from To Fly and Fight

by Clarence E. Anderson
with Joseph P. Hamelin

Clarence "Bud" Anderson (born 1922) shot down 17 German planes during World War II, when he served (with Chuck Yeager) in the U.S. Air Force's 357th Fighter Group in Europe.

The sky above was a bright crystal blue, and the land below a green-on-green checkerboard divided by a silver-blue ribbon. Below was occupied France, beyond the river lay Germany, and it all looked the same, rolling and peaceful and bursting with spring.

But this was an overpoweringly sinister place. From our perch six miles up, we couldn't see the enemy, some huddling over their guns taking aim, some climbing into their airplanes to fly up and get us, and some, on the far side of the river, waiting with pitchforks and hoping we'd fall somewhere close. All we could see was the green of their fields and forests. But we knew they were there, looking up, watching us come, and thinking how they could kill us.

The day was unusually, incredibly clear. In better times, it would have been a day for splashing through trout streams with fly rods, or driving so fast that some giggling girl would beg you to slow. But these weren't those kinds of times. These were the worst times God ever let happen. And so the trout streams were left to the fish, gasoline was a thing you used sparingly, and it was just one more day for flying and fighting and staying alive, if you could, six miles high over Germany.

Staying alive was no simple thing in the skies over Europe in the spring of 1944. A lot of men couldn't. It was a bad thing to dwell on if you were a fighter pilot, and so we told ourselves we were dead men and lived for the moment with no thought of the future at all. It wasn't too difficult. Lots of us *had* no future and everyone knew it.

This particular day, out of the year I flew combat in Europe, is the one I have thought of on a thousand days since, sometimes on purpose and sometimes in spite of myself. Sometimes it's in cameo glimpses, other times in slow motion stop action, but always in Technicolor. I sit on my porch, nearly a half-century and half-world removed from that awful business, looking out over a deep, green, river-cut canyon to the snow-capped Sierra, thinking about getting tires for the Blazer or mowing the lawn or, more likely, the next backpacking trip . . . and suddenly May 27, 1944, elbows its way to the front of my thoughts like a drunk to a bar. The projectionist inside my head who chooses the films seems to love this one rerun.

We were high over a bomber stream in our P-51B Mustangs, escorting the heavies to the Ludwigshafen-Mannheim area. For the past several weeks the Eighth Air Force had been targeting oil, and Ludwigshafen was a center for synthetic fuels. Oil was everything, the lifeblood of war. Nations can't fight without oil. All through my training, and all through the war, I can't remember ever being limited on how much I could fly. There always was fuel enough. But by 1944, the Germans weren't so fortunate. They were feeling the pinch from the daily bombardments. Without fuel and lubricant, their war machine eventually would grind to a stop. Now that the Mustang fighters were arriving in numbers, capable of escorting the bombers all the way to their targets and back, Germany's oil industry was there for the pounding.

The day would come, and it would be soon, when the German Air Force, the Luftwaffe, would begin picking its spots, contesting some missions and not others; or concentrating on isolated bomber formations, to the exclusion of all the rest, largely at random from what we could tell. The Luftwaffe's idea was to conserve fuel and pilots. But for the moment, at least, there seemed no great shortage of fighter planes between us and the target.

We'd picked up the bombers at 27,000 feet, assumed the right flank, and almost immediately all hell began breaking loose up ahead of us. This was early, still over France, long before we'd expected the German fighters to come up in force. You maintained radio silence until you engaged the enemy, and after that it didn't much matter since they knew you were there, and so people would chatter. They were chattering now, up ahead, and my earphones were crackling with loud, frantic calls: "Bandits, 11 o'clock low! . . . Two o'clock high, pick him up! . . . Blue leader break left!" It sounded as though the Messerschmitts and Focke-Wulfs were everywhere.

You knew how it was up ahead, and you knew it would be like that for you any minute now, the German single-seat Fw 190s and Me 109s coming straight through the bombers, mixing it up with the Mustangs, the hundreds of four-engined heavies and the hundreds of fighters scoring the crystal blue sky with their persistent white contrails.

The Germans liked to roar through the bombers head on, firing long bursts, and then roll and go down. They would circle around to get ahead of the bomber stream, groping for altitude, avoiding the escorts if possible, then reassemble and come through head on again. When their fuel or ammunition was exhausted, they would land and refuel and take off again, flying mission after mission, for as long as there were bombers to shoot at. They seldom came after us. Normally, they would skirmish the escorts only out of necessity. We were an inconvenience, best avoided. It was the bombers they wanted, and the German pilots threw themselves at them smartly and bravely. It was our job to stop them.

It seemed we were always outnumbered. We had more fighters than they did, but what mattered was how many they could put up in one area. They would concentrate in huge numbers, by the hundreds at times. They would assemble way up ahead, pick a section of the bomber formation, and then come in head on, their guns blazing, sometimes hitting the bombers below us before we knew what was happening.

In the distance, a red and black smear marked the spot where a B-17 and its 10 men had been. Planes still bearing their bomb loads erupted and fell, trailing flame, streaking the sky, leaving gaps in the bomber formation that were quickly closed up. Through our headsets we could hear the war, working its way back toward us, coming straight at us at hundreds of miles per hour. The adrenaline began gushing, and I scanned the sky frantically, trying to pick out the fly-speck against the horizon that might have been somebody coming to kill us, trying to see him before he saw me, looking, squinting, breathless . . .

Over the radio: "Here they come!"

They'd worked over the bombers up ahead and now it was our turn.

Things happen quickly. We get rid of our drop tanks, slam the power up, and make a sweeping left turn to engage. My flight of four Mustangs is on the outside of the turn, a wingman close behind to my left, my element leader and his wingman behind to my right, all in finger formation. Open your right hand, tuck the thumb under, put the fingers together, and check the fingernails. That's how we flew, and fought. Two shooters, and two men to cover their tails. The Luftwaffe flew that way, too. German ace Werner Mölders is generally credited with inventing the tactic during the Spanish Civil War.

Being on the outside of the turn, we are vulnerable to attack from the rear. I look over my right shoulder and, sure enough, I see four dots above us, way back, no threat at the moment, but coming hard down the chute. I start to call out, but . . .

"Four bogeys, five o'clock high!" My element leader, Eddie Simpson, has already seen them. *Bogeys* are unknowns and *bandits* are hostile. Quickly, the dots close and take shape. They're hostile, all right. They're Messerschmitts.

We turn hard to the right, pulling up into a tight string formation, spoiling their angle, and we try to come around and go at them head on. The Me 109s change course, charge past, and continue on down, and we wheel and give chase. There are four of them, single-seat fighters, and they pull up, turn hard, and we begin turning with them. We are circling now, tighter and tighter, chasing each other's tails, and I'm sitting there wondering what the hell's happening. These guys want to hang around. Curious. I'm wondering why they aren't after the bombers, why they're messing with us, whether they're simply creating some kind of a diversion or what. I would fly 116 combat missions, engage the enemy perhaps 40 times, shoot down 16 fighters, share in the destruction of a bomber, destroy another fighter on the ground, have a couple of aerial probables, and over that span it would be us bouncing them far more often than not. This was a switch.

We're flying tighter circles, gaining a little each turn, our throttles wide open, 30,000 feet up The Mustang is a wonderful airplane, 37 feet wingtip to wingtip, just a little faster than the smaller German fighters, and also just a little more nimble. Suddenly the 109s, sensing things are not going well, roll out and run, turning east, flying level. Then one lifts up his nose and climbs away from the rest.

We roll out and go after them. They're flying full power, the black smoke pouring out their exhaust stacks. I'm looking at the one who is climbing, wondering what he is up to, and I'm thinking that if we stay with the other three, this guy will wind up above us. I send Simpson up after him. He and his wingman break off. My wingman, John Skara, and I chase the other three fighters, throttles all the way forward, and I can see that we're gaining.

I close to within 250 yards of the nearest Messerschmitt—dead astern, 6 o'clock, no maneuvering, no nothing—and squeeze the trigger on the control stick between my knees gently. *Bambambam-bambam!* The sound is loud in the cockpit in spite of the wind shriek and engine roar. And the vibration of the Mustang's four .50-caliber machine guns, two in each wing, weighing 60-odd pounds apiece, is pronounced. In fact, you had to be careful in dogfights when you were turning hard, flying on the brink of a stall, because the buck of the guns was enough to peel off a few critical miles per hour and make the Mustang simply stop flying. That could prove downright embarrassing.

But I'm going like hell now, and I can see the bullets tearing at the Messerschmitt's wing root and fuselage. The armor-piercing ammunition we used was also incendiary, and hits were easily visible, making a bright flash and puff. Now the 109's trailing smoke thickens, and it's something more than exhaust smoke. He slows, and then suddenly rolls over. But the plane doesn't fall. It continues on, upside down, straight and level! What the hell . . . ?

The pilot can't be dead. It takes considerable effort to fly one of these fighter planes upside down. You have to push hard on the controls. Flying upside down isn't easy. It isn't something that happens all by itself, or that you do accidentally. So what in the world is he doing?

Well. It's an academic question, because I haven't the time to wait and find out. I pour another burst into him, pieces start flying off, I see flame, and the 109 plummets and falls into a spin, belching smoke. My sixth kill.

The other two Messerschmitt pilots have pulled away now, and they're nervous. Their airplanes are twitching, the fliers obviously straining to look over their shoulders and see what is happening. As we take up the chase again, two against two now, the trailing 109 peels away and dives for home, and the leader pulls up into a sharp climbing turn to the left. This one can fly, and he obviously has no thought of running. I'm thinking this one could be trouble.

We turn inside him, my wingman and I, still at long range, and he pulls around harder, passing in front of us right-to-left at an impossible angle. I want to swing in behind him, but I'm going too fast, and figure I would only go skidding on past. A Mustang at speed simply can't make a square corner. And in a dogfight you don't want to surrender your airspeed. I decide to overshoot him and climb.

He reverses his turn, trying to fall in behind us. My wingman is vulnerable now. I tell Skara, "Break off!" and he peels away. The German goes after him, and I go after the German, closing on his tail before he can close on my wingman. He sees me coming and dives away with me after him, then makes a climbing left turn. I go screaming by, pull up, and he's reversing his turn—man, he can fly!—and he comes crawling right up behind me, close enough that I can see him distinctly. He's bringing his nose up for a shot, and I haul back on the stick and climb even harder. I keep going up, because I'm out of alternatives.

This is what I see all these years later. If I were the sort to be troubled with nightmares, this is what would shock me awake. I am in this steep climb, pulling the stick into my navel, making it steeper, steeper . . . and I am looking back down, over my shoulder, at this classic gray Me 109 with black crosses that is pulling up too, steeper, steeper, the pilot trying to get his nose up just a little bit more and bring me into his sights.

There is nothing distinctive about the aircraft, no fancy markings, nothing to identify it as the plane of an ace, as one of the "dreaded yellow-noses" like you see in the movies. Some of them did that, I know, but I never saw one. And in any event, all of their aces weren't flamboyant types who splashed paint on their airplanes to show who they were. I suppose I could go look it up in the archives. There's the chance I could find him in some *gruppe's* log book, having flown on this particular day, in this particular place, a few miles northwest of the French town of Strasbourg that sits on the Rhine. There are fellows who've done that, gone back and looked up their opponents. I never have. I never saw any point.

He was someone who was trying to kill me, is all.

So I'm looking back, almost straight down now, and I can see this 20-millimeter cannon sticking through the middle of the fighter's propeller hub. In the theater of my memory, it is enormous. An elephant gun. And that isn't far wrong. It is a gun designed to bring down a bomber, one that fires shells as long as your hand, shells that explode and tear big holes in metal. It is the single most frightening thing I have seen in my life, then and now.

But I'm too busy to be frightened. Later on, you might sit back and perspire about it, maybe 40–50 years later, say, sitting on your porch

7,000 miles away, but while it is happening you are just too damn busy. And I am extremely busy up here, hanging by my propeller, going almost straight up, full emergency power, which a Mustang could do for only so long before losing speed, shuddering, stalling, and falling back down; and I am thinking that if the Mustang stalls before the Messerschmitt stalls, I have had it.

I look back, and I can see that he's shuddering, on the verge of a stall. He hasn't been able to get his nose up enough, hasn't been able to bring that big gun to bear. Almost, but not quite. I'm a fallen-down-dead man almost, but not quite. His nose begins dropping just as my airplane, too, begins shuddering. He stalls a second or two before I stall, drops away before I do.

Good old Mustang.

He is falling away now, and I flop the nose over and go after him hard. We are very high by this time, six miles and then some, and falling very, very fast. The Messerschmitt had a head start, plummeting out of my range, but I'm closing up quickly. Then he flattens out and comes around hard to the left and starts climbing again, as if he wants to come at me head on. Suddenly we're right back where we started.

A lot of this is just instinct now. Things are happening too fast to think everything out. You steer with your right hand and feet. The right hand also triggers the guns. With your left, you work the throttle, and keep the airplane in trim, which is easier to do than describe.

Any airplane with a single propeller produces torque. The more horsepower you have, the more the prop will pull you off to one side. The Mustangs I flew used a 12-cylinder Packard Merlin engine that displaced 1,649 cubic inches. That is 10 times the size of the engine that powers an Indy car. It developed power enough that you never applied full power sitting still on the ground because it would pull the plane's tail up off the runway and the propeller would chew up the concrete. With so much power, you were continually making minor adjustments on the controls to keep the Mustang and its wing-mounted guns pointed straight.

There were three little palm-sized wheels you had to keep fiddling with. They trimmed you up for hands-off level flight. One was for the little trim tab on the tail's rudder, the vertical slab which moves the plane left or right. Another adjusted the tab on the tail's horizontal elevators that raise or lower the nose and help reduce the force you had to apply for hard turning. The third was for aileron trim, to keep your wings level, although you didn't have to fuss much with that one. Your left hand was down there a lot if you were changing speeds, as in combat . . . while at the same time you were making minor adjustments with your feet on the rudder pedals and your hand on the stick. At first it was awkward. But, with experience, it was something you did without thinking, like driving a car and twirling the radio dial.

It's a little unnerving to think about how many things you have to deal with all at once to fly combat.

So the Messerschmitt is coming around again, climbing hard to his left, and I've had about enough of this. My angle is a little bit better this time. So I roll the dice. Instead of cobbing it like before and sailing on by him, I decide to turn hard left inside him, knowing that if I lose speed and don't make it I probably won't get home. I pull back on the throttle slightly, put down 10 degrees of flaps, and haul back on the stick just as hard as I can. And the nose begins coming up and around, slowly, slowly. . . .

Hot damn! I'm going to make it! I'm inside him, pulling my sights up to him. And the German pilot can see this. This time, it's the Messerschmitt that breaks away and goes zooming straight up, engine at maximum power, without much alternative. I come in with full power and follow him up, and the gap narrows swiftly. He is hanging by his prop, not quite vertically, and I am right there behind him, and it is terribly clear, having tested the theory less than a minute ago, that he is going to stall and fall away before I do.

I have him. He must know that I have him.

I bring my nose up, he comes into my sights, and from less than 300 yards I trigger a long, merciless burst from my Brownings. Every fifth bullet or so is a tracer, leaving a thin trail of smoke, marking the path of the bullet stream. The tracers race upward and find him. The bullets chew at the wing root, the cockpit, the engine, making bright little flashes. I hose the Messerschmitt down the way you'd hose down a campfire, methodically, from one end to the other, not wanting to make a mistake here. The 109 shakes like a retriever coming out of the water, throwing off pieces. He slows, almost stops, as if parked in the sky, his propeller just windmilling, and he begins smoking heavily.

My momentum carries me to him. I throttle back to ease my plane alongside, just off his right wing. Have I killed him? I do not particularly want to fight this man again. I am coming up even with the cockpit, and although I figure the less I know about him the better, I find myself looking in spite of myself. There is smoke in the cockpit. I can see that, nothing more. Another few feet. . . .

And then he falls away suddenly, left wing down, right wing rising up, obscuring my view. I am looking at the 109's sky blue belly, the wheel wells, twin radiators, grease marks, streaks from the guns, the black crosses. I am close enough to make out the rivets. The Messerschmitt is right there and then it is gone, just like that, rolling away and dropping its nose and falling (flying?) almost straight down, leaking coolant and trailing flame and smoke so black and thick that it has to be oil smoke. It simply plunges, heading straight for the deck. No spin, not even a wobble, no parachute, and now I am wondering. His ship seems a death ship—but is it?

Undecided, I peel off and begin chasing him down. Did I squander a chance here? Have I let him escape? He is diving hard enough to be shedding his wings, harder than anyone designed those airplanes to dive, 500 miles an hour and more, and if 109s will stall sooner than Mustangs going straight up, now I am worrying that maybe their wings stay on longer. At 25,000 feet I begin to grow nervous. I pull back on the throttle, ease out of the dive, and watch him go down. I have no more stomach for this kind of thing, not right now, not with this guy. Enough. Let him go and to hell with him.

Straight down he plunges, from as high as 35,000 feet, through this beautiful, crystal clear May morning toward the green-on-green checkerboard fields, leaving a wake of black smoke. From four miles straight up I watch as the Messerschmitt and the shadow it makes on the ground rush toward one another . . .

. . . and then, finally, silently, merge.

Eddie Simpson joins up with me. Both wingmen, too. Simpson, my old wingman and friend, had gotten the one who'd climbed out. We'd bagged three of the four. We were very excited. It had been a good day.

I had lived and my opponent had died. But it was a near thing. It could have been the other way around just as easily, and what probably made the difference was the airplane I flew. Made in America. I would live to see the day when people would try to tell me the United States can't make cars like some other folks do. What a laugh.

I didn't wonder if I'd just made a new bride a widow, or if he might have had kids, any more than I would have wondered about a snake's mate and offspring. I may have given some thought to how many of my friends he had killed, or might have killed in the future, or how many bombers he might have shot down had he lived. But that's as far as it went. From what I could tell, he hadn't been overly concerned about me.

People ask about that all the time. People usually ask it hesitantly, as tactfully as they can, but they ask it. Did I wonder and worry about the mothers and children and wives of the men I shot down? Did I carry any guilt or regret?

No.

Not then, and not now.

World War Two was a total thing, *us against them*, when being against *them* was unquestionably the right thing to be. I flew for my country, and was proud I could help in any way that I could.

Besides, all of my opponents were trying to kill me. And frankly, I always was elated they hadn't.

This one had almost gotten a bead on me. He'd come as close as anyone would. When it was done, the 480 hours of combat flying in P-51s, and another 25 or so missions in Vietnam, almost all of those in F-105s, I never once suffered a hit in air-to-air combat. The sum total of the damage all my aircraft absorbed amounted to one small-arms round that found one of my wings during a strafing run after D-Day. It bored a hole the size of my little finger. It didn't even go all the way through, just punctured the underside's skin. Nobody noticed it until the next day. Needing a patch the size of a coin, that's exactly what my crew used—a British shilling.

People on the ground often shot at me. Flak batteries. Machine gunners. Foot soldiers with rifles and pistols. There may have been some who threw rocks, who can say? But this man, on that day, was the only opponent who was ever behind me, and he couldn't quite bring me into his sights, and never did fire.

To my knowledge, I never was fired upon by an airplane in combat.

Skill had something to do with that, I suppose. But there was certainly something more to it than skill. Lots of hot pilots never came home. I guess I was lucky. Or blessed.

That night, back at our Leiston base, in the "half-pipe" Nissen hut where the flight leaders bunked, we stoked our little stove with coke and made toasted cheese sandwiches. And afterward, after twirling the poker through the coals until it glowed, we ceremonially burned two more little swastikas beneath my name on the hut's wooden door.

O'Bee O'Brien's name was up there, Ed Hiro's, Jim Browning's, Don Bochkay's, Daddy Rabbit Peters'. Chuck Yeager, who three years later would become the first man to fly through the sound barrier, would have his name up there too, along with some others. Already, there were a lot of little swastikas burned into that door. Fortunately, there was still lots of room. It would be a long war.

There would be a lot more.

from # Yeager

by Chuck Yeager
and Leo Janos

Chuck Yeager (born 1923) was a model for generations of flyers after World War II. He shot down 13 German planes during that war—destroying five in a single mission on October 12, 1944—and went on to become a legendary test pilot. Yeager by his 1975 retirement had flown some 10,000 hours in more than 330 aircraft models. Those craft included the Bell X-1, which Yeager flew to break the sound barrier on October 14, 1947.

FIRST POWERED FLIGHT: AUGUST 29, 1947

Shivering, you bang your gloved hands together and strap on your oxygen mask inside the coldest airplane ever flown. You're being cold-soaked from the hundreds of gallons of liquid oxygen (LOX) fuel stored in the compartment directly behind you at minus 296 degrees. No heater, no defroster; you'll just have to grit your teeth for the next fifteen minutes until you land and feel that wonderful hot desert sun. But that cold saps your strength: it's like trying to work and concentrate inside a frozen food locker.

That cold will take you on the ride of your life. You watched the X-I get its 7:00 a.m. feeding in a swirling cloud of vapor fog, saw the frost form under its orange belly. That was an eerie sight; you're carrying six hundred gallons of LOX and water alcohol on board that can blow up at the flick of an igniter switch and scatter your pieces over several counties. But if all goes well, the beast will chug-a-lug a ton of fuel a minute.

Anyone with brain cells would have to wonder what in hell he was doing in such a situation—strapped inside a live bomb that's about to be dropped out of a bomb bay. But risks are the spice of life, and this is the kind of moment that a test pilot lives for. The butterflies are fluttering, but you feed off fear as if it's a high-energy candy bar. It keeps you alert and focused.

You accept risk as part of every new challenge; it comes with the territory. So you learn all you can about the ship and its systems, practice flying it on ground runs and glide flights, plan for any possible contingency, until the odds against you seem more friendly. You like the X-1; she's a sound airplane, but she's also an experimental machine, and you're a researcher on an experimental flight. You know you can be hammered by something unexpected, but you count on your experience, concentration, and instincts to pull you through. And luck. Without luck . . .

You can't watch yourself fly. But you know when you're in sync with the machine, so plugged into its instruments and controls that your mind and your hand become the heart of its operating system. You can make that airplane talk, and like a good horse, the machine knows when it's in competent hands. You know what you can get away with. And you can be wrong only once. You smile reading newspaper stories about a pilot in a disabled plane that maneuvered to miss a schoolyard before he hit the ground. That's crap. In an emergency situation, a pilot thinks only about one thing—survival. You battle to survive right down to the ground; you think about nothing else. Your concentration is riveted on what to try next. You don't say anything on the radio, and you aren't even aware that a schoolyard exists. That's exactly how it is.

There are at least a dozen different ways that the X-1 can kill you, so your concentration is total during the preflight check procedures. You load up nitrogen gas pressures in the manifolds—your life's blood because the nitrogen gas runs all the internal systems as well as the flaps and landing gear. Then you bleed off the liquid oxygen manifold and shut it down. All's in order.

Half an hour ago, we taxied out to takeoff in the mother ship. Because of the possibility of crashing with so much volatile fuel, they closed down the base until we were safely off the ground. That's the only acknowledgment from the base commander that we even exist. There's no interest in our flights because practically nobody at Muroc gives us any chance for success. Those bastards think they have it all figured. They call our flights "Slick Goodlin's Revenge." The word is that he knew when to get out in one piece by quitting over money.

One minute to drop. Ridley flashes the word from the copilot's seat in the mother ship. We're at 25,000 feet as the B-29 noses over and starts its shallow dive. Major Cardenas, the driver, starts counting backwards from ten.

C-r-r-ack. The bomb shackle release jolts you up from your seat, and as you sail out of the dark bomb bay the sun explodes in brightness. You're looking into the sky. *Wrong!* You should be dropped level. The dive speed was too slow, and they dropped you in a nose-up stall. You blink to get your vision, fighting the stall with your control wheel, dropping toward the basement like an elevator whose cable snapped. You're three thousand pounds heavier than in those glide flights. Down goes that nose and you pick up speed. You level out about a thousand feet below the mother ship and reach for that rocket igniter switch.

The moment of truth: if you are gonna be blown up, this is likely to be when. You light the first chamber.

Whoosh. Slammed back in your seat, a tremendous kick in the butt. Nose up and hold on. Barely a sound; you can hear your breathing in the oxygen mask—you're outracing the noise behind you—and for the first time in a powered airplane you can hear the air beating against the windshield as the distant dot that is Hoover's high chase P-80 grows ever bigger. You pass him like he's standing still, and he reports seeing diamond-shaped shock waves leaping out of your fiery exhaust. Climbing faster than you can even think, but using only one of four rocket chambers, you turn it off and light another. We're streaking up at .7 Mach; this beast's power is awesome. You've never known such a feeling of speed while pointing up in the sky. At 45,000 feet, where morning resembles the beginning of dusk, you turn on the last of the four chambers. God, what a ride! And you still have nearly half your fuel left.

Until this moment, you obeyed the flight plan to the letter: firing only one chamber at a time, to closely monitor the chamber pressures; if you use two or more, there's too much to watch. If you fire all four, you may accelerate too rapidly, be forced to raise your nose to slow down, and get yourself into a high-speed stall.

Now the flight plan calls for you to jettison remaining fuel and glide down to land. But you're bug-eyed, thrilled to your toes, and the fighter jock takes over from the cautious test pilot. Screw it! You're up there in the dark part of the sky in the most fabulous flying machine ever built, and you're just not ready to go home. The moment calls for a nice slow roll, and you lower your wing, pulling a couple of Gs until you're hanging upside down in zero Gs and the engine quits. As soon as the X-1 rights itself it starts again, but you've been stupid. At zero Gs the fuel couldn't feed the engine, and you might have been blown up. But the X-I is forgiving—this time.

You know what you're supposed to do, but you know what you're gonna do. You turn off the engine, but instead of jettisoning the remaining fuel, you roll over and dive for Muroc Air Base. We blister down, shit-heavy, .8 Mach in front of the needle, a dive-glide faster than most jets at full power. You're thinking, "Let's show those bastards the real X-1."

Below 10,000 feet is the danger zone, the limit for jettisoning fuel with enough maneuver time to glide down to a safe landing. But we're below 5,000, lined up with Muroc's main runway. And we're still in a dive.

We whistle down that main runway, only 300 feet off the ground, until we are parallel with the control tower. You hit the main rocket switch. The four chambers blow a thirty-foot lick of flame. Christ, the impact nearly knocks you back into last week. That nose is pointed so straight up that you can't see the blue sky out the windshield. We are no longer an airplane: we're a skyrocket. You're not flying. You're holding on to the tiger's tail. Straight up, you're going .75 Mach! In one minute the fuel is gone. By then you're at 35,000 feet, traveling at .85 Mach. You're so excited, scared, and thrilled that you can't say a word until the next day.

But others said plenty. The NACA team thought I was a wild man. Dick Frost chewed me out for doing that slow roll. Even Jack Ridley shook his head. He said, "Any spectators down there knew damned well that wasn't Slick rattling those dishes. Okay, son, you got it all out of your system, but now you're gonna hang tough." Colonel Boyd fired a rocket of his own. "Reply by endorsement about why you exceeded .82 Mach in violation of my direct orders." I asked Ridley to write my reply. "Bullshit," he said. "You did it. You explain it."

I wrote back: "The airplane felt so good and flew so well that I felt certain we would have no trouble going slightly above the agreed speed. The violation of your direct orders was due to the excited state of the undersigned and will not be repeated."

A few days later, the old man called me. "Damn it, I expect you to stick to the program and do what you are supposed to. Don't get overeager and cocky. Do you want to jeopardize the first Air Corps research project?"

"No, sir."

"Well, then obey the goddamn rules."

From then on I did. But on that first powered flight I wanted to answer those who said we were doomed in the attempt to go faster than sound. My message was, "Stick it where the sun don't shine."

Going out to .85 Mach put the program out on a limb because it carried us beyond the limits of what was then known about high-speed aerodynamics. Wind tunnels could only measure up to .85 Mach, and as Walt Williams of NACA was quick to point out to me, "From now on, Chuck, you'll be flying in the realm of the unknown." Ridley and I called it "the Ughknown."

Whatever happened, I figured I was better off than the British test pilots who had attempted supersonic flights in high-powered dives. If they got into trouble, that was it—especially in a tailless airplane like *The Swallow*. All my attempts would be made in climbs—the power of the rocket over the jet—and that way, if I encountered a problem, I could quickly slow down. But the price of rocket power was flying with volatile fuel. Running four chambers, my fuel lasted only two and a half minutes; it lasted five minutes on two chambers and ten minutes on one. Each minute of climbing we got lighter and faster, so that by the time we had climbed up and over at 45,000 feet, we were at max speed.

Who would decide the max speed of a particular flight? This was an Air Corps research project, but the seventeen NACA engineers and technicians used their expertise to try to control these missions. They were there as advisers, with high-speed wind tunnel experience, and were performing the data reduction collected on the X-1 flights, so they tried to dictate the speed in our flight plans. Ridley, Frost, and I always wanted to go faster than they did. They would recommend a Mach number, then the three of us would sit down and decide whether or not we wanted to stick with their recommendation. They were so conservative that it would've taken me six months to get to the barrier.

I wanted to be careful, but I also wanted to get it over with. Colonel Boyd sided with NACA caution, going up only two-hundredths of a Mach on each consecutive flight. Once I flew back with Hoover to see if I could get the old man to agree to speed things up. We met in the evening at his home. But Bob led off by trying to explain why he had been forced to crash-land a P-80 a few days before. I could tell the old man wasn't buying Bob's explanations; those thick eyebrows were bunching up. But ol' Hoover pushed on, becoming emotional to the point where he accidentally spat a capped tooth onto the old man's lap. I decided to have my say at another time.

So I flew in small increments of speed. On October 5, I made my sixth powered flight and experienced shock-wave buffeting for the first time as I reached .86 Mach. It felt like I was driving on bad shock absorbers over uneven paving stones. The right wing suddenly got heavy and began to drop, and when I tried to correct it my controls were sluggish. I increased my speed to .88 Mach to see what would happen. I saw my aileron vibrating with shock waves, and only with effort could I hold my wing level.

The X-1 was built with a high tail to avoid air turbulence off the wings; the tail was also thinner than the wings, so that shock waves would not form simultaneously on both surfaces. Thus far, the shock waves and buffeting had been manageable, and because the ship was stressed for eighteen Gs, I never was concerned about being shaken apart. Also, I was only flying twice a week, to give NACA time to reduce all the flight data and analyze it. Special sensing devices pinpointed the exact location of shock waves on any part of the airframe. The data revealed that the airplane was functioning exactly as its designers planned.

But on my very next flight we got knocked on our fannies. I was flying at .94 Mach at 40,000 feet, experiencing the usual buffeting, when I pulled back on the control wheel, and Christ, nothing happened! The airplane continued flying with the same attitude and in the same direction.

The control wheel felt as if the cables had snapped. I didn't know what in hell was happening. I turned off the engine and slowed down. I jettisoned my fuel and landed feeling certain that I had taken my last ride in the X-1. Flying at .94, I lost my pitch control. My elevator ceased to function. At the speed of sound, the ship's nose was predicted to go either up or down, and without pitch control, I was in a helluva bind.

I told Ridley I thought we had had it. There was no way I was going faster than .94 Mach without an elevator. He looked sick. So did Dick Frost and the NACA team. We called Colonel Boyd at Wright, and he flew out immediately to confer with us. Meanwhile, NACA analyzed the telemetry data from the flight and found that at .94 Mach, a shock wave was slammed right at the hinge point of the elevator on the tail, negating my controls. Colonel Boyd just shook his head. "Well," he said, "it looks to me like we've reached the end of the line." Everyone seemed to agree except for Jack Ridley.

He sat at a corner of the conference table scribbling little notes and equations. He said, "Well, maybe Chuck can fly without using the elevator. Maybe he can get by using only the horizontal stabilizer." The stabilizer was the winglike structure on the tail that stabilized pitch control. Bell's engineers had purposely built into them an extra control authority because they had anticipated elevator ineffectiveness caused by shock waves. This extra authority was a trim switch in the cockpit that would allow a small air motor to pivot the stabilizer up or down, creating a moving tail that could act as an auxiliary elevator by lowering or raising the airplane's nose. We were leery about trying it while flying at high speeds; instead, we set the trim on the ground and left it alone.

Jack thought we should spend a day ground testing the hell out of that system, learn everything there was to know about it, then flight test it. No one disagreed. There was no other alternative except to call the whole thing quits, but Jack got a lot of "what if" questions that spelled out all the risks. What if the motor got stuck in a trim up or trim down position? Answer: Yeager would have a problem. What if the turbulent airflow at high speed Mach overwhelmed the motor and kept the tail from pivoting? Answer: Yeager would be no worse off than he was during the previous mission. Yeah, but what if that turbulent air ripped off that damned tail as it was pivoting? Answer: Yeager better have paid-up insurance. We were dealing with the Ughknown.

Before returning to Wright, Colonel Boyd approved our ground tests. We were to report the results to him, and then he'd decide whether to proceed with a flight test. Then the old man took me aside. "Listen," he said, "I don't want you to be railroaded into this deal by Ridley or anyone else. If you don't feel comfortable with the risks, I want you to tell me so. I'll respect your decision. Please don't play the hero, Chuck. It makes no sense getting you hurt or killed."

I told him, "Colonel Boyd, it's my ass on the line. I want us to succeed but I'm not going to get splattered doing it."

So, Ridley and I ground tested that stabilizer system every which way but loose. It worked fine, and provided just enough control (about a quarter of a degree change in the angle of incidence) so that we both felt I could get by without using the airplane's elevator. "It may not be much," Ridley said, "and it may feel ragged to you up there, but it will keep you flying." I agreed. But would the system work at high Mach speed? Only one way to find out. Colonel Boyd gave us the go ahead.

No X-1 flight was ever routine. But when I was dropped to repeat the same flight profile that had lost my elevator effectiveness, I admit to being unusually grim. I flew as alert and precisely as I knew how. If the damned Ughknown swallowed me up, there wasn't much I could do about it, but I concentrated on that trim switch. At the slightest indication that something wasn't right, I would break the record for backing off.

Pushing the switch forward opened a solenoid that allowed high-pressure nitrogen gas through the top motor to the stabilizer, changing its angle of attack and stabilizing its upward pitch. If I pulled back, that would start the bottom motor, turning it in the opposite direction. I could just beep it and supposedly make pitch changes. I let the airplane accelerate up to .85 Mach before testing the trim switch. I pulled back on the switch, moving the leading edge of the stabilizer down one degree, and her nose rose. I retrimmed it back to where it was, and we leveled out. I climbed and accelerated up to .9 Mach and made the same change, achieving the same result. I retrimmed it and let it go out to .94 Mach, where I had lost my elevator effectiveness, made the same trim change, again raising the nose, just as I had done at the lower Mach numbers. Ridley was right: the stabilizer gave me just enough pitch control to keep me safe. I felt we could probably make it through without the elevator.

I had her out to .96 at 43,000 feet and was about to turn off the engine and begin jettisoning the remaining fuel, when the windshield began to frost. Because of the intense cabin cold, fogging was a continual problem, but I was usually able to wipe it away. This time, though, a solid layer of frost quickly formed. I even took off my gloves and used my fingernails, which only gave me frostbite. That windshield was lousy anyway, configured to the bullet-shaped fuselage and affording limited visibility. It was hard to see out during landings, but

I had never expected to fly the X-I on instruments. I radioed Dick Frost, flying low chase, and told him the problem. "Okay, pard," he said, "I'll talk you in. You must've done a lot of sweating in that cockpit to ice the damned windshield." I told him, "Not as much as I'm gonna do having you talk me in. You better talk good, Frost." He laughed. "I know. A dumb bastard like you probably can't read instruments."

The X-1 wasn't the Space Shuttle. There were no on-board computers to line you up and bring you down. The pilot was the computer. Under normal flight conditions, I'd descend to 5,000 feet above the lakebed and fly over the point where I wanted to touch down, then turn and line up downwind, lowering my landing gear at around 250 mph. The X-1 stalled around 190 mph, so I held my glide speed to around 220 and touched down at around 190. The ship rolled out about three miles if I didn't apply the brakes. Rogers Dry Lake gave me an eight-mile runway, but that didn't make the landing untricky. Coming in nose-high, you couldn't see the ground at all. You had to feel for it. I was sensitive to ground effect, and felt the differences as we lowered down. There was also that depth perception problem, and a lot of pilots bent airplanes porpoising in, or flaring high then cracking off their landing gears. My advantage was that I had landed on these lakebeds hundreds of times. Even so, the X-1 was not an easy-landing airplane. At the point of touchdown, you had to discipline yourself to do nothing but allow the ship to settle in by itself. Otherwise you'd slam it on its weak landing gear.

So, landing blind was not something you'd ever want to be forced to do. I had survived the Ughknown only to be kicked in the butt by the Unexpected. But that was a test pilot's life, one damned thing after another. Frost was a superb pilot, who knew the X-l's systems and characteristics even better than I did. I had plenty of experience flying on instruments, and in a hairy deal like this, experience really counted. Between the two of us we made it look deceptively easy, although we both knew that it wasn't exactly a routine procedure. Frost told me to turn left ten degrees, and I followed by using my magnetic compass, monitoring my rate of turn by the needle and ball. I watched the airspeed and rate of descent, so I knew how fast I was coming down from that and the feel of the ground effect. I followed his directions moving left or right to line up on the lakebed, which was also five miles wide, allowing him to fly right on my wing and touch down with me.

He greased me right in, but my body sweat added another layer of frost to the windshield. "Pard," Dick teased, "that's the only time you haven't bounced her down. Better let me hold your hand from now on."

Before my next flight, Jack Russell, my crew chief, applied a coating of Drene Shampoo to the windshield. For some unknown reason it worked as an effective antifrost device, and we continued using it even after the government purchased a special chemical that cost eighteen bucks a bottle.

Despite the frosted windshield, I now had renewed confidence in the X-1. We had licked the elevator problem, and Ridley and I phoned Colonel Boyd and told him we thought we could safely continue the flights. He told us to press on. This was on Thursday afternoon. The next scheduled flight would be on Tuesday. So we sat down with the NACA team to discuss a flight plan. I had gone up to .955 Mach, and they suggested a speed of .97 Mach for the next mission. What we didn't know until the flight data was reduced several days later, was that I had actually flown .988 Mach while testing the stabilizer. In fact, there was a fairly good possibility that I had attained supersonic speed.

Instrumentation revealed that a shock wave was interfering with the airspeed gauge on the wing. But we wouldn't learn about this until after my next flight.

All I cared about was that the stabilizer was still in one piece and so was I. We were all exhausted from a long, draining week, and quit early on Friday to start the weekend. I had promised Glennis that I would take her to Elly Anderson's, in Auburn, for a change of scene and to get her away from the kids. As cautiously as we were proceeding on these X-1 flights, I figured that my attempt to break the barrier was a week or two away. So I looked forward to a relaxed few days off. But when I got home, I found Glennis lying down, feeling sick. We canceled the babysitter and called Elly. By Sunday she was feeling better, so we went over to Pancho's place for dinner. On the way over, I said to Glennis, "Hey, how about riding horses after we eat?" She was raised around horses and was a beautiful rider.

Pancho's place was a dude ranch, so after dinner we walked over to the corral and had them saddle up a couple of horses. It was a pretty night and we rode for about an hour through the Joshua trees. We decided to race back. Unfortunately there was no moon, otherwise I would have seen that the gate we had gone out of was now closed. I only saw the gate when I was practically on top of it. I was slightly in the lead, and I tried to veer my horse and miss it, but it was too late. We hit the gate and I tumbled through the air. The horse got cut and I was knocked silly. The next thing I remember was Glennis kneeling over me, asking me if I was okay. I was woozy, and she helped me stand up. It took a lot to straighten up, feeling like I had a spear in my side.

Glennis knew immediately. "You broke a rib," she said. She was all for driving straight to the base hospital. I said, no, the flight surgeon will ground me. "Well, you can't fly with broken ribs," she argued. I told her, "If I can't, I won't. If I can, I will." Monday morning, I struggled out of bed. My shoulder was sore, and I ached generally from bumps and bruises, but my ribs near to killed me. The pain took my breath away. Glennis drove me over to Rosemond, where a local doctor confirmed I had two cracked ribs, and taped me up. He told me to take it easy. The tape job really helped. The pain was at least manageable and I was able to drive myself to the base that afternoon.

I was really low. I felt we were on top of these flights now, and I wanted to get them over with. And as much as I was hurting, I could only imagine what the old man would say if I was grounded for falling off a horse. So, I sat down with Jack Ridley and told him my troubles. I said, "If this were the first flight, I wouldn't even think about trying it with these busted sumbitches. But, hell, I know every move I've got to make, and most of the major switches are right on the control wheel column."

He said, "True, but how in hell are you gonna be able to lock the cockpit door? That takes some lifting and shoving." So we walked into the hangar to see what we were up against.

We looked at the door and talked it over. Jack said, "Let's see if we can get a stick or something that you can use in your left hand to raise the handle up on the door to lock it. Get it up at least far enough where you get both hands on it and get a grip on it. We looked around the hangar and found a broom. Jack sawed off a ten-inch piece of broomstick, and it fit right into the door handle. Then I crawled into the X-1 and we tried it out. He held the door against the frame, and by using that broomstick to raise the door handle, I found I could manage to lock it. We tried it two or three times, and it worked. But finally, Ridley said, "Jesus, son, how are you gonna get down that ladder?"

I said, "One rung at a time. Either that or you can piggyback me."

Jack respected my judgment. "As long as you really think you can hack it," he said. We left that piece of broomstick in the X-1 cockpit.

NINTH POWERED FLIGHT OCTOBER 14, 1947

Glennis drove me to the base at six in the morning. She wasn't happy with my decision to fly, but she knew that Jack would never let me take off if he felt I would get into trouble. Hoover and Jack Russell, the X-1 crew chief, heard I was dumped off a horse at Pancho's, but thought the only damage was to my ego, and hit me with some "Hi-Ho Silver" crap, as well as a carrot, a pair of glasses, and a rope in a brown paper bag—my bucking bronco survival kit.

Around eight, I climbed aboard the mother ship. The flight plan called for me to reach .97 Mach. The way I felt that day, .97 would be enough. On that first rocket ride I had a tiger by the tail; but by this ninth flight, I felt I was in the driver's seat. I knew that airplane inside and out. I didn't think it would turn against me. Hell, there wasn't much I could do to hurt it; it was built to withstand three times as much stress as I could survive. I didn't think the sound barrier would destroy her, either. But the only way to prove it was to do it.

That moving tail really bolstered my morale, and I wanted to get to that sound barrier. I suppose there were advantages in creeping up on Mach 1, but my vote was to stop screwing around before we had some stupid accident that could cost us not only a mission, but the entire project. If this mission was successful, I was planning to really push for a sound barrier attempt on the very next flight.

Going down that damned ladder hurt. Jack was right behind me. As usual, I slid feet-first into the cabin. I picked up the broom handle and waited while Ridley pushed the door against the frame, then I slipped it into the door handle and raised it up into lock position. It worked perfectly. Then I settled in to go over my checklist. Bob Cardenas, the B-29 driver, asked if I was ready.

"Hell, yes," I said. "Let's get it over with."

He dropped the X-1 at 20,000 feet, but his dive speed was once again too slow and the X-1 started to stall. I fought it with the control wheel for about five hundred feet, and finally got her nose down. The moment we picked up speed I fired all four rocket chambers in rapid sequence. We climbed at .88 Mach and began to buffet, so I flipped the stabilizer switch and changed the setting two degrees. We smoothed right out, and at 36,000 feet, I turned off two rocket chambers. At 40,000 feet, we were still climbing at a speed of .92 Mach. Leveling off at 42,000 feet, I had thirty percent of my fuel, so I turned on rocket chamber three and immediately reached .96 Mach. I noticed that the faster I got, the smoother the ride.

Suddenly the Mach needle began to fluctuate. It went up to .965 Mach—then tipped right off the scale. I thought I was seeing things! We were flying supersonic! And it was as smooth as a baby's bottom: Grandma could be sitting up there sipping lemonade. I kept the speed off the scale for about twenty seconds, then raised the nose to slow down.

I was thunderstruck. After all the anxiety, breaking the sound barrier turned out to be a perfectly paved speedway. I radioed Jack in the B-29. "Hey, Ridley, that Machmeter is acting screwy. It just went off the scale on me."

"Fluctuated off?"

"Yeah, at point nine-six-five."

"Son, you is imagining things."

"Must be. I'm still wearing my ears and nothing else fell off, neither."

The guys in the NACA tracking van interrupted to report that they heard what sounded like a distant rumble of thunder: my sonic boom! The first one by an airplane ever heard on earth. The X-1 was supposedly capable of reaching nearly twice the speed of sound, but the Machmeter aboard only registered to 1.0 Mach, which showed how much confidence they had; I estimated I had reached 1.05 Mach. (Later data showed it was 1.07 Mach—700 mph.)

And that was it. I sat up there feeling kind of numb, but elated. After all the anticipation to achieve this moment, it really was a let-down. It took a damned instrument meter to tell me what I'd done. There should've been a bump on the road, something to let you know you had just punched a nice clean hole through that sonic barrier. The Ughknown was a poke through Jello. Later on, I realized that this mission had to end in a let-down, because the real barrier wasn't in the sky, but in our knowledge and experience of supersonic flight.

I landed tired, but relieved to have hacked the program. There is always strain in research flying. It's the same as flying in combat, where you never can be sure of the outcome. You try not to think about possible disasters, but fear is churning around inside whether you think of it consciously or not. I thought now that I'd reached the top of the mountain, the remainder of these X-1 experimental flights would be downhill. But having sailed me safely through the sonic barrier, the X-1 had plenty of white-knuckle flights in store over the next year. The real hero in the flight test business is a pilot who manages to survive.

And so I was a hero this day. As usual, the fire trucks raced out to where the ship had rolled to a stop on the lakebed. As usual, I hitched a ride back to the hangar with the fire chief. That warm desert sun really felt wonderful. My ribs ached.

from # Kamikaze
by Yasuo Kuwahara
and Gordon T. Allred

Yasuo Kuwahara was 15 years old when he joined the

Japanese Air Force in 1943. Kuwahara was trained as a

fighter pilot, and flew several missions as an escort for the

kamikaze pilots who made suicide attacks on American

ships. He knew that his turn would eventually come. One

day in the summer of 1944, he returned to his air base

after visiting a young woman named Toyoko Akimoto.

Early in the morning I left for the base—not knowing that I would never see Toyoko Akimoto again.

The streets and lanes were quiet, and clouds were blotching part of the sky. In the fields, and between the houses, the wind swirled dust and bits of paper. It was one of those rare summer mornings, one of those strange reminders, even in the midst of heat and greenery, that winter will come again some day.

Nearing the base, I felt an empty tingling. Today I would be flying another escort mission. Okinawa. We had been briefed yesterday and would receive final instructions today. Okinawa. Who would it be this time? Another fifteen or twenty men. Lately I hadn't been checking the names. It was better that way, better, too, that I hadn't formed any close friendships at Ôita.

Already, as I flashed my pass for the gate MP, the base was beginning to vibrate. Overhead, almost out of sight, a plane cried, and I began walking fast. It was almost time for formation.

The formation over, I hurried to the mess hall, planning to eat quickly, then check over my fighter. I was more cautious in this regard than most, always making sure the mechanics had everything primed. At least I had confidence in my own flying ability now, and I was determined not to leave this world because of some trivial oversight.

Months of grueling practice were behind me—a series of dog fights, most of them hit-and-run affairs, but several good skirmishes. I was no longer the green pilot who had followed his lieutenant into battle. I had two of the enemy to my credit—verified kills. And at Ôita I had been promoted to corporal, a rank not easily attained by Japanese enlisted men.

And now, grim as the task was, I was a leader—leading *Kamikaze* pilots through the enemy fighter screen, defending them to that last dive, then returning with the facts. That was my job. Who else had a more important job?

And at night? There would be Toyoko. Toyoko had said she loved me, and that was enough for the time being. I couldn't die now. Something would happen to save me. I would be invincible. A time would come when Toyoko would give me all her love, and it would be right. She would be my wife.

Today Nakamura was to fly the same mission with me. That made everything better. I had spotted him in the mess hall, ahead of me in line. My plate and bowl filled, I followed him to a table.

"*Yai, tomadachi*, pal!" I roughed his head playfully. "Seen Tatsu this morning?"

Unsmiling, Nakamura looked up. "Yes, I've seen Tatsuno."

"Well, what's the matter? Where is he?"

"Getting ready."

"Going with us? Escort now?"

"Going with us—yes. Escort—no."

Something filled my chest like a lead slab. "He's lucky," Nakamura said. "No more worries, not after noon today. You and I—we still have to wait."

As if it were a very important matter, I placed my chopsticks carefully on the table. "When did he find out? Why didn't somebody tell me before so I could have at least been with him? Why didn't you tell me?"

"It only happened day before yesterday. And you haven't been the most available man in the world this last month—you know that. You should try reading the orders sometime, Kuwahara. You don't want to miss your own name."

I locked my fingers and clamped one knuckle between my teeth, staring through the table into nothingness. "And I've hardly even seen him, lately. Since we left Hiro, I haven't even been a friend to Tatsuno! Where have I been? What have I been thinking?" Fiercely I bit my knuckle. That was the only thing that felt good just then—my teeth cutting into the knuckle.

"I tried to find you last night," Nakamura said. "I went to your girl's apartment about ten, but you weren't there."

"We were down at the beach."

"Nice! A lot nicer than being with—"

"Stop it!" I banged my fists on the table, grated my chair back, and stumbled blindly out of the mess hall. Where was Tatsuno? I'd find him. I'd tell him I would die with him. I'd cover him all the way down, all the way to the ship. We'd go together. No, Tatsuno wouldn't go alone. Not my friend! I ran for nearly a quarter of a mile across the base, then stopped before I ever got to his barrack. He and his fated companions would be getting their final briefing now.

I turned and shuffled bleakly toward my own quarters. Two hours before take-off time—an hour before our last instructions. Nothing to do but wait. I wouldn't even check my Hayabusa now, not until time to go. Nakamura was waiting when I entered my billet, sitting on my cot.

Without speaking, I sat beside him. Nakamura drew a deep breath and clapped me on the leg. "I'm sorry, Yasbei," he said. "I didn't know what I was saying. I'm about ready to crack up. I really am." I gripped his arm hard.

"Don't feel bad, Yasbei," he muttered. "Tatsuno wouldn't have wanted it any different—not with you. It's just as he told me last night. We're all going to the same place, and we're going soon. It's only a few days, one way or the other—no matter how you look at it. These last days . . . You've done the best thing, Yasbei. You've found somebody worth spending the time with. Something, no matter what happens."

"But not even to see him!" I choked. "Tatsuno! Do you know how long we've known each other?"

"Ever since you were about four—Tatsu told me. You couldn't have done him any good hanging around here anyway. We'd all be getting on each other's nerves. I haven't seen Tatsu much myself. He's been up in the mountains with the priest anyway."

I had to ask the next: "How's he taking it?"

"Perfectly!" Nakamura said. "Perfectly! Anyway," Nakamura continued, "I have a funny feeling about today. Today maybe we'll all get it. Today we'll all go down burning—we'll repay the emperor. I've a feeling in my bones."

Somehow the remaining time passed. It was as if there had been a blank space, then I found myself standing on the airfield, suited up, waiting to fly. There were sixteen pilots all told—four of us escorts, the remaining dozen never to return. The twelve had just grouped for final directions before an officer with a map.

We all stood at attention, respectfully listening to the commanding officer now—his parting words. A short distance away I could see Tatsuno, but he didn't look real—just a facsimile. His spirit . . . It had already gone like the wind among the lanterns.

Around the shaved skull of each *Kamikaze* was bound a small flag, the crimson rising sun over his forehead. These departures were never conducted in a perfunctory manner. There was much ceremony, much show, toasts and valiant speeches—most of which I had already learned by rote.

Boys and girls, drafted from school to work on the base, were allowed to assemble with the squadron on these occasions. Among the fringe of onlookers a knot of girls began to weep, and then grew quiet. It was time for the commanding officer's speech.

Yes, the same words, the words I had heard so often on this runway during the past weeks—the voice droning nasally for several minutes, and then the conclusion: "And so, valiant comrades, smile as you go. . . . There is a place prepared for you in the esteemed presence of your ancestors . . . guardian warriors . . . *samurai* of the skies. . . ."

And at last it was time to sing the battle song:

> The Airman's color is the color of the cherry blossom.
> Look, the cherry blossoms fall on the hills of Yoshino.
> If we are born proud sons of the Yamato race,
> Let us die fighting in the skies.

Then the final toast. The *sake* glasses were raised and the cry surged: *Tennoheika Banzai!* (Long live the Emperor). The *Kamikaze* were saying *sayonara* now, laughing and joking as they climbed into their obsolete planes—antiquated fighters, even trainers. The old planes didn't matter, though. It was a one-way trip. The smiles? They might remain on some of these faces to the very last. For others, those smiles began to fade as they settled into their cockpits. Maybe for a few the fear cloud would not settle until the enemy convoy loomed. And what was courage? I never knew. Who was the most courageous—the man who felt the least fear or the man who felt the most? But just then I could think of only one man.

There he was with Nakamura, walking toward me. He didn't look real. That was right; the spirit had left already. His body would mechanically fulfill the duty. What a strange smile carved on that waxen face. *Tell him! Tell him you'll cover him all the way that you'll die with him. But no, he doesn't want it, and something, something strangles all words. Your time will come soon enough, Kuwahara. Yes, by repeating* those words, I could ease the sensation of guilt. I was no friend; I hadn't been for weeks. And never once had he presumed to suggest that we see each other more often.

The lead slab in my chest was heavy now, weighing me down, crushing the words. "Tatsuno . . . I . . ." Our hands met in an icy clasp. Nakamura stood by, looking down. Nakamura, a better friend than I, was giving me this final moment.

"Remember . . ." the words came, "how we always wanted to fly together?" I looked into his eyes and bowed my head.

"I will follow you soon," I whispered.

Then he gave me something. "Here," he said, "take care of this for me. It's not much to send, but take care of it."

Quickly I looked away. Tatsuno had just given me his little finger. Our doomed men always left something of themselves behind, a lock of hair, fingernails, an entire finger—for cremation. The ashes were sent home to repose in the family shrine. There, in a special alcove, the ashes would reside with the pictures of ancestors. Once yearly, a priest would enter that room to pray.

The first motors were beginning to rev, and I held onto Tatsuno as if by holding on I might preserve him. "*Sayonara*, Yasuo," he said. We fell toward each other embracing.

Without looking back, I broke away and stumbled to my Hayabusa. Not knowing how I got there, I found myself seated, fastening my safety belt, feeling the controls, adjusting my goggles. The whole base was grumbling in final preparation.

I checked the prop mixture, then pressed the starter button. One cylinder caught, a high coughing explosion, then another and another. . . . The motor blared, and shifted into a steady grumble. We were moving out—lethargic, winged beasts coming to life. Uno, a veteran with five kills, was in the lead; I was close behind him—signals coming from the control tower. Already the onlookers were in another world, withdrawn. A ring fading from the prop blasts hurled back the air, sand, bits of straw and paper.

The commanding officer, students, other pilots, the mechanics who had come to bid good-by to the ships they had nutured—all began shrinking as the strip sank beneath us.

It was good flying weather. The seasonal rains had subsided, leaving a clear dome of blue. Within minutes, we had left the mainland behind, left the mountains, and I was thinking how Japan itself is little more than a conglomeration of mountains, great, rolling remnants of the past, when islands reared and sank like stricken monsters, when fires burst from nature's hidden furnaces. We left the shores. The shores of four islands, and the slopes that housed over seventy million people in the crust of black-brown dwellings.

There was the re-fueling stop at Kagoshima on the island of Kyushu, about an hour after take-off. For twelve men, the last glimpse of their homeland. For twelve men, the three-hour flight to Okinawa would be their last hours on earth. Oka and Yamamoto had left three weeks ago.

A few minutes off Kagoshima we spotted a flight of B-29's escorted by Grummans, traveling toward Shikoku. Altering our course slightly, we faded into a skein of wispy cirrus clouds, and cruised on at a moderate speed. Below, the Pacific rolled, a deep, scalloped green, glinting further out under the sun, like a billion holiday sparklers.

I thought of many things during that flight to Okinawa. Home was a dream, an old wound that throbbed faintly, and not so often as it had. Toyoko? I saw her countless times, in countless ways. Sometimes just a silver face, unreal in the garden moonlight—or glowing softly beneath a lantern gateway. Sometimes the clear eyes, as they had looked at me on our first meeting. Little movements—the way she walked in her tight kimono, such dainty steps, one foot placed directly in front of the other.

But always there was a great void within me, and I kept hearing Nakamura's fateful augury from a few hours back in the other world; "Today we will fulfill our obligation to the emperor. I have a feeling in my bones." Nakamura, the recruit who had first befriended me during the beginning days of basic—those frightening times my loquacious friend, a practical man and a strong one.

I remembered a day long, long ago when Tatsuno and I had run laughing through the streets of Onomichi, swatting at each other with our caps. Always the pensive one, Tatsuno, the rare friend in whom one could always confide, whose understanding went so far below the surface. "Tatsuno, Tatsuno . . ." I repeated the name, and moved on in a dream.

The waters turned back, and far ahead the clouds were merging. "One hour left," Uno's words crackled in the intercom. I glanced at him, ahead, off my right wing, and signaled acknowledgment. Uno was a squat, sinewy sergeant in his early twenties, who had known only a farmer's life and had been transformed into a cunning sky fighter. Soon, if he was lucky, he would be an ace.

Ahead, the clouds were heavier, cutting off the sparklers beneath them. Off somewhere amid that darkening water. . . .

Our *Kamikaze* were traveling in wedges of three—lethal arrows slicing toward the American ships. On and on, we cut deeper into the day. The time was close at hand and, as it drew nearer, the dry-plaster feeling in my mouth increased—something that always happened. My hands were clenching and opening—the inevitable sweating. "You're too taut, Kuwahara," I kept saying. Quick glimpses of Toyoko again. "Wait for me, Toyoko. Wait for me."

Strange how so many irrelevant thoughts kept pecking at me. They were part of my defense mechanism—sedatives against fear. Soon these last sedatives would wear off.

Long since, we had passed the small islands of Yaku and Togara, and now with Amami fading in our wake, we looked ahead. Okinawa! It was looming before us, brooding, and a throbbing in my head had started. I craned my neck, then came the jolt. Sergeant Uno waggled his wings. Far off, I saw the swaths of the first American ships. I began counting those water trails—*ichi, ni, san, shi*—twenty-five in all, and there, no bigger than seeds for the moment, in the center of that task force was our quarry, four carriers, guarded by battleships and a perimeter of destroyers.

Uno signaled again and our twelve *Kamikaze* crept ahead of us at full bore—moving into the strike at ten thousand feet. The four of us climbed slightly, following. Moments sliding by, the ships growing . . . growing . . . growing. They were beginning to open up!

At last the waiting was over. I even welcomed the fear. It would all happen fast now. Then we could return and make our reports as usual. It would be no more dangerous than ever.

Tatsuno was leading the last V in an all-but-defunct navy plane—a Mitsubishi, Type 96.

Already the twelve had opened their cockpits, and fluttered their silk scarves in the wind. Always the wind—the divine wind. Ahead and beneath them the first flak was beginning to burst in soft, black puffs, and the tracers were red lines reaching for the heavens.

Now . . . we seem to be almost on top of them! I am sweating, watching. The lead *Kamikaze* dives, dropping vertically into a barbed-wire entanglement of flak. He'll never make the carriers; that seems obvious. Instead, he's heading for a cruiser near the fringe. For a moment it looks as if he'll make it. But no—he's hit, and it's all over. His plane is a red flare fading, dropping from sight.

Everything is a blur now—a mixture of sound and color. Two more of them go the same way, exploding in mid-air. A fourth is luckier. He screams unscathed through the barrage, leveling inside the flak umbrella near the water. A hit! He's struck a destroyer right at the water line. A bellowing explosion, then another and another. It's good! It's good! The ship is in its death throes. It can't stay afloat—water plunging over the bow, stifling it. It up-ends and is gone.

Now I'm losing track of the flights. They've been scattered. The two trailing formations are forging in through the lethal blossoms. Everywhere, incredible sound and confusion. One of our planes is skimming low across the water, gunfire kicking up a thousand spouts around him. He's closing the gap, aiming straight for a carrier. Straight in—he'll score a direct bit. No, no, they got him. He's bashing into the stern, inflicting little damage.

The defense is almost impregnable. Only a gnat could penetrate that fire screen now. Two more suicides stab at the same carrier and disintegrate, splattering the water. Others have dropped like firebrands into the sea. Impossible to keep track at all now. So far I can be certain that we have sunk only one ship.

Already, only a few planes left. It's hard to discern some of them against the murky horizon. Two planes, an advanced trainer and a Mitsubishi fighter, have swerved back toward us. We circle above them, watch them complete their arcs and head back in. That Mitsubishi! It's Tatsuno! Yes, I'm positive. He was in the last V—the only navy plane!

The two of them are diving, knifing for the convoy's core. Suddenly the trainer plane next to him is hit, virtually clubbed from the sky. His wing and tail rip off, and he corkscrews insanely away, out of my line of vision.

Tatsuno is alone now, still unhit, making a perfect run, better than they ever taught us in school. Tatsuno! Tatsuno! Fire spouts from his tail section, but he keeps going. The orange fingers reach out. His plane is a moving sheet of flame, but they can't stop him. Tatsuno! A tanker looms, ploughing the leaden liquid. They're closing! A hit! An enormous explosion rocks the atmosphere. For a curious instant embers seem to roll and dance. Now a staccato series of smaller bursts and one mighty blast, shaking the sea like a blanket. The tanker is going down. Gone. No trace but the widening shroud of oil.

The Pilot's Tale

by Matthew Klam

Matthew Klam (born 1964) is best known for his short stories. Klam in 1998 visited his friend Doug Hamilton on the aircraft carrier U.S.S. Dwight D. Eisenhower, where Hamilton served as a fighter pilot. Klam's article describing the visit was published in the February 1999 issue of Harper's.

I. The Flight Deck

Standing on the newly resurfaced deck of the USS *Dwight D. Eisenhower* sixty miles off the coast of Norfolk, Virginia, last spring, I watched a group of F/A-18 Hornets approach from the southeast, three black crosses against a pale sky. The enormous ocean lay flat and gray in the morning haze, and as the three crosses assumed their more familiar and menacing shapes, I tried to imagine the reverse perspective of the pilots intending to do well what almost no one can do at all—land a jet on a ship. I had come to see Lieutenant Commander Doug Hamilton, an old college friend, undergo two days of landing exercises, and although I'd been aboard the carrier for only a short time I'd begun to appreciate the odds in favor of a fatal accident.

More than three football fields long, the deck spreads across four and a half acres, as do the decks of the Navy's seven other Nimitz-class carriers, the largest warships in the world. The ship's "island" rises from the starboard side to the height of a seven-story building, housing the flight tower and observation platform and capped by seven radar antennae, one of them the size of a minivan. Bigger and heavier than the *Titanic* and longer than the Chrysler Building is tall, the *Eisenhower* is powered by two nuclear reactors that will run for at least twenty years before the uranium needs to be changed. Six thousand sailors live onboard, nearly half of them providing support for the pilots, like roadies for the Rolling Stones; the hangar deck holds at least sixty aircraft. Commissioned in 1977, the *Eisenhower* cost $5 billion to build. Adding the cost of the planes (another $2 billion) as well as the guided-missile cruisers, frigates, and maybe a nuclear submarine, the carrier and its battle group come at a price well beyond the combined annual military expenditures of the "rogue nations" of Iran, Iraq, North Korea, Cuba, Syria, and Libya.

Beginning with Doug's first landing and continuing over the next forty-eight hours, the pilots of the *Eisenhower*[1] would have to prove their skill by performing both day and night landings. The *Eisenhower* and its battle group then was scheduled to run through a quick, three-day simulated war, using Air Force and other Navy fighter squadrons as adversaries, before starting a four-month patrol of the Mediterranean Sea—first to the Adriatic to threaten Yugoslavia's rusting yet intact Serbian Army and then, for the final two months of its deployment, the ship would steam to the Suez Canal and the Red Sea to take over the patrol of Iraq's southern no-fly zone from the carrier USS *Stennis*.

As the carrier turned slowly into the wind, the angle of the sun shifted, and my attention focused on Doug, who would have to land on a deck moving thirty miles an hour away from him, into what the pilots call the "trap," zeroing in on a target eighteen inches long. The "arrested landing" is a seemingly crazy idea: a twenty-ton plane moving 170 miles an hour snags its four-foot titanium "tail hook" onto a giant cable connected to hydraulic cylinders below-decks,[2] and stops in a mere 300 feet.

Even a single bad landing exposes the pilot to the heckling of his squadronmates. More serious landing mishaps, when the pilot must eject from the airplane, often result in sudden death and an unrecoverable body; or, if the pilot survives, three separate Navy investigations and the possible termination of the pilot's career.[3]

Doug broke off his flight pattern directly overhead the *Eisenhower* and turned in a steeply banked oval at an altitude of 600 feet. The ship increased its speed to "catch" as he lined his plane up with the enormous wake and glided toward the flight deck's center line. His wheels touched down, and the hook from his plane snagged the number 3 arresting wire. Landing—perfect.

But the plane was still moving, still rocketing toward us, fifteen feet tall, fifty-six feet long, roaring so loudly that even through my foam earplugs and ear protectors, I felt the sound rattling my chest, vibrating my teeth, and, worse, crackling my eardrums like cellophane. I stumbled backward, and the safety officer grabbed my arm.[4]

After the plane came to a stop, Doug taxied it a hundred yards to the giant, steam-powered bow catapult and dropped the jet's launch bar, a white piece of alloy the size of a piano leg. A sailor in a bright green jersey kicked it hard with the heel of his boot a few times to make sure it sat firmly against the catapult's holdback; then he signaled to the flight-deck crew chief, who signaled up to Doug, who locked his left elbow to push the engine to full power. White cans of fire flamed out the back of the jet, blackening the twelve-ton blast deflector, which lifted up out of the deck like a barn door. The crewman in green did a dance of hand and body signals, his left hand swinging up as if he were throwing a lariat. He whacked the deck with the flat of his hand, signaling another man to release the catapult, then BOOM, Doug rocketed off the catapult so loud, so fast, so maximum, that it looked like speeded-up film, his two tailpipe engine exhausts dilating and closing, adjusting the flow of oxygen to the flames in the jet's engines.

Another plane landed, trapped a wire, and launched, then another and another. The ocean air became a numbing wind filled with jet fuel; it got in my eyes, I tasted it.[5] A forty-knot wind flattened the front of my windbreaker. Doug landed a second time, fulfilling his daytime requirement. He halted ten feet from where I stood. Sunlight reflected on the plane's canopy in an odd reddish-green tint, like the filmy rainbow on a soap bubble.[6] He sat up inside the cockpit at roughly the height of a tall lifeguard chair, his head helmeted and visored behind a tight rubber oxygen mask.

I hadn't seen Doug in a long time. We met in 1982, in college. After we graduated and he'd begun his flight training in 1986 I consoled myself that he hadn't known what he was doing when he joined the Navy, that he was some nonpolitical flyboy and had backed into his profession for the pure joy of flying. We attempted to stay close through our early thirties by exchanging letters and e-mails, but as time passed, what I read in the newspapers about our American military contradicted what I thought I knew about Doug, and what little he said in his letters revealed only mystery and paradox. I knew, for example, that he was called Hambone by the other pilots, that he used such phrases as "implications our job has on the world's security" and "as we stabilize this hemisphere." But I was perplexed. If the birth of his new son made him so obsessed with safety, why was he constantly risking his life? If he only lived to serve our country, why had his ego grown to the size of a cathedral? When Doug explained that he could get permission for me to come onboard the *Eisenhower*, I sensed not just an opportunity to see Doug's world and answer my questions but also a chance to find out whether I still, really, knew him at all.

I knew that being a carrier pilot required extraordinary ability. Doug had always been an athlete, a great downhill and water-skier, and since joining the Navy he'd become a nationally ranked triathlete. After going through aviation officer candidate school and learning to fly, he began to practice for carrier landings at the Naval Air Station in Kingsville, Texas, dropping his plane onto a runway painted like a ship's deck. Then Doug had his first try at the real thing, a carrier off the coast of Florida, and failed. He caught the number 1 wire twice, which means that he was landing too short. He was given three more weeks of practice, 150 landings. In need of a friend, he wrote me a letter then, telling me that if he were to catch the number 1 wire again, his career would be over. No more practice, no third chance, no Navy commission, no job as a pilot of lesser status, no wings, nothing. He would have to leave the Navy and start from scratch.

Never again would Doug come so close to failure. He returned to the ship and passed with honors at the top of his class. At the conclusion of advanced training, he again earned top honors in his carrier qualification. In his first assignment in the fleet, flying the two-seater A-6 bomber, he again came out at the top of his "nugget" class, and was called up by an A-6 squadron going right to sea that was in need of a pilot.

He first wrote to me from the *Eisenhower* in 1992, while the ship was patrolling in the north Arabian Gulf just after the Persian Gulf War. He wrote again while trapped above Norway in a hurricane in the North Sea, when a storm called a polar low had overwhelmed his carrier battle group, sending the small ships (nuclear subs and frigates) into the fjords for protection while Doug and his A-6 bomber squadron were required to fly their airplanes in the midst of snow, sleet, and sixty-knot hurricane winds, trying to land with four-story waves crashing over the ship's bow. He wrote to me in 1994 from the carrier *George Washington*, after the fiftieth anniversary commemoration of the Allied landing in Normandy, where he starred in the "missing man" formation broadcast on CNN—the one lone jet vectoring off slowly as the other five flew past President Clinton at the ceremony. Doug spent a total of forty-two days at home in 1994; the rest of the year he was on deployment or training. He and his wife, Sarah, tried to honeymoon in Europe while Doug's carrier was deployed in the Mediterranean, but the ship never showed up at scheduled ports of call. After crisscrossing Europe, Sarah went home alone. The ship moved to the Adriatic and Doug patrolled the skies over Bosnia. "I flew a mission last night and they shot at me," he wrote while participating in the U.N.'s Operation Deny Flight. "They pay us 150 bucks extra for getting shot at. Sounds pretty reasonable."

Now I watched Doug walk slowly across the deck, and although I sensed his relief, I knew also that his perfect daytime landing only delivered him to the much more difficult task of a night landing. The Navy practices these landings in order to be able to complete night strikes, which are more likely to surprise an enemy and are less susceptible to aircraft loss. The night attack, theoretically, paralyzes a shocked and terrified population beneath the full fury of an American bombardment.

For months Doug had hoped that the two night landings required of him would take place at dusk, when visual clues outside his canopy would help in the final moments before touchdown. Night over the ocean bears no relation to the night of anywhere over the land. Unable to discern the horizon dividing the sky from his target bobbing on the water, the carrier pilot relies on such cutting-edge magic as "synthetic aperture" ground-mapping radar, but the instruments lag fractions of a second behind real time at a moment when inches divide the safe landing from the lethal one. When Doug first found out that his night landings would be under a new moon—which is the absence of moon—he told me, "I hate night landings. Flying around the carrier in the dark is an act of insanity." For good measure, he added, "We're all scared of it. Not just me."[7]

II. Ready Room 3, Deck 03

I found Doug filling up his coffee cup in the ready room, the Blasters' one place to conduct meetings, receive instructions, make flight plans, debrief, read the paper. He greeted me with the swagger he's learned since he became a fighter pilot, smiling, his blue eyes glowing. Doug has a prominent jaw and brown hair cut to make his head look square. I could see gray flecks of stubble and heavy lines across his forehead and around his eyes, blood-black circles underneath. A strange crease ran across his face from the rubber gasket of the oxygen mask that had been tightly clamped over his nose and mouth for the last couple of hours. We normally exchange a quick and manly bear hug like men do these days, but the Uniform Code of Military Justice forbids any physical show of affection while in uniform. We shook hands.

Ready room 3 is set up like a small movie theater, and every pilot has a nicely padded armchair that looks as if it were unbolted from the inside of a 1940s airliner, with a Blue Blasters insignia and the pilot's name sewn onto the headrest. A television monitor in the front of the room airs the ship's channel, the five cameras of which provide grainy black-and-white coverage of takeoffs and landings on deck. When there are no flight operations, the channel shows the ocean in front of the bow and a piece of the railing for perspective. Despite its importance, the ready room offers no sanctuary from the ship's endless noise, the sound of an eighteen-wheeler constantly revving its engines, or perhaps a thousand industrial refrigerators humming at once. The roar is draining, because you can't help but pay attention to it, and that's just the background noise. The catapult above us that launches the planes causes the entire ship to shudder, and when planes land, it sounds like bulldozers being dropped from a great height. Except for their quarters, where the pilots can sleep or watch movies, or the wardroom, where they can eat, or their jets, they have no other place to go, suffering, it seemed to me, a form of shipboard incarceration.

Another pilot, C. C. "Heater" Heaton IV, introduced himself.[8] Like the others, he moved and spoke with a stiff confidence, immediate and robotic; even though his squadronmates ran the gamut of personality and looks, and even though they could be charming or pensive or joking, it was impossible to penetrate what an individual man might have felt about something deeply—such as being called sir all day or the off-chance of disappearing in a fireball.

The fighter pilot derives his swagger in part from his privileged position in the Navy. Fighter pilots, who comprise less than one percent of the Navy's population, make more money than their nonflying peers, and unlike anyone but a ship's captain, have command over their vessel. They're privy to all sorts of highly classified information and combat rooms. They enjoy their reputation, and star in the very public show up on the flight deck. Everyone inside the ship seems to keep track of each feat or botched landing.

In preparation for the coming three-day simulated war, a map at the front of the room was laid out with fake countries identical to those in the northern Arabian Gulf but with such names as "Kowonka" and "Ladam" superimposed over a map of the eastern U.S. seaboard. The squadron was already planning dogfighting and bombing scenarios. Beneath the television, Lieutenant Mike "Crusher" Barger quizzed Lieutenant Phil "Stork" Poliquin, about dogfighting strategy.

"What's your mission?" he asked.

"Pre-strike sweep."

"What's that mean?"

"Kill anything that comes out."

Hearing this, Crusher sat back and cracked his knuckles, all of the knuckles, even the thumb knuckle, even the tip of his pinkie.

III. Wardroom 3, Deck 3

Some of the other pilots joined Doug and me for lunch. Phil Poliquin led the way down the long, narrow corridor through the ship to wardroom 3; he was followed by Commander Chip Miller known as "Bullet" then Lieutenant Commander Barry "Butch" Wilmore—Doug's roommate—Lieutenant Commander Peter "Pepe" Harris, and Lieutenant "Heater." Every seven steps we stepped over a one-foot-high bulkhead. Some of the bulkheads have regular doors with doorknobs; others have watertight porthole doors that have to be unbolted and then bolted shut behind you.

Even though 6,000 sailors live and work on the *Eisenhower*'s seventeen decks, all the flight operations take place in one section of Deck 03, and for pilots this means living, eating, seeing about repairs, changing out of their G suits, and sleeping all in a fairly tight corner among the same faces day in and day out. I'd go back and forth through those corridors, six or seven strides, from my stateroom to the ready room to eat or watch the jets, step up through a bulkhead, let two-way traffic pass, do it again, day and night, and I began to dread the walks, adopting a strut and a mask of efficiency.

The wardroom is one of three where the pilots can eat. There are

also a number of enormous enlisted people's messes on the decks
below us, a captain's mess (I met him once; he appeared to be in his
late forties, haggard and overburdened), and an admiral's mess (the
admiral heads the whole battle group frigates, cruisers, submarines—
and looked trouble-free and fit, as if fresh from a tennis court perhaps, and ready to run for the Senate).

In the food line Phil warned me away from the pukish trough of
green vegetable liquid but gave a thumbs up to the meat loaf, which
he'd tested earlier in the day, and the macaroni and cheese, which was
predictably delicious. Wardroom 3 was the favorite mess of the 120
pilots of the air wing, and they were pouring out of the food line now,
bumping into one another, looking for a place to sit. A steady stream
of pilots—Tomcat, Hornet, Prowler, Hawkeye, and helicopter pilots—
came by our table in their tight flight suits with their special patches to
designate squadrons and plane type. Because their numbers were few
and their training took so long and needed constant updating, they
crossed paths throughout their careers, at bases in Florida, Texas, Mississippi, and Nevada. They called hello, passing on greetings from
somebody named "Bronco," yelling "Hey homo," from across the
room or sidling up and asking about the family with a glass of milk in
one hand and a classified-weapons binder in the other. Here were the
best-trained, best-equipped pilots in the world, professional athletes
standing at the farthest promontory of American power, ready at a
moment's notice to bring down the pain of death on as many of their
designated enemies as happened to stand in the way of a political purpose or military objective, and yet who reminded me somehow—with
their powerful builds, their mustaches, and their short haircuts—of
Chippendale dancers.

Among Doug's Blue Blasters, ten of the eighteen had become new
fathers within the last year. Despite the dull conversation, the
slouching, the silences filled by chewing noises and stupid
Lewinsky/Clinton jokes, a brotherly closeness marks their group, as
with a professional sports team who are forced to travel the poky back-
waters of the world in close quarters but who still like to play ball

together, except that these guys are trained to fight in the air and drop bombs that blow things up and kill people. Every pilot Doug introduced me to was "a great guy" and "an old friend," but I could see the stress of competition. Pilots are ranked within the squadron on every imaginable statistic, from bombing accuracy to staying on the correct frequency to the grace of landings.

Some of the younger pilots from the squadron walked into the wardroom with trays of meat loaf and joined the table. Still new to the Blasters, they tended to stick together. They appeared smaller and more innocent, a couple of them not yet filling out their flight suits, and bore diminutive nicknames given to them as part of their invitation into the squadron—Cubby, Odie, Fetus—in contrast to the tough call signs of the older pilots—Bullet, Bone, Crusher, Dirt, Fingers, Rocky, and Butch. The senior officers were discussing something called a FLIR pod, a forward-looking infrared sensor. Looking like a giant Q-tip under the plane's wing, the FLIR costs an ungodly amount of money but, Cubby explained, helps the pilot designate an enemy's radar, which can then be blown up with HARM, high-speed anti-radiation missiles. Cubby discussed its use the way someone might explain a leaf blower, rather than as a device that denudes a country of air defenses in preparation for getting hit with gigantic explosives.

The younger pilots finished eating in five minutes, wiping up their gravy with stale rolls. Doug explained privately that they were still learning the most minute details of flying and the risks they would have to suffer every day, and had only the vaguest understanding that they were being studied intently by the senior men at the other end of the table.

Doug asked Phil if he thought there'd be any residual light cast from Virginia this far out into the ocean, to define the horizon. Phil said, "I don't think so."

From the beginning of his Navy career, Doug filled his letters to me with detailed descriptions of how it feels to perform the carrier landing at night. The pilot stares blindly into a "black void," then comes aboard at a high speed, crash-like, at a steep angle for accuracy of hook position, almost out of gas—the plane can carry only a small amount of gas because if it is overburdened with fuel, it might break apart on landing. "Whoever invented the night cat/trap is a lunatic," he wrote. "As soon as I launch, I'm worrying about the landing when I get back."

I wondered why he spent so much energy telling me his fears of landing at night. No other aspect of the job bothered him; the drudgery of military life, wondering whether the targets you're ordered to bomb are "military, you hope, and not too close to civilians," the endless trips far away from home, the endless risk. Why should landing at night bother him so much? Doug is a typical daredevil: this fear seemed like an anomaly, a hysterical concoction, but I couldn't figure out to what end. He talked about the anxiety, the adrenaline that rushed through him during the final moments before touchdown, the sleeplessness, the misery and humiliation of counting days until the moon comes back out. Night-carrier landings are by nature intimate: the pilot reaches back to an intuitive, athletic marriage of instinct and faith in order to land. By last spring, Doug had performed 360 carrier landings, 115 of them at night. Since the birth of his son Craig, though, he'd begun to obsess even more than usual about safety and proficiency. Things seemed to have gotten worse. "None of us likes to fly at night," he told me. "I hate it and I wish I didn't have to go through it."

IV. Bomb Magazine, Deck 6

I was curious to see what a bomb looks like up close, and so Doug introduced me to a crewman called a gunner, who carries a key shaped like a gun barrel with interlocking chinks cut out of it on a chain around his neck. We followed him through an enlisted people's mess. There, two strides from the salad bar, he unlocked an enormous steel hatch and lifted a hinged, quadruple-bolted cover that appeared to weigh hundreds of pounds. We descended by a ladder, then through an even tighter hatch, down another ladder. At the bottom we stood in a rectangular shaft that had no exit except a small door mounted in front of us like a wall safe. The bomb magazines are locked, as prevention against terrorists, surely, but also for the simple reason that if any unhappy sailor gets into a magazine he might start igniting things or accidentally knock a bomb over and set it off; one man could potentially hold the entire ship hostage or blow it up. The gunner slipped in his key, the door swung open, and we squeezed through the opening into a vast, silent, unmanned warehouse full of bombs.

Before us stood eight-foot-high stacks of bombs on wooden pallets, missiles on dollies, oil drums with bomb parts, and fuses, tail fins, firing pins. This was a small magazine, one of the thirty-five inside the ship. The *Eisenhower*'s well carries enough destructive capability to decapitate a medium-sized country. No other country can project such destructive capability. Britain and France sport a handful of small carriers, and China may someday, but with the former Soviet fleet sold for scrap or rusting at berth in Sevastopol, no other country poses even a popgun's threat to American global sovereignty. We run NATO, we control much of the world's airspace, we run the Atlantic and Pacific Oceans. We are, we know and assume, alone.[9]

Now the gunner grew more animated as he strolled between the high rows of bombs, talking nonstop. He popped open an oil drum whose contents were packed in Styrofoam. Unfused warheads. He handled them the way a butcher handles meat. I envisioned the three of us vanishing in an accidental explosion, blown into peach-colored vapor. Each bomb was wired with a paper tag showing its date of manufacture. Some were Vietnam-era, built in the early Seventies, still usable. The gunner showed us how bombs were assembled on the bomb table. "Six men on a side, we build one in a minute and a half." He showed us where each sailor stood and what each man did, moving on the balls of his feet like a basketball coach sketching out a play. He pointed out one missile about ten feet long that weighed 900 pounds. "This bomb has a bunch of little bombs come out," he explained. "We call them bomblets. There's like 280-something in each bomb, and they'll spread themselves around. You wouldn't want to be under that." His hands opened to imitate the bomb's fuselage. "The pilots really love to drop these and watch them spread." He looked at Doug, who remained unresponsive, his hands hanging at his sides. The crewman touched the bomb's flanks. "I like bombs and missiles and torpedoes, I like all ordnance," he said, "so this is a good job for me." Rubbing the bomb and smiling, he said, "This bomb's got a sister bomb, called Hydra." He looked at another bomb. "This one here's called Gale." He noted items that were part of the "standard missile family." He knew the name, number, payload, and fusing options of every single weapon in the room. He was courteous and attentive to us, and he appeared to perform his responsibilities with vigor. It occurred to me that someone in the Navy, very clever and dark, had identified his special talents and put him there, had understood what type of a person not only survives locked in a roomful of bombs for years at sea but thrives there, believes he is in heaven.

The sight of Doug's discomfort was a relief to me. He was acting like the man I thought I knew, and so, for fifteen or twenty seconds, here in the belly of the ship full of bombs, it felt as if we stood on the same side of the fence, suffering the same alienations, looking at this freaky bomb guy.

But it wasn't that simple. Having spent a total of three years on carriers in his various deployments, Doug had never visited the bomb magazine before. I saw now that this wasn't an accident. He already knew everything there was to know about the size and shape and weight and capability and fusing option of every single weapon. What I mistook for Doug's alienation was, I now suspect, a much more personal and intimate moment about his choice in life, about associations of his job he probably didn't choose to dwell on.

Doug cleared his throat. "Thanks," he said to the crewman. On the way back up eight flights of stairs, Doug and I didn't speak.

But, naturally, I wondered about those bombs and what Doug could do with them. I remembered the phony targets on the eastern U.S. coast in the Blasters' ready room. What if they were real? The Hornet can be outfitted from a vast menu of weapons, twenty-five different types of bombs and missiles (it also carries a six-barrel cannon in its nose that shoots 570 rounds of eight-inch bullets in twenty seconds). On a typical bombing mission, a Hornet will carry air-to-air missiles—Sparrows, Sidewinders—and, depending on how deeply defended the target is, will also carry high-tech "smart" bombs with TV cameras in the nose so that they may, at least theoretically, be targeted by the pilot (or another pilot nearby, via datalink) into something as small as an open window. But the bulk of bombing is accomplished with general-purpose "dumb" bombs, iron casings filled with explosives, with tail fins that allow the bomb to fall in a smooth, definite curve to the target, instead of tumbling through the air.

My Washington, D.C., neighborhood consists of two rows of eight red-brick houses facing one another. The street is lined with eighty-year-old ginkgo trees. If Doug were ordered to attack my neighborhood, he explained to me, it wouldn't take much of his arsenal to destroy it. He'd use 1,000-pound MK 83 or 2,000-pound MK 84 bombs. His divebombing skills had been honed on the bombing ranges of a 108,000-acre air station in Fallon, Nevada, so the bombs would fall within just twenty yards of their target. En route to the target Doug would program the type of bomb and fuse setting into the computer in his cockpit. Given the size of the target he's being sent to destroy—in this case, two rows of two-story houses a block long—he'd set up a program in the air-to-ground mode of the computer so that the bombs would strike the houses in a pattern, say, twenty-five feet apart. He'd follow the heading on his navigational instruments to a spot overhead and, in a steep descent, lay them down on the houses on one side of the street; then he'd turn and lay them down on the other side.

A structure like a house, not reinforced against attack, would be leveled by the smallest bomb he carries. The 2,000-pound bomb would blow up a standard airplane hangar and everything in it, or a block-wide apartment building or a barge or a row of houses. Doug might also consider using some horrifying weapon like the FAE, or fuel air explosive, a canister that disperses huge amounts of fuel into the air that are then ignited to create a vacuum that literally turns human beings inside out and knocks a non-reinforced structure flat. Doug carries enough ordnance on a single run—6,000 pounds—to blow up every man-made structure in sight of my house. The general-purpose bombs, though not designed for penetration, carry enough penetration ability to shred the street and sidewalk and fling pavement into chunks. The ginkgo trees would be defoliated and sheared to stumps. The fire hydrants would explode, sewers would be cut open, electrical wires would come down.

After flying back to the ship, having successfully placed his bombs on target, Doug could be given new orders to conduct another mission, in which case he'd refuel, have new bombs loaded on his wings, and take off again. Returning to this area, he'd view the damage as if for the first time—fire, smoke, dead dogs, blown-up propane tanks, impassable roads.

If some of my neighbors in the next target area were putting up a fight with an antiaircraft artillery gun, he would go after them first. Because of superior U.S. intelligence and detailed satellite photos he would have seen before launching, and with the help of a three-dimensional map of every part of the earth hooked up to the global positioning system inside his cockpit, Doug would know exactly where that artillery gun had been positioned, and he'd draw a line from the eyes of the artillery gunner to the sun and set his angle of attack on that line so that his jet would come out of the sun and this enemy would have to stare directly into it to spot him. He could pinpoint the artillery gun with a supersonic missile, steered by a different pilot headed outside the threat envelope, using a datalink hooked up to the second plane's frequency, steered by a tiny thumbsized mouse on his rudder control stick. Doug would then drop another five tons of bombs. If on his return to the ship he was told that a military facility disguised as the presidential palace or a hospital or a cruise ship or a vegetable farm or a bingo club was his next strike target, he'd bomb it too; he'd execute his orders as many times as they told him to until my whole town was smoldering rubble, mud, and corpses.

• • •

V. An Unauthorized Stroll

Doug was scheduled to fly at 10:00 p.m. and wanted to take a nap, so I left him and roamed the ship. It was vital that I looked like I knew where I was going, because I was absolutely not supposed to be wandering anywhere alone.

I passed the rest of the ready rooms, moving through "Officers' country"—the hallways with blue linoleum floors and wooden handrails on the stairs, where enlisted people were not allowed to walk—and into the regular hallways of basic stainless steel. I hoped that anyone who saw me would think I was one of the private contractors or engineers from General Dynamics, Lockheed Martin, or General Electric who ran complex computer programs and dressed in civilian clothing and joined the ship for the entire cruise, carrying black briefcases and wearing ID badges around their necks that gave them clearance into places otherwise locked. I passed the ship's jail, a small cell painted black, with one innocent bench inside. I found a weight room, one of four, painted bright white with new red vinyl benches and machines, and unbolted a watertight door to enter the cavernous main deck, where planes are stored. Every inch of the ship is a zone belonging to someone, a different fiefdom with its own rules of conduct, and as I stepped between jets a mechanic eyed me. Enlisted people didn't even think of asking me what I was doing; they were just trying to finish their jobs without getting yelled at ("Listen up, shithead," and "Get the fuck off my deck!" were two ways I heard officers addressing sailors). The mechanic had the guts of an F-14 laid out on the floor and was running something deafening that sounded like a vacuum. I knew he'd get in trouble if I stepped on anything, and I'd get in trouble if he asked why I was there, so I queasily tiptoed past him.

I slipped around aileron fins and the folded wings of parked airplanes. In the middle of the main deck sat two huge wood-paneled pleasure boats belonging to the admiral and the captain for use in foreign ports with dignitaries and also to transport officers back and forth for port visits. What a strange sight: two boats in a hangar of planes, inside a ship. The fighter planes had Sidewinders and other missiles loaded onto their wings, with demure little canvas covers on the warhead of what was either a live or a dummy explosive. Sea air blew into this cavern through the house-size bay door; the air felt good after the closeness inside the ship and I could see the ocean beneath the setting sun.

Back inside the narrow corridors I passed along one freezing hallway whose bolted doors said NO ENTRANCE, RESTRICTED ACCESS. I cut across the interior of the ship and walked down another corridor toward the keel, where the air was suddenly 130 degrees, and passed some deafening machinery, which sounded like a roomful of printing presses.

Then I found a "gee dunk," one of the two 7-Eleven-type stores on the ship. A line had formed outside. As I watched, an officer in khakis who outranked everybody else simply cut the line and entered. The file of enlisted people stood by. The store sold aspirin, Timex watches, shampoo, baby powder, pens and paper, hats and pins and decals emblazoned with the *Eisenhower* CVN 69 insignia, Zippos with same, phone cards, Saltines, gym shorts, Norelco electric razors, Barney videos, flavored lollipops, Obsession cologne by Calvin Klein, batteries, Herpecin lip balm, cameras, film, cheese in a can, Tastykakes, ginger snaps, Paco Rabanne face lotion, khaki uniforms, Chicken-in-a-Biscuit crackers, Fig Newtons, cigarettes, tampons. No beer. Nor was any pornography for sale, but the pilots told me that every single man on the *Eisenhower* received the Victoria's Secret catalogue in the mail.

I heard something unintelligible over the loudspeaker, and tried to make it out. At lunch Chip had told me, "if you hear general quarters called and you can't find our ready room quickly, wherever you happen to be, just freeze, because you will soon find a Marine sticking the barrel of his M-16 in your face and asking you what you're doing on the ship."

The tone of the bustle around me seemed unchanged, however, so I moved on, found a staircase, and went down again. I still wanted to find the engine room, perhaps, or the chapel, the two barbershops, the dry cleaner. I found another staircase and went down. Doug said, "You don't want to go down to the lower area where the enlisted people berth," ostensibly because as many as 250 live in one room, sleep on cots in cubbyholes the size of bookshelves, and an officer, like Doug, would disrupt their privacy. But, more important, he explained, I shouldn't walk among enlisted folks because "you don't want to be in places where you're not supposed to be." When I asked for clarification, he said that I could "end up disappeared." One could get attacked. Anyone, even officers, could get beaten and thrown overboard. Maybe this was true, maybe not.

Some crewmen went by carrying a desk. I passed many closed porthole doors, then began to feel lost and doubled back through an enlisted people's rec room/weight room. Music was playing in a much more rough-and-ready atmosphere than the officers' weight room. Guys sat around in sweats watching CNN sports headlines. Nothing felt dangerous. I looked up at the numbers, called a bull's-eye, painted above the doorway, and above every doorway in the ship, which allow people to identify exactly where they are on the ship. I had no idea where I was.

An officer in khakis and a black sweater turned a corner and stared up at the bull's-eye, then at me, and told me unsmilingly that I was not where I should be.

VI. The Pilot's Stateroom

I knocked on Doug's door. He lay on his bunk in the dark, not sleeping. He asked me to flip on the light. Pale fluorescent bulbs came on. His "stateroom" was as ugly and barren as a high school locker room, the furniture and walls constructed of that same thin, dented metal they use to make lockers, with paint chipping on the ceiling; beside the door was a list of phone numbers and a heavy black intership telephone. The room was like the inside of a steel crate, two strides across, and, like the rest of the ship, it shook with vibration.

The bathrooms were no better. Doug had told me to be sure to bring shower shoes "for the scupper trout," because the plumbing got funky onboard sometimes and forced shit back up the shower drains.

And you couldn't find a worse shower—tepid water dribbling out of those water-saver showerheads, cold wind blowing through the stall. When the ship was in port, he said, it couldn't dump sewage, and the whole ship stank. I was onboard for two and a half days, and after the second day, even though we were out on the Atlantic and could dump waste all we wanted, every toilet I visited made my eyes burn.

He started taping a photo of his baby on the metal bureau. "I want to be home more. That's the effect that little bastard has," he said. Aware that soon he would have to perform the night landing, he waved to the face in the photo, stepped across the room, and grabbed his flight suit off a hook on the wall.

I watched Doug carefully in an attempt to understand how he felt about being a father and, potentially, a killer. The answer began to emerge in a conversation with his roommate, Barry, who, in his high-pitched Tennessee cadence said, "We don't train to kill people, we train to stop aggression—to alter things that we as a country see as immoral, like invading Kuwait." Barry had flown twenty-one missions during the Persian Gulf War off the carrier USS *Kennedy* in 1991. His voice quavered with earnestness as he tried to resolve the thrill of flying combat with the remorse he felt for killing. "We don't train to kill people. That's just kind of a by-product, and that's kind of a bummer. It stinks, it really does. People actually die and lose limbs, and it's horrible. Certainly at the moment it's exhilarating—they're shooting at you, you're dodging this, dodging that, and you successfully put your bombs on target. But the reality of it is people die."

I imagined Barry in the months following the Persian Gulf War: a lowly lieutenant junior grade who had, by the war's end, been at sea for two whole years, trying to make sense of the unfinished feelings he'd encountered there. I pictured him standing before a crowd at the local Lions Club or at his church. I imagined him developing some of the phrases he used to describe his bombings, and I saw how over time he might have been able to turn his own actions into a kind of victimization. I saw his struggle as a way to create order out of chaos, to explain rationally the irrational act of killing people.

He described his very first night mission of the war, when Iraqi weaponry had not yet been vaporized and the enemy was offering up an enormous defense. His strike group dodged bombs and missiles the size of telephone poles, flew through dense clouds of antiaircraft artillery; he dropped his bombs on the target and watched them explode and then on the way back to the ship had four missiles fired at him in a span of ninety seconds, tracking the heat signature of his plane's exhaust; he dodged and flipped upside-down, spitting out flares and chaff (flares, if someone's shooting a heat-seeking missile; chaff, to defeat enemy radar). Planes thirty miles in front of him from a different strike were also spitting out flares, which were indistinguishable from the missiles coming at him in the night sky; other pilots in Hawkeyes and Prowlers and Tomcats and Hornets thousands of feet above him watched the scene unfold, calling out warnings. Barry got so flustered he ended up heading back toward the antiaircraft artillery he'd just passed through.

Doug said, "I think there is an enlightenment to dropping live bombs on people that I have not experienced."

They were a strange pair. Doug, whom I knew well and who hardly spoke, wanted to tell me the secrets in his heart but could not. Barry, whom I didn't want to interview, seemed suspicious of me yet would not stop confessing and explaining himself. I think of these two men, sitting in that stateroom, trying to make sense of their lives, of the drudgery and possible loss of life, and I think of how through them the United States maintains stability over the world. The fact and image and idea of the American pilot and his jet is one of the ways America explains itself to its citizenry and to the rest of the world, friend and foe alike. Barry and Doug figure, somehow, in the stable price of crude oil, the primacy of the New York Stock Exchange, the national anthem sung at the Super Bowl. They are the ever-sharp knife in Secretary of Defense William Cohen's silk pocket, they are the darkest undertone of Secretary of State Madeleine Albright's stern posturing. At night when I listen to the C-Span State Department press conference on the radio, and hear State Department spokesman James Rubin lecture that "the use of force" might be "the desired and best outcome" in "furtherance" of international objectives, I think of Barry and Doug in their room, living inside this concept, the threat of "force." When President Clinton says, "All options remain on the table" in Kosovo or Iraq, he's referring to Doug and his colleagues. When he asserted, as he did in his December 16 announcement of the bombing of Iraq, "We are delivering a powerful message to Saddam," his words were made of the flesh of pilots.

Doug explained that the risks were known—one in four died during a twenty-year career—and he kept a will on file with the squadron, in case of a mishap. He had had talks with Sarah; she was always very strong about such things, though in the last conversation, "She got a little edgy," because now they had a son.

I mentioned that I'd read that Naval aviation was safer now.

"Safer than what?" Doug asked. "I personally know ten guys—these are guys I flew in the same airplane with, students and instructors—who died in crashes in my twelve years in the Navy." Barry sat calmly and listened, nodding along. "Not just people I'd met or knew—that number is much higher. But these are names written in my flight log." Later he told me, "My roommate on my first cruise, a guy named 'Wild Bill,' was killed because of a mechanical problem in an F-14. They fixed that problem after it killed him. My T-2 instructor, Victor, had a bird strike a few years after he taught me, and the bird came through the canopy and killed him. Randy didn't fuel his plane properly, and it rolled over on him on takeoff. His student ejected and walked away. Craig flew into the water two years ago. A kid I taught in Kingsville, I forget what happened to him. Eric flew into a mountain in Japan. Rob flew into a mountain in Virginia. His bombardier navigator was killed, too. XO and Chet had a midair and were killed."[10]

Doug went on, "The most disturbing one was a Harrier pilot, a Marine guy I trained with, who was lost at sea. He just never showed up back at the ship."

I asked Doug what his father thought of all this.

"Every time I go home my dad cries."

Barry interrupted. "Your dad, too?"

VII. The Cat Seat

After dinner Doug and I entered the Carrier Air Traffic Control Center, which Doug called the "cat seat"—a cool, dark room where dull green lights glowed in the ceiling and a bank of radar screens and floor-to-ceiling clear Plexiglas backlit status boards formed a wall in front of us. Doug joined Chip and Pepe Harris to help with any emergencies the other Blasters might have in the air that night. All the other airborne squadrons had their own representatives, so the two long benches were almost full. A large man in khakis sat in the center of the room, coffee mug on the arm of his chair, staring straight ahead at the screens. A woman in a headset stood before the Plexiglas status board filling in boxes so that for each type of plane, we could see exactly how much gas the plane had, what the plane weighed, where it was in the sky, and projected times when it would have to refuel at the airborne tanker if it ran out of gas. She wrote numbers quickly in white grease pencil and because she stood on the wrong side of the Plexiglas, she wrote backwards.

The control rooms were placed all together here in the center corridor of the ship. Behind the Carrier Air Traffic Control Center was a larger dark room with a six-foot-tall triptych of computer projections showing a map of the world displayed on a wall, the purpose of which was to track any important ship or aircraft positions around the globe.[11] Behind that room was one that relayed attack plans to everyone airborne and tracked air activity within 100 miles of the ship; another room specialized in tracking submarine and torpedo threats, another watched vessels on the water, another positioned the ship in a fight, another positioned the whole battle group, telling the subs and missile cruisers and frigates where to go to meet up with the Air Force and Marine and Army ground troops, coordinating those movements with the movements of our NATO allies.

Each room was manned by skinny young sailors staring at screens in semi-darkness, sitting beside other sailors speaking on telephones in monotone streams of acronyms. In front of them their supervising officers sat in swivel chairs. If and when it came time to fight a war, control of the actual combat would descend in a pyramid shape of commands with surveillance and intelligence redundantly overlapping. The crew here on the *Eisenhower* would be compiling and sharing information simultaneously with the ship's captain upstairs on the bridge, and with the admiral of the battle group, who also had a dark room like this around the corner. (He never went anywhere without his "admiral's aide," who was young and blond and handsome. Somebody at lunch called him "towel boy.") They in turn would be in contact with CINCLANT—the commander in chief of the Atlantic fleet, based in Norfolk, Virginia, and with generals and strategists at the Pentagon, who with the help of modern technology might be able to run the next war in their pajamas.

As to whether aircraft carriers are still necessary, the answer, of course, depends on who is being asked. Because "forward deployment" of American military resources is supposed to "deter and prevent foreign aggression," Army strategists ask how a carrier, which does not come into contact with a population, can provide as much preventative "influence" as the 37,000 American troops that have been stationed in Seoul for the last forty years. The Air Force, in turn, argues that in the three regions where U.S. military deployments are most likely—the Middle East, Europe, and northeast Asia—military access is already assured and that, moreover, there are only a handful of countries on the planet that wouldn't welcome us to refuel bombers in their territory; if our military decides to shoot a Tomahawk missile across, say, Syria's airspace, we only need to ask Syria's permission. Yet the Navy insists that forward deployment comes down to intimidation. A soldier is just a man; an Air Force plane is here and then zoom, gone. Navy posters call a carrier "90,000 tons of diplomacy" and "four and a half acres of sovereign U.S. territory, when it's needed." Or, as Steve Fleischmann, a former State Department intelligence officer, admitted to me, "Nobody knows what the carrier is out there for. We just know it's big."

The longer I stayed on the carrier and the more I learned about the ship's capabilities, the more threatening the world became—like a big, bug-infested peach—and the safer I felt aboard. More than once I imagined a full-scale invasion of the United States by some unspecified aggressor and how safe I'd be here, and thought of my girlfriend back home, poor soul, innocent and trusting enough to sleep at night without a helmet. Unprotected, unarmed people of America seemed farcical to me, unbelievably naive and misguided dummies. Every few minutes I learned about some other amazing weapon: the radar-guided Phalanx Gatling gun on each comer of the ship that can fire fifty rounds a second at the front end of a missile the diameter of a pie plate approaching the ship at 500 miles an hour and obliterate it in midair. Others were too fantastic to believe: a secret radar so powerful it bounces off the moon and fries the electronics of anything airborne, causing it to drop out of the sky. Hearing about these weapons gave me the same dull cushiony feeling I had when I took Dilaudid, synthetic morphine, after having my wisdom teeth ripped out. Nothing could happen to me out here, nothing could touch me, nobody in the world. I come from a family of very paranoid people—if you wake one of us up in the middle of the night we jump to our feet in karate position—and this was the first time in my life that I was surrounded by people far more paranoid than I am.

The lighting in the cat seat reminded me of a dark, late-night bar lounge, except that the days of drinking and smoking in here were gone and nothing about this room was relaxing. Each landing began with the pilot's voice playing loudly over the speaker, "Two-oh-six-Hornet-ball-four-point-five," signaling his plane's approach and the beginning of dread. Then we'd all look up on the black-and-white TV screen in the corner to see how the approach looked, and although every pilot watching beside me stayed cool, by the micro-mumblings and grunts or bits of laughter you could get a sense of whether the pilot on approach would make his landing. I also noticed a kind of bull's-eye on the TV screen that after a few landings helped gauge whether the plane would hit home in the right spot on the deck, whether it was coming in high or low (the best pilots could also get a sense of glide slope, velocity, relative position of the jet to the center line off the television). The pilots were all business, and their reaction to a bad landing attempt was always the same disgust. It was what separated them from their nightmares.

Then there was the noise, through the ceiling, of the planes crashing onto the deck. The arresting wires laced through the surrounding walls and were connected to the tractor-trailer-size hydraulics two rooms away. Every fifty seconds you heard, first, a whistling, which was the approaching jet; followed by a shudder as the jet hit the ship; a loud clacking, which was the arresting cable paying out, sounding like an enormous broken torque wrench pinging and banging against metal; a hollow steel sound like a washing machine flailing with broken gears; followed by anvil-size booming hammer blows pounding down on the ceiling just above us. Pepe sat on the far side of Chip with a clipboard on his lap reading the status boards, making notations. Doug and Chip watched the planes on the TV screen. Everyone ignored the noise.

So far the Blasters were having a perfect night. Then Phil Poliquin came over the loudspeaker as he approached. In the view of the fuzzy TV monitor he looked to be high at the ship's ramp, the nose of the plane up, and he "boltered" (landing beyond the area where the arresting cables lay before touching down, his dragging hook making an awful sound, missing the fourth wire); off he accelerated for another try (otherwise he would have dropped into the ocean). A pilot from another squadron sitting behind us muttered, "That was ugly," and laughed. A minute later Phil came around again, this time too close to the ramp with his nose pointed too steeply down, adding power in a burst at the end to keep from flying into the back of the ship, and caught a number 1 wire, hitting the deck with an enormous thump. Chip turned and said, "Ouch." Phil was done for the night. The essential ingredient in night carrier landings is an intangible— which Phil had lost tonight, going from too long on the first pass to too short on the second. Pepe wrote something down on his clipboard. Doug folded his hands around the coffee cup in his lap and watched the screen.

Fetus caught a number 2 and then a number 3 wire. It sounded each time like he was crashing through the ceiling. Latka called over the radio, right behind Fetus; he was mysteriously low on fuel. The Hornet burns 100 pounds (15 gallons) of fuel a minute on approach, and Latka was 1,000 pounds short. The problem was serious. Latka had only two more chances to try to land before he would need to go to the airborne refueling tanker or head to the mainland.

Latka came in high and shallow, and boltered. Two bolters for the Blasters. Chip got up and stretched his short legs, sat back down, and rubbed his bald head. Doug said, "It's no big deal. This shit happens all the time." A minute later over the loudspeaker Latka called in his altitude and fuel status; five minutes of flying time before he'd have to head to land or get more gas.

The pointy nose of his F/A-18 came into view on the TV. Another bad approach and he bolstered again; the mood in the room shifted. Pepe exited the cat seat to see when Latka began his flight. Doug figured out exactly how many minutes of fuel Latka had left to keep him airborne. The officer in front of us called the boss in "primary flight," air-traffic control, in the tower; who called the airport in Oceana, Virginia, to see what time they closed in case Latka had to coast to a landing on fumes. (When a pilot has real trouble getting aboard he goes to the tanker as many times as is needed; compared to the $35 million plane and the $2 million cost of a pilot's training, fuel is the cheapest expendable out here. The reach for a seaside airport is a final option if the carrier is too far, but if the ship is in, say, the Kara Sea, 250 miles from shore, or if the weather is bad, there may not be a safe way to land.)

They announced over the deck loudspeaker that Latka was "Bingo on the ball"—his fuel status was dire. One pass away from bad trouble. Doug looked at me matter-of-factly and said, "He's trick or treat." He added, somewhat more compassionately, "Latka's tired and ashamed and is going to be beating himself up hard right now, inside his jet, and that'll just make everything worse." Doug said, "Latka's solid, no question. But if he shows any kind of a trend, develops any kind of a pattern, he'll be removed and retired."

Pepe returned and looked at his clipboard and said, "The whole schedule is backed up now." Then Latka came in very smoothly on the TV monitor and caught a number 2 wire. Chip turned to Doug and said, "It's a good thing I'm already bald."

VIII. On the Flight Deck at Night

Doug looked at his watch. It was almost time to fly. He suddenly seemed fragile. He hadn't slept well the night before and complained how he wasn't yet in the groove of life on the ship, how it would only get worse, how this first week always felt like a month, the first month felt like a year. I wondered if the lack of sleep would bother him when he was flying. He hung his head and said, "Sometimes they fly us all night just to stress us." The fear in his face reminded me of who he used to be. Then it was 9:00 p.m., and he said he was going to head to his rack for a few minutes, to get into his "box"—not some coffin he kept handy, but the common term for the inviolable time before flying. From the time he left the cat seat until he reached his jet at 10:00 p.m., if anybody wanted to speak to him he'd say, "I'm in my box," and they would have to wait until later. He went to his crappy stateroom and closed the door, and in anticipation of landing his jet on the ship, did something to his mind.

A few minutes before ten, he dressed in his flight gear. It seems appropriate that when he's at work he wears an elaborate costume, a strange form-fitting G suit, like a giant external jockstrap, with its rubber air bladders that inflate when he flies to keep the blood pressure up in the top half of his body so that he won't faint while doing what he has to do; the white helmet, the tight rubber oxygen mask, fireproof gloves. He went up to the deck. After his plane captain signed off as the final inspector of number 205, Doug did his own preflight check, looking for any oddity, maybe a blown hydraulic line leaking on the graphite and epoxy skin of the jet. At the end of the tail-hook bar, tucked up between the Hornet's two jet engines, Doug examined an ordinary looking nut and bolt the size of a quarter, made of titanium, that held the hook onto the bar. Notched through the nut and bolt was an inch-long cotter pin, folded over on one side. Before every flight Doug grabbed the pin and pulled on it. If the pin were to break or fall out, or if, by a deck strike or some other bad coincidence the hook came off, there wouldn't be any way for him to snag the wire to arrest his landing.

Heater took me out to the flight deck to watch. We wore earplugs and flameproof life vests and ski hats, and he pulled out a little flash-light with a red lens. Then we were on the outside platform that rims the deck of the ship. I didn't know it until I saw water shooting by beneath my feet through a steel grate. This was the darkness I'd been hearing about. Heater pointed the light down where I stepped, making sure I didn't trip, and we moved carefully along the edge of the flight deck—you couldn't see the edge at all—toward a small, exposed spot off to one side of the landing strip, the LSO (landing signal officers') platform. From there the LSOs—pilots themselves—helped the air-borne pilots to land, while grading each attempt. Behind us hung a huge rubber safety net, stretching seven stories above the water; if a plane came crashing toward us, we were supposed to jump into that.

We were in the middle of the ocean, without the moon, whipping along as fast as a water-ski boat. A jet came invisibly out of the dark-ness and landed, kicking up dislodged pieces of rubber from the newly tarred deck, and in the momentary light I saw that there were five or six people up here besides Heater and myself: two female helicopter pilots, one with a French-braided ponytail, the other wearing a long wool ski hat with a pom-pom on the end, and a couple of LSOs from other squadrons. When the plane passed it got dark again. I couldn't see my hand in front of my face.

Up at the catapult, Doug pushed the throttle up, watching the plane captain for signals, waiting for the engines to spool up, watching the RPMs, temperature, fuel flow, hydraulic pressure. He didn't have the same fears about night launches that he had about landings. "I guess I put faith in all that engineering. If it works, it's gonna work. If it doesn't work, you're gonna die, there's nothing you can do about it." He cleared his head and did a quick emergency procedure, touching the thick braided loop of the ejection handle between his legs, and a second later the whole ship shook and off he went.

After a while a few stars became visible. On nights like this, Heater told me, it was just as confusing for the LSOs as it was for the pilots. They have the same problem orienting themselves to the horizon line. Heater said, "It feels like you're wearing a baseball hat that goes on forever. Sometimes they'll throw a flare in the water just off the stern of the ship to give everyone a relative sense of things."

Depending on the cycle of the moon and the altitude of the cloud ceiling, the pilot's view in the final seconds of approach is the ship's minuscule landing-strip light, a dull sodium beacon. At 4,000 feet, three miles, and a mere forty-five seconds away, the huge ship is a dot of light the size of a pinhead held at arm's length. (The ship, painted matte, is designed to be invisible at night.) The sensation in pitch darkness, one pilot told me, is that one is sitting still while the tiny glowing pinhead of light becomes, in a disorienting and unnatural rush, the deck of the carrier. Doug's fear, I knew, caught him like a bowling ball rising in his throat. He got terrified enough to try to give a name to all that void in his mind. But the only thing for the pilot to see inside the void is the pilot. It is the fact of his total aloneness that draws out the conflicts in his identity. This is when he is most clear about the unpleasantness of himself. He's forced to contemplate himself. But any thought, if you repeat it enough times, even if it's the truth, begins to sound like nothing. The essence of one's paradoxical nature goes poof, and the fear stops scaring you.

Doug's mind locked onto the target, the ship speeding ahead. Sloping downward, he got squarely behind the stern and backed off his airspeed. A good pilot, Doug told me, can sense acceleration in his chest. Now Doug intuited his closing speed, making fine corrections with the stick, and nudged the nose up, the gently rolling deck rising up out of the dark in front of him. His unconscious athleticism married all his senses, and in that last twenty seconds the actual features of the deck became visible to him. Beside me the woman with the wool pom-pom hat stared up into the black sky with binoculars, unable to see anything other than three colored lights, and spoke to Doug by radio, coughing up commands every half second: "Power." "Right." "Don't go low." He came over the landing area, and it disappeared beneath him. His landing gear took the intense shock, and I stepped forward as he went by and watched him pull the number 3 wire right to the edge of the deck.

Landing—perfect. Of course.

I found Doug afterward, that line from the mask indenting his cheek again, a grin of relief on his face. He'd made his second landing without incident. He poured some coffee (it was almost midnight), and as we headed down to the wardroom for one last meal of meat loaf, he mentioned that when he'd climbed into his jet at ten, he noticed that two of the cockpit instruments that help the pilot with his approach, the "needles" and the "bull's-eye," were broken. A third navigational instrument, the least desirable of the three, still worked. Doug, trained for less than perfect conditions, took off anyway.

In the wardroom we found Latka lost in thought, eating in a corner by himself. He looked spooked, as if he were trying to hold it together. Doug and I sat with our food trays, and they spoke about fuel problems. Latka took his fork and knife and cleared a space on the blue tablecloth to show Doug how, after taking on fuel, he got stuck sitting behind a Tomcat waiting to launch and couldn't get around him, and didn't get any help from the tower, both planes running their engines, the Tomcat blowing exhaust into Latka's air intake as he sat there for thirty minutes, second in line. This was why he'd come back aboard so low on fuel—it was the Tomcat, it was the tower. Doug listened. He was patient but explained, "It's your fault. I know what you're thinking but you're wrong."

"Two bolters are a lot worse than one. It sucks," Latka said. "The worst part is that everybody's laughing at you." For the rest of the meal Latka quietly bit his fingernails.

Doug grabbed some cake and strutted stiffly out, still somehow my longtime friend, yet also the man in the visored helmet and tight oxygen mask, now and forever unknown to me.

Notes

1 The ship carries 120 pilots divided into nine squadrons, three of which—the Sunliners, the Rams, and Doug's group, the Blue Blasters—fly F/A-18 Hornets. The other squadrons fly F-14 fighters, radar-jamming EA-6B Prowlers, anti-submarine S-3B Vikings, and radar communications E-2C Hawkeyes as well as SH-60 helicopters. A C-2 Greyhound ferries mail and personnel back and forth.

2 There are four two-inch-thick steel cables suspended five inches high across the back of the flight deck. Number 1 is closest to the stern. Number 3 is preferred because it's safely away from the edge of the stern. Hitting the edge is called a "rampstrike." The plane folds in half at the belly and explodes.

3 Fighter planes sometimes plunge into the ocean without warning, and I'd read about jet engines capriciously catching fire, about crash landings, infernos tumbling across the flight deck. In ejection, the canopy blows off the plane and then the pilot shoots straight out in his rocket-powered ejection seat. Seats today are "zero-zero" capable, meaning that at zero altitude and zero ground speed, the seat will send a pilot high enough for his parachute to deploy effectively. Two months before my visit, one of the F/A-18 pilots, Tom "Big Comet" Halley, had to eject after a weak launch. Halley survived, but his $35 million jet was lost. The Navy doesn't retrieve planes that fall into the ocean unless doing so aids its investigation of the incident.

4 If I had fallen, I could have clung to the safety officer's pant leg and taken him with me. Perhaps we would have survived the seven-story fall and a helicopter would have had to pluck us out. But people disappear on carriers; sometimes there's an explanation, sometimes not. I'd been warned, in both written and verbal form, about the jet exhaust that could knock you off your feet or fry you dead where you stood. The air intakes on the jets could suck you in whole. Propellers, especially at

night, are quiet and invisible. The arresting cables on the landing strip sometimes snap during arrestment and whip across the deck, razoring sailors in half the way a knife cuts through butter. An ensign told me a few days later that when someone goes off the deck unseen, his disappearance might not be noted until the next roll call, which could be as long as twelve hours later. By then the ship could be 300 miles away.

5 Military-grade jet fuel burns at a rate of between $1,000 and $4,000 an hour in the F/A-18. Over Doug's twelve years, the gas for his 3,000 flight hours cost perhaps $4,000,000.

6 Doug later explained that the tint was designed to filter out certain parts of the light spectrum for pilots using night-vision goggles. I tried the goggles on in a dark closet in the squadron's equipment room; weighing about twenty ounces, and at a cost of tens of thousands of dollars, they made everything appear to glow green, as if I were peering through a jar of mint jelly.

7 I found his fear notable, given the fighter pilot's gift for intuiting the relationship of the three spatial dimensions, moving objects, and time. I am reminded that in college one night my friend Jim was at the wheel of his tired red Subaru driving recklessly on a hard snowpacked road in New Hampshire. Doug sat in the passenger seat and I was in the back. As a five-ton municipal sand dumptruck approached, our car went into a skid. "Lift your foot off the brake, Jim," Doug commanded. We stopped skidding, and Doug actually helped Jim steer the car away from the oncoming truck. It was over in a flash, and he may have saved our lives.

8 The pilots' nicknames seemed to me transparently supermacho, and I couldn't say "Hi, Heater," with a straight face, but the pilots' use of them suggests not just a willful conformity of identity but a de facto recognition of their own interchangeability and perishability.

[9] The cost of this supremacy is staggering, so large as almost to be invisible to the average citizen—except, of course, if you happen to be standing on a tiny fraction of it steaming across the Atlantic at a cost to taxpayers of $444 million a year, or $51,000 an hour. America's 1999 military budget—$271 billion—is more than triple that of Russia, which has the next highest, and greater than the total expenditures of the next six biggest military spenders. Despite the current lack of a real threat, the Pentagon continues to believe that the military must be capable of fighting two wars simultaneously; for example, in North Korea and in the Persian Gulf.

[10] At the very moment we were speaking, a few doors away, Doug's old friend Ronald "Rhino" Wise was readying for his nighttime landing. Thirty-six, married, father of three, he'd be redeploying with Doug and Barry to the Mediterranean, and on July 30, ten weeks later, he'd be killed after ejecting from his plane following a midair collision with another F-14 during a training flight off Turkey's coast. By September the air wing had suffered three disastrous mishaps, losing two F/A-18s and one F-14; one involved Heater. At the end of the month, new Navy statistics revealed that pilots were crashing their planes at twice the previous year's rate. The rise was attributed to the fact that Navy pilots are increasingly overworked.

[11] A huge sailor with the face of Rodney Dangerfield showed me a book filled with codes for every vessel in the NATO alliance; it looked like a big-city telephone book, with thousands of names and numbers, Italian submarines, Swedish helicopter gunships, Turkish amphibious landing crafts. The codes were changed every few weeks, and the old book would be thrown away.

from The Right Stuff
by Tom Wolfe

John Glenn made America's first manned orbital flight in February, 1962. The mission did not go quite as planned. Tom Wolfe (born 1931) described Glenn's ride in The Right Stuff.

At the outset neither Glenn nor his wife, Annie, foresaw the sort of excitement that was going to build up over his flight. Glenn regarded Shepard as the winner of the competition, since he looked at it the way pilots had always looked at it on the great ziggurat of flying. Al had been picked for *the first flight,* and there was no getting around that. He had been the first American to go into space. It was as if he were the project pilot for Mercury. The best Glenn could hope for was to play Scott Crossfield to Shepard's Chuck Yeager. Yeager had broken the sound barrier and become the True Brother of all the True Brothers, but at least Crossfield had gone on to become the first man to fly Mach 2 and, later on, the first man to fly the X-15.

Not even when reporters began arriving in New Concord, Ohio, his old hometown, and pushing his parents' doorbell and roaming and foaming over the town like gangs of strays, looking for anything, scraps, morsels of information about John Glenn—not even then did Glenn fully realize just what was about to happen. The deal with *Life* kept all but *Life* reporters away from him, and so the other fellows were out trying to root up whatever they could. That seemed to be the explanation. The Cape hadn't turned into a madhouse yet. As late as December, Glenn could go out to the strip on Route A1A in Cocoa Beach with Scott Carpenter, who was training with him as backup man, out to that little Kontiki Village joint, whatever the name of it was, and listen to the combo play "Beyond the Reef." John got a kick out of "Beyond the Reef." By early January, however, it was madness to try to go to the Kontiki joint or anywhere else in Cocoa Beach. There were now reporters all over the place, all of them rabid for a glimpse of John Glenn. They would even pile into the little Presbyterian church when John went there on Sunday and turn the service into a sort of muffled melee, with the photographers trying to keep quiet and muscle their way into position at the same time. They were really terrible. So John and Scott now stuck pretty much to the base, working out on the procedures trainer and the capsule itself. At night, in Hangar S, John would try to answer the fan mail. But it was like trying to beat back the ocean with a hammer. The amount of mail he was getting was incredible.

Nevertheless, the training regimen created a curtain around John, and he didn't really have as clear an idea of the storm of publicity . . . and the *passion* of it all . . . as his wife did. At their house in Arlington, Virginia, Annie was getting the whole storm, and she had practically no protection from it and few happy distractions. John's flight was first scheduled for December 20, 1961, but bad weather over the Cape kept forcing postponements. He was finally set to go on January 27. He was inserted into the capsule before dawn. Annie was in a state. She was petrified. This had little to do with fear for John's life, however. Annie could take that kind of pressure. She had been through the whole course of worrying over a pilot. John had flown in combat in the Pacific Theater in the Second World War and then in Korea. In Korea he was hit seven times by flak. Annie had also been through just about everything that Pax River had to inflict upon a pilot's wife, short of the visit of the Friend of Widows and Orphans at her own door. But one thing she had never done. She had never had to step outside after one of John's flights and say a few words on television. She knew that would be coming up when John flew, and she was already dreading the moment. Some of the other wives were at her house for the Danger Wake, and she asked them to bring some tranquilizers. She wouldn't need them for the flight. She would take them before she had to step outside for the ordeal with the TV people. With her ferocious stutter . . . the thought of millions of people, or even hundreds, or even five . . . seeing her struggling on television . . . She had been in front of microphones with John before, and John always knew how to step in and save the day. She had certain phrases she had no trouble with—"Of course," "Certainly," "Not at all," "Wonderful," "I hope not," "That's right," "I don't think so," "Fine, thank you," and so on— and most of the questions from the television reporters were so simpleminded she could handle them with those eight phrases, plus "yes" and "no"—and John or one of the children would chime in if any amplification was called for. They were a great team that way. But today she would have to solo.

Annie could see the impending catastrophe easily enough. All she had to do was look at the television screen. Any channel . . . it didn't matter . . . she could count on seeing some woman holding a microphone covered in black foam rubber and giving a declamation on the order of:

"Inside this trim, modest suburban home is Annie Glenn, wife of Astronaut John Glenn, sharing the anxiety and pride of the entire world at this tense moment but in a very private and very crucial way that only she can understand. One thing has prepared Annie Glenn for this test of her own courage and will sustain her through this test, and that one thing is her faith: her faith in the ability of her husband, her faith in the efficiency and dedication of the thousands of engineers and other personnel who provide his guidance system . . . and her faith in Almighty God . . ."

In the picture on the screen all you could see was the one TV woman, with the microphone in her hand, standing all by herself in front of Annie's house. The curtains were pulled, somewhat unaccountably, inasmuch as it was nine o'clock in the morning, but it all looked very cozy. In point of fact, the lawn, or what was left of it, looked like Nut City. There were three or four mobile units from the television networks with cables running through the grass. It looked as if Arlington had been invaded by giant toasters. The television people, with all their gaffers and go-fers and groupies and cameramen and couriers and technicians and electricians, were blazing with 200-watt eyeballs and ricocheting off each other and the assembled rabble of reporters, radio stringers, tourists, lollygaggers, policemen, and free-lance gawkers. They were all craning and writhing and rolling their eyes and gesturing and jabbering away with the excitement of the event. A public execution wouldn't have drawn a crazier mob. It was the kind of crowd that would have made the Fool Killer lower his club and shake his head and walk away, frustrated by the magnitude of the opportunity.

Meanwhile, John is up on top of the rocket, the Atlas, a squat brute, twice the diameter of the Redstone. He's lying on his back in the human holster of the Mercury capsule. The count keeps dragging on. There's hold after hold because of the weather. The clouds are so heavy they will make it impossible to monitor the launch properly. Every day for five days Glenn has psyched himself up for the big event, only to have a cancellation because of the weather. Now he has been up there for four hours, four and a half, five hours—he has been stuffed into the capsule, lying on his back, for five hours, and the engineers decide to scrub the flight because of the heavy cloud cover.

He's drained. He makes his way back to Hangar S, and they start taking the suit off and unwiring him. John is sitting there in the ready room with just the outer covering of the suit off—he still has on the mesh lining underneath and all the sensors attached to his sternum and his rib cage and his arms—and a delegation from NASA comes trooping in to confront him with the following message from on high:

John, we hate to trouble you with this, but we're having a problem with your wife.

My wife?

Yes, she won't cooperate, John. Perhaps you can give her a call. There's a phone hookup right here.

A call?

Absolutely befuddled, John calls Annie. Annie is inside their house in Arlington with a few of the wives, a few friends, and Loudon Wainwright, the writer from *Life*, watching the countdown and, finally, the cancellation on television. Outside is the bedlam of the reporters baying for scraps of information about the ordeal of Annie Glenn—and resenting the fact that *Life* has exclusive access to the poignant drama. A few blocks away, on a quaint Arlington side street, in a limousine, waits Lyndon Johnson, Vice-President of the United States. Kennedy had appointed Johnson his special overseer for the space program. It was the sort of meaningless job that Presidents give Vice-Presidents, but it had a symbolic significance now that Kennedy was presenting manned space flight as the very vanguard of his New Frontier (version number two). Johnson, like many men who have had the job of Vice-President before him, has begun suffering from publicity deprivation. He decides he wants to go inside the Glenn household and console Annie Glenn over the ordeal, the excruciating pressure of the five-hour wait and the frustrating cancellation. To make this sympathy call all the more memorable, Johnson decides it would be nice if he brought in NBC-TV, CBS-TV, and ABC-TV along with him, in the form of a pool crew that will feed the touching scene to all three networks and out to the millions. The only rub—the only rub, to Johnson's way of thinking—is that he wants the *Life* reporter, Wainwright, to get out of the house, because his presence will antagonize the rest of the print reporters who can't get in, and they will not think kindly of the Vice-President.

What he does not realize is that the only ordeal that Annie Glenn has been going through has been over the possibility that she was going to have to step outside at some point and spend sixty seconds or so stammering a few phrases. And now . . . various functionaries and secret-service personnel are calling on the telephone and banging on the door to inform her that the Vice-President is already in Arlington, in a White House limousine, waiting to pull up and charge in and pour ten minutes of hideous Texas soul all over her on nationwide TV. Short of the rocket blowing up under John, this is the worst thing she can imagine occurring in the entire American space program. At first Annie is trying to deal with it gracefully by saying that she can't possibly ask *Life* to leave, not only because of the contract, but because of their good personal relationship. Wainwright, being no fool, doesn't particularly care to get caught in the middle like this and so he offers to bow out, to leave. But Annie is not about to give up her *Life* shield at this point. Her mind is made up. She's getting angry. She tells Wainwright: "You're *not leaving* this house!" Her anger does wonders for her stutter. It flattens it right out temporarily. She's practically ordering him to stay. Annie's stutter often makes people underestimate her, and Johnson's people didn't realize that she was a Presbyterian pioneer wife living in full vitality in the twentieth century. She could deal with any five of them with just a few amps from the wrath of God when she was angry. Finally, they're getting the picture. She's too much for them. So they start trying to bend arms at NASA to get someone to *order* her to play ball. But it has to be done very rapidly. Johnson is sitting out there a few blocks away in his limousine, fuming and swearing and making life hell for everyone within earshot, wondering, in so many words, why the fuck there isn't anybody on his staff who can deal with a *housewife*, f'r chrissake, and his staff is leaning on NASA, and NASA is bucking the problem up the chain, until in a matter of minutes it's at the top, and the delegation is trooping into Hangar S to confront the astronaut himself.

So there's John, with half his mesh underlining hanging off his body and biosensor wires sprouting from out of his thoracic cage . . . there's John, covered with sweat, drawn, deflated, beginning to feel very tired after waiting for five hours for 367,000 pounds of liquid oxygen to explode under his back . . . and the hierarchy of NASA has one thing on its mind: keeping Lyndon Johnson happy. So John puts in the call to Annie, and he tells her: "Look, if you don't want the Vice-President or the TV networks or anybody else to come into the house, then that's it as far as I'm concerned, they are *not* coming in—and I will back you up all the way, one hundred percent, and you tell them that. I don't want Johnson or any of the rest of them to put so much as *one toe* inside our house!"

That was all that Annie needed, and she simply became a wall. She wouldn't even discuss the matter any further, and there was no question any longer about Johnson getting in. Johnson, of course, was furious. You could hear him bellowing and yelling over half of Arlington, Virginia. He was talking about his aides. *Pansies! Cows! Gladiolas!* Webb could scarcely believe what was going on. The astronaut and his wife had shut the door in the Vice-President's face. Webb had a few words with Glenn. Glenn wouldn't back down an inch. He indicated that Webb was *way out of line.*

Way out of line! What the hell was this? Webb couldn't figure out what was happening. How could the number-one man, himself, the administrator of NASA, be *way out of line?* Webb called in some of his top deputies and described the situation. He said he was considering changing the order of the flight assignments—i.e., putting another astronaut in Glenn's place. This flight required a man who could comprehend the broader interests of the program better. His deputies looked at him as if he were crazy. He'd never get away with it! *The astronauts* wouldn't stand for it! . . . They had their differences, but on something like this the seven would stand together like an army . . . Webb was beginning to see something he had never quite figured out before. The astronauts were not *his* men. They were in a category new to American life. They were single-combat warriors. If anything, *he* was *their* man.

One could imagine what would happen if Webb tried to exercise his authority nonetheless . . . Here comes the showdown . . . the seven Mercury astronauts on the TV . . . explaining that in the very moments when their lives are on the line, he, Webb, is meddling, trying to curry favor with Lyndon Johnson, being vindictive because John Glenn's wife, Annie, would not let the hideous hand-wringing Texan into her living room to emote all over her on nationwide television . . . He sits in his office suite in Washington while their hides are up on the tip of the rocket . . . One could see the lines drawn in just that way. Webb would be issuing denials, furiously . . . Kennedy would be the umpire— and it wasn't too hard to figure out which way the decision would go. The changing of the assignments was never mentioned again.

Not long thereafter an old friend visited Webb in his corner office, and Webb unburdened himself.

"Look at this office," he said, making a grand gesture across a room with all the trappings of Cabinet-level rank known to the General Services Administration syllabus. "And I . . . *cannot . . . get . . . a . . . simple . . . order . . . carried out!*"

But in the next moment his mood changed. "All the same," he said, "I love those guys. They're putting their lives on the line for their country."

Dryden and Gilruth decided to postpone the launch for at least two weeks, to the middle of February. Glenn made a statement to the press about the delays. He said that anybody who knew the first thing about "the flight test business" expected delays; they were all part of it; the main thing was not to involve people who became "panicky" when everything didn't go just right . . . Glenn went home to Arlington for a three-day weekend. While he was there, President Kennedy invited him to the White House for a private get-together. He did not invite Webb or Johnson to join them.

On February 20 Glenn was once again squeezed inside the Mercury capsule on top of the Atlas rocket, lying on his back, whiling away the holds in the countdown by going over his checklist and looking at the scenery through the periscope. If he closed his eyes it felt as if he were lying on his back on the deck of an old ship. The rocket kept creaking and twisting, shaking the capsule this way and that. The Atlas had 4.3 times as much fuel as the Redstone, including 80 tons of liquid oxygen. The liquid oxygen, the "lox," had a temperature of 293 degrees below zero, so that the shell and tubing of the rocket, which were thin, kept contracting and twisting and creaking. Glenn was at the equivalent of nine stories up in the air. The enormous rocket seemed curiously fragile, the way it moved and creaked and whined. The contractions created high-frequency vibrations and the lox hissed in the pipes, and it all ran up through the capsule like a metallic wail. It was the same rocket lox wail they used to hear at dawn at Edwards when they fueled the D-558-2 many years before.

Through the periscope Glenn could see for miles down the Banana River and the Indian River. He could just barely make out the thousands of people along the beaches. Some of them had been camping out along there in trailers since January 23, when the flight was first scheduled. They had elected camp mayors. They were having a terrific time. A month in a Banana River trailer camp was not too long to wait to make sure you were here when an event of this magnitude occurred.

There they were, thousands of them, off on the periphery as Glenn looked out. He could only see them through the periscope. They looked very small and far away and far below. And they were all wondering with a delicious shudder what it must be like to be in his place now. How frightened is he! *Tell us! That's all we want to know!* The fear and the gamble. Never mind the rest. Lying on his back like this, with his legs jackknifed up above him, stuffed blind into the holster, with the hatch closed, he couldn't help but be aware of his own heartbeat from time to time. Glenn could tell that his pulse was slow. Out loud, if the subject ever came up, everyone said that pulse rates didn't matter; it was a very subjective thing; many variables; and so on. It had only been within the past five years that biosensors had ever been put on pilots. They resented them and didn't care to attach any importance to them. Nevertheless, without saying so, everyone knew that they provided a rough gauge of a man's emotional state. Without saying so—not a word!—everyone knew that Gus Grissom's pulse rate had been *somewhat panicky*. It kept jumping over 100 during the countdown and then spurted up to 150 during the lift-off and stayed that high throughout his weightless flight, then jumped again, all the way to 171, just before the retro-rockets went off. No one—certainly not out loud—no one was going to draw any conclusions from it, but . . . it was not a sign of the right stuff. Add to that his performance in the water . . . In his statement about people who get panicky over the flight test business, Glenn had said you had to know how to control your emotions. Well, he was as good as his word. Did any yogi ever control his heartbeat and perspiration better! (And, as the biomedical panels in the Mission Control room showed, his pulse never went over 80 and was holding around 70, no more than that of any normal healthy bored man having breakfast in the kitchen.) Occasionally he could feel his heart skip a beat or beat with an odd electrical sensation, and he knew that he was feeling the tension. (And at the biomedical panels the young doctors looked at each other in consternation—and then shrugged.) Nevertheless, he was aware that he was feeling no fear. He truly was not. He was more like an actor who is going out to perform in the same play yet once again—the only difference being that the audience this time is enormous and highly prestigious. He knew every sensation he would feel once the event began. The main thing was not to . . . "foul up." Please, dear God, don't let me foul up. In fact, there was little chance that he would forget so much as a word or a single move. Glenn had been the backup pilot—everyone said *pilot* now—for both Shepard and Grissom. During the charade before the first flight, he had gone through all of Shepard's simulations, and he had repeated most of Grissom's. And the simulations he had gone through as prime pilot for the first orbital flight had surpassed any simulations ever done before. They had even put him in the capsule on top of the rocket and *moved the gantry* away from the rocket, because Grissom had reported the odd sensation of perceiving the gantry as *falling over*, as he witnessed the event through his periscope, just before lift-off. Therefore, this feeling would be *adapted out* of Glenn. They put him in the capsule on top of the rocket and instructed him to watch the gantry move away through his periscope. *Nothing* must be novel about the experience! On top of all that, he had Shepard's and Grissom's descriptions of variations from the simulations. "On the centrifuge you feel thus-and-such. Well, during the actual flight it feels like that but with this-and-that difference." No man had ever lived an event so completely ahead of time. He was socketed into the capsule, lying on his back, getting ready to do precisely what his enormous Presbyterian Pilot self-esteem had been dying to do for fifteen years: demonstrate to the world his righteous stuff.

Exactly that! The Presbyterian Pilot! Here he is!—within twenty seconds of lift-off, and the only strange thing is how little adrenalin is pumping when the moment comes . . . He can hear the rumble of the Atlas engines building up down there below his back. All the same, it isn't terribly loud. The huge squat rocket shakes a bit and struggles to overcome its own weight. It all happens very slowly in the first few seconds, like an extremely heavy elevator rising. They've lit the candle and there's no turning back, and yet there's no surge inside him. His pulse rises only to 110, no more than the minimum rate you should have if you have to deal with a sudden emergency. How strange that it should be this way! He has been more wound up for a takeoff in an F-102.

"The clock is operating," he said. "We're underway."

It was all very smooth, much smoother than the centrifuge . . . just as Shepard and Grissom said it would be. He had gone through the same g-forces so many times . . . he hardly noticed them as they built up. It would have bothered him much more if they had been less. Nothing novel! No excitement, please! It took thirteen seconds for the huge rocket to reach transonic speed. The vibrations started. It was just as Shepard and Grissom said: it was much gentler than the centrifuge. He was still lying flat on his back, and the g-forces drove him deeper and deeper into the seat, but it all felt so familiar. He barely noticed it. He kept his eyes on the instrument panel the whole time . . . All quite normal, every little needle and switch in the right place . . . No malevolent instructor feeding *Abort* problems into the loop . . . As the rocket entered the transonic zone, the vibration became intense. The vibrations all but obliterated the roar of the engines. He was entering the area of "max q," maximum aerodynamic pressure, in which the pressure of the shaft of the Atlas forcing its way through the atmosphere at supersonic speed would reach almost a thousand pounds per square foot. Through the cockpit window he could see the sky turning black. Almost 5 g's were driving him back into his seat. And yet . . . *easier than the centrifuge* . . . All at once he was through *max q*, as if through a turbulent strait, and the trajectory was smooth and he was supersonic and the rumble of the rocket engines was more muffled than ever and he could hear all the little fans and recorders and the busy little kitchen, the humming little shop . . . The pressure on his chest reached 6 g's. The rocket pitched down. For the first time he could see clouds and the horizon. In a moment—*there it was*—the Atlas rocket's two booster engines shut down and were jettisoned from the side of the shaft and his body was slammed forward, as if he were screeching to a halt, and the g-forces suddenly dropped to 1.25, almost as if he were on earth and not accelerating at all, but the central sustainer engine and two smaller engines were still driving him up through the atmosphere . . . A flash of white smoke went up past the window . . . *No! The escape tower was firing early—but the* JETTISON TOWER LIGHT WASN'T ON! . . . He didn't see the tower go . . . Wait a minute . . . There went the tower, on schedule . . . The JETTISON TOWER light came on green . . . The smoke must have been from the booster rockets as they left the shaft . . . The rocket pitched back up . . . going straight up . . . The sky was very black now . . . The g-forces began pushing him back into his seat again . . . 3 g's . . . 4 g's . . . 5 g's . . . Soon he would be forty miles up . . . the last critical moment of powered flight, as the capsule separated from the rocket and went into its orbital trajectory . . . or didn't . . . *Hey!* . . . All at once the whole capsule was whipping up and down, as if it were tied to the end of a diving board, a springboard. The g-forces built up and the capsule whipped up and down. Yet no sooner had it begun than Glenn knew what it was. The weight of the rocket on the launch pad had been 260,000 pounds, practically all of it rocket fuel, the liquid oxygen. This was being consumed at such a furious rate, about one ton per second, that the rocket was becoming merely a skeleton with a thin skin of metal stretched over it, a tube so long and light that it was flexing. The g-forces reached six and then he was weightless, just like that. The sudden release made him feel as if he were tumbling head over heels, as if he had been catapulted off the end of that same springboard and was falling through the air doing forward rolls. But he had felt this same thing on the centrifuge when they ran the g-forces up to seven and then suddenly cut the speed. At the same moment, right on schedule . . . a loud report . . . the posigrade rockets fired, throwing the capsule free of the rocket shaft . . . the capsule began its automatic turnabout, and all the proper green lights went on in front of him, and he knew he was "through the gate," as they said.

"Zero-g and I feel fine," he said. "Capsule is turning around . . ."

Glenn knew he was weightless. From the instrument readings and through sheer logic he knew it, but he couldn't feel it, just as Shepard and Grissom had never felt it. The turn-around brought him up to a sitting position, vertical to the earth, and that was the way he felt. He was sitting in a chair, upright, in a very tiny cramped quiet little cubicle 125 miles above the earth, a little metal closet, silent except for the humming of its electrical system, the inverters, the gyros, the cameras, the radio . . . *the radio* . . . He had been specifically instructed to violate the Fighter Jock code of No Chatter. He was supposed to radio back every sight, every sensation, and otherwise give the taxpayers the juicy stuff they wanted to hear. Glenn, more than any of the others, was fully capable of doing the job. Yet it was an awkward thing. It seemed unnatural.

"Oh!" he said. "That view is tremendous!"

Well, it was a start. In fact, the view was not particularly extraordinary. It was extraordinary that he was up here in orbit about the earth. He could see the exhausted Atlas rocket following him. It was tumbling end over end from the force of the small rockets throwing the capsule free of it.

He could hear Alan Shepard, who was serving as capcom in the Mercury Control Center at the Cape. His voice came in very clearly. He was saying, "You have a go, at least seven orbits."

"Roger," said Glenn. "Understand Go for at least seven orbits . . . This is *Friendship 7*. Can see clear back, a big cloud pattern way back across toward the Cape. Beautiful sight."

He was riding backward, looking back toward the Cape. It must be tremendous, it must be beautiful—what else could it be? And yet it didn't look terribly different from what he had seen at 50,000 feet in fighter planes. He had no greater sense of having left the bonds of earth. The earth was not just a little ball beneath him. It still filled his field of consciousness. It slid by slowly underneath him, just the way it did when you were in an airplane at forty or fifty thousand feet. He had no sense of being a *star voyager*. He couldn't see any stars at all. He could see the Atlas booster tumbling behind him and beginning to grow smaller, because it was in a slightly lower orbit. It just kept tumbling. There was nothing to stop it. Somehow the sight of this colossal great tumbling cylinder, which had weighed more than the average freighter while it was on the ground and which now weighed nothing and had been discarded like a candy wrapper—somehow it was more extraordinary than the view of earth. It shouldn't have been, but it was. The earth looked the way it had looked to Gus Grissom. Shepard had seen a low-grade black-and-white movie. Through his window Glenn could see what Grissom saw, the brilliant blue band at the horizon, a somewhat wider band of deeper blues leading into the absolutely black dome of the sky. Most of the earth was covered in clouds. The clouds looked very bright, set against the blackness of the sky. The capsule was heading east, over Africa. But, because he was riding backward, he was looking west. He saw everything after he had passed over it. He could make out the Canary Islands, but they were partly obscured by clouds. He could see a long stretch of the African coast . . . huge dust storms over the African desert . . . but there was no sense of taking in the whole earth at a glance. The earth was eight thousand miles in diameter and he was only a hundred miles above it. He knew what it was going to look like in any case. He had seen it all in photographs taken from the satellites. It had all been flashed on the screens for him. Even the view had been simulated. *Yes . . . that's the way they said it would look* . . . Awe seemed to be demanded, but how could he express awe honestly? He had lived it all before the event. How could he explain that to anybody? The view wasn't the main thing, in any case. The main thing . . . *was the checklist!* And just try explaining that! He had to report all his switch and dial readings. He had to put a special blood-pressure rig on the arm of his pressure suit and pump it up. (His blood pressure was absolutely normal, 120 over 80—*perfect stuff!*) He had to check the manual attitude-control system, swing the capsule up and down, side to side, roll to the right, roll to the left . . . and there was nothing novel about it, not even in orbit, a hundred miles above the earth. *How could you explain that!* When he swung the capsule, it felt the same as it did in a one-g state on earth. He still didn't feel weightless. He merely felt less cramped, because there were no longer any pressure points on his body. He was sitting straight up in a chair drifting slowly and quietly around the earth. Just the hum of his little shop, the background noises in his head-set, and the occasional spurt of the hydrogen-peroxide jets.

"This is *Friendship 7*," he said. "Working just like clockwork on the control check, and it went through just about like the procedures-trainer runs."

Well, that was it. The procedures trainer and the ALFA trainer and the centrifuge . . . He noticed that, in fact, he seemed to be moving a little faster than he had been on the ALFA trainer. When you sat in the trainer, cranking your simulated hydrogen-peroxide thrusters, they ran films on the screen of the earth rolling by below you, just the way it would be in orbital flight. "They didn't roll it by fast enough," he said to himself. Not that it mattered particularly . . . The sensation of speed was no more than that of being in an airliner and watching a cloud bank slide by far below . . . The world demanded awe, because this was a voyage through the stars. But he couldn't feel it. The backdrop of the event, the stage, the environment, the true orbit . . . was not the vast reaches of the universe. It was the simulators. *Who could possibly understand this?* Weightless he was, in the vacuum of space, humming around the earth . . . but his center of gravity was still back in that Baptist hardtack Low Rent stretch of sand and palmetto grass in Florida.

Ahhhh—but now this was truly something. Forty minutes into the flight, as he neared the Indian Ocean, off the east coast of Africa, he began sailing into the night. Since he was traveling east, he was going away from the sun at a speed of 17,500 miles an hour. But because he was riding backward, he could see the sun out the window. It was sinking the way the moon sinks out of sight as seen on earth. The edge of the sun began to touch the edge of the horizon. He couldn't tell what part of the earth it was. There were clouds everywhere. They created a haze at the horizon. The brilliant light over the earth began to dim. It was like turning down a rheostat. It took five or six minutes. Very slowly the lights were dimming. Then he couldn't see the sun at all, but there was a tremendous band of orange light that stretched from one side of the horizon to the other, as if the sun were a molten liquid that had emptied into a tube along the horizon. Where there had been a bright-blue band before, there was now the orange band; and above it a wider dimmer band of oranges and reds shading off into the blackness of the sky. Then all the reds and oranges disappeared, and he was on the night side of the earth. The bright-blue band reappeared at the horizon. Above it, stretching up about eight degrees, was what looked like a band of haze, created by the earth's atmosphere. And above that . . . for the first time he could make out the stars. Down below, the clouds picked up a faint light from the moon, which was coming up behind him. Now he was over Australia. He could hear Gordon Cooper's voice. Cooper was serving as the capcom at the tracking station in the town of Muchea, out in the kangaroo boondocks of western Australia. He could hear Cooper's Oklahoma drawl.

"That sure was a short day," said Glenn.

"Say again, *Friendship 7*," said Cooper.

"That was about the shortest day I've ever run into," said Glenn. Somehow that was the sort of thing to say to old Oklahoma Gordo sitting down there in the middle of nowhere.

"Kinda passes rapidly, huh?" said Gordo.

"Yessir," said Glenn.

The clouds began to break up over Australia. He could make out nothing in the darkness except for electric lights. Off to one side he could make out the lights of an entire city, just as you could at 40,000 feet in an airplane, but the concentration of lights was terrific. It was an absolute mass of electric lights, and south of it there was another one, a smaller one. The big mass was the city of Perth and the smaller one was a town called Rockingham. It was midnight in Perth and Rockingham, but practically every living soul in both places had stayed up to turn on every light they had for the American sailing over in the satellite.

"The lights show up very well," said Glenn, "and thank everybody for turning them on, will you?"

"We sure will, John," said Gordo.

And he went sailing on past Australia with the lights of Perth and Rockingham sliding into the distance.

He was over the middle of the Pacific, about halfway between Australia and Mexico, when the sun began to come up behind him. This was just thirty-five minutes after the sun went down. Since he was traveling backward, he couldn't see the sunrise through the window. He had to use the periscope. First he could see the blue band at the horizon becoming brighter and brighter. Then the sun itself began to slide up over the edge. It was a brilliant red—not terribly different from what he had seen at sunrise on earth, except that it was rising faster and its outlines were sharper.

"It's blinding through the scope on clear," said Glenn. "I'm going to the dark filter to watch it come on up."

And then—*needles!* A tremendous layer of them—Air Force communications experiment that went amok . . . Thousands of tiny needles gleaming in the sun outside the capsule . . . But they couldn't be needles, because they were luminescent—they were like snowflakes—

"This is *Friendship 7*," he said. "I'll try to describe what I'm in here. I am in a big mass of some very small particles that are brilliantly lit up like they're luminescent. I never saw anything like it. They're round, a little. They're coming by the capsule, and they look like little stars. A whole shower of them coming by. They swirl around the capsule and go in front of the window and they're all brilliantly lighted. They probably average maybe seven or eight feet apart, but I can see them all down below me also."

"Roger, *Friendship 7*." This was the capcom on Canton Island out in the Pacific. "Can you hear any impact with the capsule? Over."

"Negative, negative. They're very slow. They're not going away from me more than maybe three or four miles per hour."

They swirled about his capsule like tiny weightless diamonds, little bijoux—no, they were more like fireflies. They had that lazy but erratic motion, and when he focused on one it would seem to be lit up, but the light would go out and he would lose track of it, and then it would light up again. That was like fireflies, too. There used to be thousands of fireflies in the summers, when he was growing up. These things were like fireflies, but they obviously couldn't be any sort of organism . . . unless all the astronomers and all the satellite recording mechanisms had been fundamentally wrong . . . They were undoubtedly particles of some sort, particles that caught the sunlight at a certain angle. They were beautiful, but were they coming from the capsule? That could mean trouble. They must have been coming from the capsule, because they traveled along with him, in the same trajectory, at the same speed. But wait a minute, Some of them were far off, far below . . . there might be an entire field of them . . . a minute cosmos . . . something never seen before! And yet the capcom on Canton Island didn't seem particularly interested. And then he sailed out of range of Canton and would have to wait to be picked up by the capcom at Guaymas, on the west coast of Mexico. And when the Guaymas capcom picked him up, he didn't seem to know what he was talking about.

"This is *Friendship 7*," said Glenn. "Just as the sun came up, there were some brilliantly lighted particles that looked luminous that were swirling around the capsule. I don't have any in sight right now. I did have a couple just a moment ago, when I made the transmission over to you. Over."

"Roger, *Friendship 7*."

And that was it. "Roger, *Friendship 7*." Silence. They didn't particularly care.

Glenn kept talking about his fireflies. He was fascinated. It was the first true unknown anyone had encountered out here in the cosmos. At the same time he was faintly apprehensive. *Roger, Friendship 7*. The capcom finally asked a polite question or two, about the size of the particles and so on. They obviously were not carried away by this celestial discovery.

All of a sudden the capsule swung out to the right in a yaw, out about twenty degrees. Then it was as if it hit a little wall. It bounced back. Then it swung out again in the yaw and hit the little wall and bounced back. Something had gone out in the automatic attitude control. Never mind the celestial fireflies. He was sailing over California, heading for Florida. Now all the capcoms were coming alive, all right.

President Kennedy was supposed to come on the radio as Glenn came over the United States. He was going to bless his single-combat warrior as he came over the continental U.S.A. He was going to tell him the hearts of all his fellow citizens were with him. But that all went by the boards in view of the problem with the automatic controls.

Glenn went sailing over Florida, over the Cape, starting his second orbit. He couldn't see much of anything down below, because of the clouds. He no longer cared particularly. The attitude control was the main thing. One of the small thrusters seemed to have gone out, so that the capsule would drift to the right, like a car slowly skidding on ice. Then a bigger thruster would correct the motion and bounce it back. That was only the start. Pretty soon other thrusters began acting up when he was on automatic. Then the gyros started going. The dials that showed the angle of the capsule with respect to the earth and the horizon were giving obviously wrong readings. He had to line it up visually with the horizon. Fly by wire! Manual control! It was no emergency, however, at least not yet. As long as he was in orbit, the attitude control of the capsule didn't particularly matter, so far as his safety was concerned. He could be going forward or backward or could have his head pointed straight at the earth or could be drifting around in circles or pitching head over heels, for that matter, and it wouldn't change his altitude or trajectory in the slightest. The only critical point was the re-entry. If the capsule were not lined up at the correct angle, with the blunt end and the heat shield down, it might burn up. To line it up correctly, fuel was required, the hydrogen peroxide, no matter whether it was lined up automatically or by the astronaut. If too much fuel was used keeping the capsule stable while it sailed around in orbit, there might not be enough left to line it up before the re-entry. That had been the problem in the ape's flight. The automatic attitude control had started malfunctioning and was using up so much fuel they brought him down after two orbits.

Every five minutes he had to shift his radio communications to a new capcom. You couldn't receive and send at the same time, either. It wasn't like a telephone hookup. So you spent half the time just making sure you could hear each other.

"*Friendship 7, Friendship 7*, this is CYI." That was the Canary Islands capcom. "The time is now 16:32:26. We are reading you loud and clear; we are reading you loud and clear. CYI."

Glenn said: "This is *Friendship 7* on UHF. As I went over recovery area that time, I could see a wake, what appeared to be a long wake in the water. I imagine that's the ships in our recovery area."

"*Friendship 7* . . . We do not read you, do not read you. Over."

"*Friendship 7*, this is Kano. At G.M.T. 16:33:00. We do not . . . This is Kano. Out."

"*Friendship 7, Friendship 7*, this is CYI Com Tech. Over."

Glenn said: "Hello, Canary. *Friendship 7*. Receive you loud and a little garbled. Do you receive me? Over."

"*Friendship 7, Friendship 7*, this is CYI Com Tech. Over."

"Hello, Canary, *Friendship 7*. I read you loud and clear. How me? Over."

"*Friendship 7, Friendship 7*, this is CYI, CYI Tech. Over."

"Hello, CYI Com Tech. *Friendship 7*. How do you read me? Over."

"*Friendship 7, Friendship 7*, this is CYI, CYI Com Tech. Do you read? Over."

"Roger. This is *Friendship 7*, CYI. I read you loud and clear. Over."

"*Friendship 7, Friendship 7*, this is CYI Com Tech, CYI Com Tech. Do you read? Over."

"Hello, CYI Com Tech. Roger, read you loud and clear."

"*Friendship 7*, this is CYI Com Tech. Read you loud and clear also, on UHF, on UHF. Standby."

"Roger. *Friendship 7*."

"*Friendship 7, Friendship 7, Friendship 7*, this is Canary capcom. How do you read? Over."

"Hello, Canary capcom. *Friendship 7*. I read you loud and clear. How me?"

Finally, the Canary Islands capcom said: "I read you loud and clear. I am instructed to ask you to correlate the actions of the particles surrounding your spacecraft with the actions of your control jets. Do you read? Over."

"This is *Friendship 7*. I did not read you clear. I read you loud but very garbled. Over."

"Roger. Cap asks you to correlate the actions of the particles surrounding the vehicle with the reaction of one of your control jets. Do you understand? Over."

"This is *Friendship 7*. I do not think they were from my control jets, negative. Over."

There—exactly five minutes to get one question out and one answer. Well, at least they finally showed an interest in the fireflies. They wondered if they might have something to do with the malfunctioning thrusters. Oh, but it was a struggle.

In any case, he was not particularly worried. He could control the attitude manually if he had to. The fuel seemed to be holding out. Everything hummed and whined and buzzed as usual inside the capsule. The same high background tones came over the radio. He could hear the oxygen coursing through his pressure suit and his helmet. There was no "sensation" of motion speed at all, unless he looked down at the earth. Even then it slid by very slowly. When the thrusters spurted hydrogen peroxide, he could feel the capsule swing this way and that. But it was like the ALFA trainer on earth. He still didn't feel weightless. He was still sitting straight up in his chair. On the other hand, the camera—when he wanted to reload it, he just parked it in the empty space in front of his eyes. It just floated there in front of him. Way down there were little flashes all over the place. It was lightning in the clouds over the Atlantic. Somehow it was more fascinating than the sunset. Sometimes the lightning was inside the clouds and looked like flashlights going on and off underneath a blanket. Sometimes it was on top of the clouds, and it looked like firecrackers going off. It was extraordinary, and yet there was nothing new about the sight. An Air Force colonel, David Simons, had gone up in a balloon, alone, to 102,000 feet, for thirty-two hours and had seen the same thing.

Glenn was now over Africa, riding over the dark side of the earth, sailing backward toward Australia. The Indian Ocean capcom said: "We have message from MCC for you to keep your landing-bag switch in off position. Landing-bag switch in off position. Over."

"Roger," said Glenn. "This is *Friendship 7.*"

He wanted to ask why. But that was against the code, except in an emergency situation. That fell under the heading of nervous chatter.

Over Australia old Gordo, Gordo Cooper, got on the same subject: "Will you confirm the landing-bag switch is in the off position? Over."

"That is affirmative," said Glenn. "Landing-bag switch is in the center off position."

"You haven't had any banging noises or anything of this type at higher rates?"

"Negative."

"They wanted this answer."

They still didn't say why, and Glenn entered into no nervous chatter. He now had two red lights on the panel. One was the warning light for the automatic fuel supply. All the little amok action of the yaw thrusters had used it up. Well, it was up to the Pilot now . . . to aim the capsule correctly for re-entry . . . The other was a warning about excess cabin water. It built up as a by-product of the oxygen system. Nevertheless, he pressed on with the checklist. He was supposed to exercise by pulling on the bungee cord and then take his blood pressure. The Presbyterian Pilot! He did it without a peep. He was pulling on the bungee and watching the red lights when he began sailing backward into the sunrise again. Two hours and forty-three minutes into the flight, his second sunrise over the Pacific . . . seen from behind through a periscope. But he hardly watched it. He was looking for the fireflies to light up again. The great rheostat came up, the earth lit up, and now there were thousands of them swirling about the capsule. Some of them seemed to be miles away. A huge field of them, a galaxy, a microuniverse. No question about it, they weren't coming from the capsule, they were part of the cosmos. He took out the camera again. He had to photograph them while the light was just right.

"*Friendship 7.*" The Canton Island capcom was coming in. "This is Canton. We also have no indication that your landing bag might be deployed. Over."

Glenn's first reaction was that this must have something to do with the fireflies. He's telling them about the fireflies and they come in with something about the landing bag. But who said anything about the landing bag being deployed?

"Roger," he said. "Did someone report landing bag could be down? Over."

"Negative," said the capcom. "We had a request to monitor this and to ask you if you heard any flapping, when you had high capsule rates."

"Well," said Glenn, "I think they probably thought these particles I saw might have come from that, but these are . . . there are thousands of these things, and they go out for it looks like miles in each direction from me, and they move by here very slowly. I saw them at the same spot on the first orbit. Over."

And so he thought that explained all the business about the landing bag.

They gave him the go-ahead for his third and final orbit as he sailed over the United States. He couldn't see a thing for the clouds. He pitched the capsule down sixty degrees, so he could look straight down. All he could see was the cloud deck. It was just like flying at high altitudes in an airplane. He was really no longer in the mood for sightseeing. He was starting to think about the sequence of events that would lead to the retrofiring over the Atlantic after be had been around the world one more time. He had to fight both the thrusters and the gyros now. He kept releasing and resetting the gyros to see if the automatic attitude control would start functioning again. It was all out of whack. He would have to position the capsule by using the horizon as a reference. He was sailing backward over America. The clouds began to break. He began to see the Mississippi delta. It was like looking at the world from the tail-gun perch of the bombers they used in the Second World War. Then Florida started to slide by. Suddenly he realized he could see the whole state. It was laid out just like it is on a map. He had been around the world twice in three hours and eleven minutes and this was the first sense he had had of how high up he was. He was about 550,000 feet up. He could make out the Cape. By the time he could see the Cape he was already over Bermuda.

"This is *Friendship 7*," he said. "I have the Cape in sight down there. It looks real fine from up here."

"Rog. Rog." That was Gus Grissom on Bermuda.

"As you know," said Glenn.

"Yea, verily, sonny," said Grissom.

Oh, it all sounded very fraternal. Glenn was modestly acknowledging that his loyal comrade Grissom was one of the only three Americans ever to see such a sight . . . and Grissom was calling him "sonny."

Twenty minutes later he was sailing backward over Africa again and the sun was going down again, for the third time, and the rheostat was dimming and he . . . saw *blood*. It was all over one of the windows. He knew it couldn't be blood, and yet it was blood. He had never noticed it before. At this particular angle of the setting rheostat sun he could see it. Blood and dirt, a real mess. The dirt must have come from the firing of the escape tower. And the blood . . . *bugs*, perhaps . . . The capsule must have smashed into bugs as it rose from the launch pad . . . or *birds* . . . but he would have heard the thump. It must have been bugs, but bugs didn't have blood. Or the blood red of the sun going down in front of him diffusing . . . And then he refused to think about it any more. He just turned the subject off. Another sunset, another orange band streaking across the rim of the horizon, more yellow bands, blue bands, blackness, thunderstorms, lightning making little sparkles under the blanket. It hardly mattered any more. The whole thing of lining the capsule up for retrofire kept building up in his mind. In slightly less than an hour the retro-rockets would go off. The capsule kept slipping its angles, swinging this way and that way, drifting. The gyros didn't seem to mean a thing any more.

And he went sailing backward through the night over the Pacific. When he reached the Canton Island tracking point, he swung the capsule around again so that he could see his last sunrise while riding forward, out the window, with his own eyes. The first two he had watched through the periscope because he was going backward. The fireflies were all over the place as the sun came up. It was like watching the sunrise from inside a storm of the things. He began expounding upon them again, about how they couldn't possibly come from the capsule, because some of them seemed to be miles away. Once again nobody on the ground was interested. They weren't interested on Canton Island, and pretty soon he was in range of the station on Hawaii, and they weren't interested, either. They were all wrapped up in something else. They had a little surprise for him. They backed into it, however. It took him a while to catch on.

He was now four hours and twenty-one minutes into the flight. In twelve minutes the retro-rockets were supposed to fire, to slow him down for re-entry. It took him another minute and forty-five seconds to go through all the "do you reads" and "how me's" and "overs" and establish contact with the capcom on Hawaii. Then they sprang their surprise.

"*Friendship 7*," said the capcom. "We have been reading an indication on the ground of segment 5-1, which is Landing Bag Deploy. We suspect this is an erroneous signal. However, Cape would like you to check this by putting the landing-bag switch in auto position, and seeing if you get a light. Do you concur with this? Over."

It slowly dawned on him . . . *Have been reading* . . . For how long? . . . Quite a little surprise. And they hadn't told him! They'd held it back! *I am a pilot and they refuse to tell me things they know about the condition of the craft!* The insult was worse than the danger! If the landing bag had deployed—and there was no way he could look out and see it, not even with the periscope, because it would be directly behind him—if it had deployed, then the heat shield must be loose and might come off during the re-entry. If the heat shield came off, he would burn up inside the capsule like a steak. If he put the landing-bag switch in the automatic control position, then a green light should come on if the bag was deployed. Then he would know. Slowly it dawned! . . . That was why they kept asking him if the switch were in the off position!— they didn't want him to learn the awful truth too quickly! Might as well let him complete his three orbits—then we'll let him find out about the bad news!

On top of that, they now wanted him to fool around with the switch. *That's stupid!* It might very well be that the bag had not deployed but there was an electrical malfunction somewhere in the circuit and fooling with the automatic switch might then cause it to deploy. But he stopped short of saying anything. Presumably they had taken all that into account. There was no way he could say it without falling into the dread nervous chatter.

"Okay," said Glenn. "If that's what they recommend, we'll go ahead and try it. Are you ready for it now?"

"Yes, when you're ready."

"Roger."

He reached forward and flipped the switch. Well . . . this was it—

No light. He immediately switched it back to off.

"Negative," he said. "In automatic position did not get a light and I'm back in off position now. Over."

"Roger, that's fine. In this case, we'll go ahead, and the re-entry sequence will be normal."

The retro-rockets would be fired over California, and by the time the retro-rockets brought him down out of his orbit and through the atmosphere, he would be over the Atlantic near Bermuda. That was the plan. Wally Schirra was the capcom in California. Less than a minute before he was supposed to fire the retro-rockets, by pushing a switch, he heard Wally saying: "John, leave your retropack on through your pass over Texas. Do you read?"

"Roger."

But why? The retropack wrapped around the edges of the heat shield and held the retro-rockets. Once the rockets were fired, the retropack was supposed to be jettisoned. They were back to the heat shield again, with no explanation. But he had to concentrate on firing the retro-rockets.

Next to the launch this was the most dangerous part of the flight. If the capsule's angle of attack was too shallow, you might skip off the top of the earth's atmosphere and stay in orbit for days, until long after your oxygen had run out. You wouldn't have any more rockets to slow you down. If the angle were too steep, the heat from the friction of going through the atmosphere would be so intense you would burn up inside the capsule, and a couple of minutes later the whole thing would disintegrate, heat shield or no heat shield. But the main thing was not to think about it in quite those terms. The field of consciousness is very small, said Saint-Exupéry. *What do I do next?* It was the moment of the test pilot at last. Oh, yes! *I've been here before! And I am immune! I don't get into corners I can't get out of!* One thing at a time! He could be a true flight test hero and try to line the capsule up all by himself by using the manual controls with the horizon as his reference—or he could make one more attempt to use the automatic controls. Please, dear God . . . don't let me foul up! What would the Lord answer? (Try the automatic, you ninny.) He released and reset the gyros. He put the controls on automatic. The answer to your prayers, John! Now the dials gibed with what he saw out the window and through the periscope. The automatic controls worked perfectly in pitch and roll. The yaw was still off, so he corrected that with the manual controls. The capsule kept pivoting to the right and he kept nudging it back. The ALFA trainer! One thing at a time! It was just like the ALFA trainer . . .

no sense of forward motion at all . . . As long as he concentrated on the instrument panel and didn't look at the earth sliding by beneath him, he had no sense at all of going 17,500 miles an hour . . . or even five miles an hour . . . The humming little kitchen . . . He sat up in his chair squirting his hand thruster, with his eyes pinned on the dials . . . Real life, a crucial moment—against the eternal good beige setting of the simulation. One thing at a time!

Schirra began giving him the countdown for firing the rockets. "Five, four—"

He nudged it back once more with the yaw thruster.

"—three, two, one, fire."

He pushed the retro-rocket switch with his hand.

The rockets started firing in sequence, the first one, the second one, the third one. The sound seemed terribly muffled—but in that very moment, the jolt! Pure gold! One instant, as Schirra counted down, he felt absolutely motionless. The next . . . *thud thud thud* . . . the jolt in his back. He felt as if the capsule had been knocked backward. He felt as if he were sailing back toward Hawaii. All as it should be! Pure gold! The retro-light was lit up green. It was all going perfectly. He was merely slowing down. In eleven minutes he would be entering the earth's atmosphere.

He could hear Schirra saying: "Keep your retropack on until you pass Texas."

Still no reason given! He couldn't see the pattern yet. There was only the dim sense that in some fashion they were jerking him around. But all he said was: "That's affirmative."

"It looked like your attitude held pretty well," said Schirra. "Did you have to back it up at all?"

"Oh, yes, quite a bit. Yeah, I had a lot of trouble with it."

"Good enough for government work from down here," said Schirra. That was one of Schirra's favorite lines.

"Do you have a time for going to Jettison Retro?" said Glenn. This was an indirect way of asking for some explanation for the mystery of keeping the retropack on.

"Texas will give you that message," said Schirra. "Over."

They weren't going to tell him! Not so much the thought . . . as the *feeling* . . . of the insult began to build up.

Three minutes later the Texas capcom tracking station came in: "This is Texas capcom, *Friendship 7*. We are recommending that you leave the retropackage on through the entire re-entry. This means that you will have to override the zero-point-oh-five-g switch, which is expected to occur at 04:43:53, This also means that you will have to manually retract the scope. Do you read?"

That did it.

"This is *Friendship*," said Glenn. "What is the reason for this? Do you have any reason? Over."

"Not at this time," said the Texas capcom. "This is the judgment of Cape Flight . . . Cape Flight will give you the reason for this action when you are in view."

"Roger. Roger. *Friendship 7*."

It was really unbelievable. It was beginning to fit—

Twenty-seven seconds later he was over the Cape itself and the Cape capcom, with the voice of Alan Shepard on the radio, was telling him to retract his periscope manually and to get ready for re-entry into the atmosphere.

It was beginning to fit together, he could see the pattern, the whole business of the landing bag and the retropack. This had been going on for a couple of hours now—and they were telling him nothing! Merely giving him the bits and pieces! But if he was going to re-enter with the retro-pack on, then they wanted the straps in place for some reason. And there was only one possible reason—something was wrong with the heat shield. And this they would not tell him! *Him!*—the pilot! It was quite unbelievable! It was—

He could hear Shepard's voice.

He was winding in the periscope, and he could hear Shepard's voice: "While you're doing that . . . we are not sure whether or not your landing bag has deployed. We feel it is possible to re-enter with the retropackage on. We see no difficulty at this time in that type of re-entry."

Glenn said, "Roger, understand."

Oh, yes, he understood now! If the landing bag was deployed, that meant the heat shield was loose. If the heat shield was loose, then it might come off during the re-entry, unless the retropack straps held it in place long enough for the capsule to establish its angle of re-entry. And the straps would soon burn off. If the heat shield came off, then he would fry. If they didn't want him—*the pilot!*—to know all this, then it meant they were afraid he might panic. And if he didn't even *need* to know the whole pattern—just the pieces, so he could follow orders—*then he wasn't really a pilot!* The whole sequence of logic clicked through Glenn's mind faster than he could have put it into words, even if he had dared utter it all at that moment. He was being treated like a passenger—a redundant component, a backup engineer, a boiler-room attendant—in an automatic system!—like someone who did not have that rare and unutterably righteous stuff!—as if the right stuff itself did not even matter! It was a transgression against all that was holy— all this in a single limbic flash of righteous indignation as John Glenn re-entered the earth's atmosphere.

"*Seven*, this is Cape," said Al Shepard. "Over."

"Go ahead, Cape," said Glenn. "You're ground . . . you are going out."

"We recommend that you . . ."

That was the last he could hear from the ground. He had entered the atmosphere. He couldn't feel the g-forces yet, but the friction and the ion- ization had built up, and the radios were now useless. The capsule was beginning to buffet and he was fighting it with the controls. The fuel for the automatic system, the hydrogen peroxide, was so low he could no longer be sure which system worked. He was descending backward. The heat shield was on the outside of the capsule, directly behind his back. If he glanced out the window he could see only the blackness of the sky. The periscope was retracted, so he saw nothing on the scope screen. He heard a *thump* above him, on the outside of the capsule. He looked up. Through the window he could see a strap. *From the retropack. The straps broke! And now what!* Next the heat shield! The black sky out the window began to turn a pale orange. The strap flat against the window started burning—and then it was gone. The universe turned a flaming orange. That was the heat shield beginning to burn up from the tremendous speed of the re-entry. This was something Shepard and Grissom had not seen. They had not re-entered the atmosphere at such speed. Nevertheless, Glenn knew it was coming. Five hundred, a thousand times he had been told how the heat shield would *ablate*, burn off layer by layer, vaporize, dissipate the heat into the atmosphere, send off a corona of flames. All he could see now through the window were the flames. He was inside of a ball of fire. But!—a huge flaming chunk went by the window, a great chunk of something burning. Then another . . . another . . . The capsule started buffeting . . . The heat shield was breaking up! It was crumbling—flying away in huge flaming chunks . . . He fought to steady the capsule with the hand controller. *Fly-by-wire!* But the rolls and yaws were too fast for him . . . The ALFA trainer gone amok, inside a fireball . . . The heat! . . . It was as if his entire central nervous system were now centered in his back. If the capsule was disintegrating and he was about to burn up, the heat pulse would reach his back first. His backbone would become like a length of red-hot metal. He already knew what the feeling would be like . . . and when . . . *Now!* . . . But it didn't come. There was no tremendous heat and no more flaming debris . . . Not the heat shield, after all. The burning chunks had come from what remained of the retropack. First the straps had gone and then the rest of it. The capsule kept rocking, and the g-forces built up. He knew the g-forces by heart. A thousand times he had felt them on the centrifuge. They drove him back into the seat. It was harder and harder to move the hand controller. He kept trying to damp out the rocking motion by firing the yaw thrusters and the roll thrusters, but it was all too fast for him. They didn't seem to do much good, at any rate.

No more red glow . . . he must be out of the fireball . . . seven g's were driving him back into the seat . . . He could hear the Cape capcom:

"How do you read? Over."

That meant he had passed through the ionosphere and was entering the lower atmosphere.

"Loud and clear, how me?"

"Roger, reading you loud and clear. How are you doing?"

"Oh, pretty good."

"Roger. Your impact point is within one mile of the up-range destroyer."

Oh, pretty good. It wasn't Yeager, but it wasn't bad. He was inside of one and a half tons of non-aerodynamic metal. He was a hundred thousand feet up, dropping toward the ocean like an enormous cannonball. The capsule had no aerodynamic qualities whatsoever at this altitude. It was rocking terribly. Out the window he could see a wild white contrail snaked out against the blackness of the sky. He was dropping at a thousand feet per second. The last critical moment of the flight was coming up. Either the parachute deployed and took hold or it didn't. The rocking had intensified. The retropack! Part of the retropack must still be attached and the drag of it is trying to flip the capsule . . . He couldn't wait any longer. The parachute was supposed to deploy automatically, but he couldn't wait any longer. Rocking . . . He reached up to fire the parachute manually—but it fired on its own, automatically, first the drogue and then the main parachute. He swung under it in a huge arc. The heat was ferocious, but the chute held. It snapped him back into the seat. Through the window the sky was blue. It was the same day all over again. It was early in the afternoon on a sunny day out in the Atlantic near Bermuda. Even the landing-bag light was green. There was nothing even wrong with the landing bag. There had been nothing wrong with the heat shield. There was nothing wrong with his rate of descent, forty feet per second. He could hear the rescue ship chattering away over the radio. They were only twenty minutes away from where he would hit, only six miles. He was once again lying on his back in the human holster. Out the window the sky was no longer black. The capsule swayed under the parachute, and over this way he looked up and saw clouds and over that way blue sky. He was very, very hot. But he knew the feeling. All those endless hours in the heat chambers—it wouldn't kill you. He was coming down into the water only 300 miles from where he started. It was the same day, merely five hours later. A balmy day out in the Atlantic near Bermuda. The sun had moved just seventy-five degrees in the sky. It was 2:45 in the afternoon. Nothing to do but get all these wires and hoses disconnected. *He had done it.* He began to let the thought loose in his mind. He must be very close to the water. The capsule hit the water. It drove him down into his seat again, on his back. It was quite a jolt. It was hot in here. Even with the suit fans still running, the heat was terrific. Over the radio they kept telling him not to try to leave the capsule. The rescue ship was almost there. They weren't going to try the helicopter deal again, except in an emergency. He wasn't about to attempt a water egress. He wasn't about to hit the hatch detonator. The Presbyterian Pilot was not about to foul up. His pipeline to the dear Lord could not be clearer. He had done it.

from The Last Man on the Moon
by Eugene Cernan
and Don Davis

*Eugene Cernan (born 1934) entered NASA's astronaut
program in 1963. He flew his first mission in 1966 to
attempt America's second space walk.*

The first step into the void of outer space was made by Soviet cosmonaut Alexei Leonov, on March 8, 1965, as Nikita Khruschev demanded still another space spectacular, no matter the risk. The first American to walk in space was Ed White, who went outside the *Gemini 4* spacecraft on June of that same year, because we didn't want the Soviets to do something that we couldn't.

The classic photographs of Ed are among the most famous in history. A man in helmet and protective suit, one hand grasping a wandlike device that squirted jets of gas to propel him, he seems to be having a good old time floating out there above an incredibly blue Earth, connected to the spacecraft only by a crinkly umbilical cord.

The twelve-minute Russian accomplishment, as usual, was shrouded in secrecy. The American version lasted twenty-one minutes and, as usual, was trumpeted by a blaze of publicity. Although we did not realize it at the time, neither spacewalk was what it seemed. Alexei eventually became a close friend and, although he never admitted it publicly, confided in me about his fight for his life during his brief spacewalk. Ed, a man of considerable strength, was barely able to get back into the *Gemini 4* capsule, and was exhausted by the time the hatch was closed.

More than thirty years later, it can be safely said that we didn't know diddly-squat about walking in space when I popped my hatch open on *Gemini 9*, exactly a year and two days after Ed had romped outside for a few minutes. It's a sobering reflection when I think about it now, and I thank God that I lived through the experience.

In the space program, everything was designed to advance in baby steps. A test with minimum expectations would be conducted; then another a bit more complex, and so on until the ultimate goal was reached. Each Mercury flight had extended our knowledge a little further, and the whole reason for Gemini was to lay stepping stones toward Apollo.

This careful method had gotten us safely to where we were, but political considerations and the pace of new and untested technology were starting to bend that rule of caution.

One of the first examples of how things were moving too swiftly came with my spacewalk. Ed's only jobs were to test the spacesuit, a hand-held propulsion device, and the umbilical cord that fed his life-support system from the spacecraft to his suit. Now we leaped to an unrealistic schedule of two and a half hours of hard work for me. Had Dave Scott been able to conduct his *Gemini 8* spacewalk, we would have known much more, but that had been scrubbed when the mission was terminated.

My journey was loaded with experiments and tests. The highlight would come when I strapped on the rocket-powered backpack and scooted around the universe on my own. Good idea, but faulty assumptions, overly ambitious goals, and the hurry-up attitude known as "Go fever" were about to send me walking into an unknown and dangerous environment.

Tom and I spent almost four hours Sunday morning preparing for the spacewalk. Going carefully through an eleven-page checklist, we dropped to a lower orbit, and I pulled a boxy chestpack from a shelf above my left shoulder, strapped it on, and plugged a twenty-five-foot-long umbilical into the middle. The umbilical would feed me oxygen, communications, and electrical power from the spacecraft, and relay information from medical sensors that could be monitored on the ground. Getting the umbilical out of its container in zero gravity was like setting free a twisting garden hose that wanted to worm its way throughout the small cabin. Then we helped each other lock on our helmets, shut the visors, pull the heavy gloves on over silk ones, and pressurize the suits, which went from soft to rock hard around our bodies. When I pumped my suit up to three and one half pounds of pressure per square inch, the suit rook on a life of its own and became so stiff that it didn't want to bend at all. Not at the elbow, the knee, the waist, or anywhere else. It was as if I wore a garment made of hardened plaster of paris, from fingertip to toe.

My unique suit had been rather unyielding to begin with, for a very good reason. An astronaut inside a spacecraft did not need the same amount of insulation as someone doing a spacewalk. Out where I was going, the temperature in unfiltered sunlight would be many times hotter than any desert at high noon on Earth, while the nighttime cold could freeze steel until it was as brittle as glass. Without those multiple layers of protection, I could be broiled or frozen in an instant.

We finished emptying the oxygen from the spacecraft and made sure the suits were not leaking as we rode through the night sky, coming toward a dawn that would allow my spacewalk to begin over the United States, for better visibility and communication with Houston.

Mission Control ran a final check of all systems and sent up permission for me to open the hatch. During our thirty-first revolution of the Earth, Sunday morning in Houston but still night for me, I grabbed the big handle right above my head and gave it a twist. I remembered before launch how it had taken several men to wrestle the heavy hatch closed, but in zero gravity, it moved smoothly, reacting to gentle pressure. "This is *Gemini 9*. We are now going to walk," I told everyone.

When the hatch stood open, I barely pushed against the floor of the spacecraft and my suit unfolded from the seated position. I grabbed the edges of the hatch and climbed out of my hole until I stood on my seat. Half my body stuck out of *Gemini 9*, and I rode along like a sightseeing bum on a boxcar, waiting for the Sun to come up over California.

And, oh, my God, what a sight. Nothing had prepared me for the immense sensual overload. I had poked my head inside a kaleidoscope, where shapes and colors shifted a thousand times a second.

"Hallelujah!" was the best I could muster. "Boy, it sure is beautiful out here." I did not have the words to match the scene. No one does. Outer space was dead and empty while simultaneously alive and vibrant.

Since we were rushing along at about 18,000 miles an hour, we hurried the dawn. Pure darkness gave way to a ghostly mist-gray, then a thin, pale band of fragile blue appeared along the broad and curving horizon. It changed quickly to a deeper hue over narrow bands of gold, and then the Sun, a brilliant disk, jumped up to ignite a sky where night had ruled only a moment before, and its rays slowly erased the darkness on our planet below. Blue water shimmered on both sides of the Baja peninsula beneath California and the deserts of our Southwest shone like polished brass. An ivory lacework of thin, soft clouds stretched for miles. This was like sitting on God's front porch. The heavenly canopy surrounding me was still soot black, but stars could no longer be seen, and the subfreezing cold of the space night yielded to new, broiling hot temperatures. We crossed the coast of California in the full flare of the morning Sun, and in a single glance, I could see from San Francisco to halfway across Mexico.

Time was my friend for allowing me a few moments to absorb this panorama, but it could also be an enemy. I had to tear myself away from sightseeing and get to work. While Tom held my foot to anchor me, I positioned a sixteen-millimeter Mauer movie camera on its mount and retrieved a nuclear emulsion package that recorded radiation data and measured the impact of space dust. Then I stretched forward and planted a small mirror on the nose of the spacecraft. Using it, Tom could watch when I started my trek back to the AMU.

After that, I prepared for my first big chore, evaluating something called "umbilical dynamics." I did not have the sort of space gun for mobility that Ed White had, for my job was to determine whether a person could maneuver in space just by pulling on the long umbilical tether.

So I pushed off and rose like a puppet on a string. I had been weightless for two days already, so that sensation wasn't new, but now I was moving away from my security blanket, the protective shell of *Gemini 9*. Instead of being trapped inside a claustrophobic spacecraft, I was suddenly surrounded by the limitless universe. Only two other men had ever experienced such a sensation. I did not feel lonely, for I knew the whole world was keeping up with my every move.

Some NASA shrinks had warned that when I looked down and saw the Earth speeding past so far below, I might be swamped by space euphoria, as if I was in a headlong fall. Ridiculous. My world was relative not to the Earth, but to the spacecraft, and we were bulleting along at exactly the same velocity. There was no disorientation whatsoever, and we never worried about space euphoria again.

My only connection with the real world was through the umbilical cord, which we called the "snake," and it set out to teach me a lesson in Newton's laws of motion. My slightest move would affect my entire body, ripple through the umbilical, and jostle the spacecraft. We were forced into an unwanted game of crack-the-whip, with Tom inside the Gemini and me on the other end of the snake.

Since I had nothing to stabilize my movements, I went out of control, tumbling every which way, and when I reached the end of the umbilical, I rebounded like a Bungee jumper, and the snake reeled me in as it tried to resume its original shape. I hadn't even done anything yet and was already losing the battle. There had been no advance warning on the difficulties I was having because everything I did was new. I was already beyond the experiences of White and Leonov, moving into uncharted territory. Nobody in history had ever done this before.

I felt as if I was wrestling an octopus. The umbilical cavorted with a life of its own, twirling like a ribbon, trying to trap me like a cord winding around a window shade. "Boy, that snake is really running around up here," I said. I was looping crazily around the spacecraft, ass over teakettle, as if slipping in puddles of space oil, with no control over the direction, position or movement of my body, and all the while the umbilical was trying to lasso me. I wasn't lost in space, but I was absolutely helpless. Without a stabilizing device, I had no control over the umbilical, and it pretty much did whatever it wanted. "I can't get to where I want to go," I told Tom in exasperation. "The snake is all over me."

It was not like hauling along on a taut rope, for I had to pull slowly, exactly through my center of gravity, and that was impossible. Even something as mundane as trying to unbend a kink in the umbilical would dangle me upside down or backward, and I was continuously tumbling in a slow-motion ballet. The only time I had any control at all was when I could grab tight just where the umbilical emerged from the hatch, as if holding a dog on a short leash. Otherwise the thing was rubbery as a worm and as stubborn as a curlicue telephone cord. It was flat-out mean.

I fought it for about thirty minutes before deciding that this snake was perhaps the most malicious serpent since the one Eve met in the Garden of Eden.

Having already set a record time for being outside a spacecraft, I needed a rest. I grabbed a small handrail and pawed my way back to the open hatch, a drowning man reaching for a titanium beach. Once stabilized, I took a deep breath. And burped. The briny taste of that big green pickle I devoured during the last scrub party five days ago returned and would haunt me for the rest of the spacewalk.

My aimless roller-coaster experience with the umbilical complete, I passed my conclusions on to Tom and Mission Control. Future space-walkers, when they were out where the only rules were push and pull, action and reaction, needed some means of propulsion for control, and the spacecraft needed more points and rails to grab. Without such tools, they, too, would flop around like a rag doll.

I took a short break before moving to the rear of the spacecraft, where the backpack was stowed, and again was faced with the enormity of what lay before my eyes, a feast for the senses. When viewed through the spacecraft window, outer space had been only six inches wide and eight inches high, but now . . . wow!

The naked Sun, an intense ball of gleaming white fire, stared at me, a tiny interloper in its realm. The view of Earth was incredible from my treehouse in the galaxy as my home planet swooshed beneath my boots. The blue horizon had vanished at sunrise and now was merely a tissue-thin curved band of cerulean color terminating in black space. From up where there was no weather, I looked down on the tops of thunderstorms and the giant cottony fingers of Hurricane Alma. In the open seas, I could make out the V-shape wakes of ships, and on land, the dark grids of major cities. Mountain ranges spawned graceful rivers that slid toward the oceans, and I could see the Mississippi wiggling down to New Orleans. A rainbow-wide palette of colors presented emerald rainforests and bronze deserts, sapphire water and ivory clouds, and above it all, total blackness. Try to imagine a place with no boundaries, a room with no walls, an empty well as deep and limitless as your imagination, for that is where I was. And it was going to be my home for the next few hours!

The clock was ticking and I needed to reach the rear of the space-craft while I still had sunlight, then check out the backpack and strap it on during darkness. Then I would exchange the umbilical connected to my chest pack for the power and oxygen contained within the AMU, and tether myself to the spacecraft with a 125-foot-long piece of thin nylon line. So the next time the Sun popped up, Tom would flip a switch, the single bolt holding the backpack to the Gemini would shear, and I'd be off, rocketing around on my own, the first human to be an independent satellite. Master of the Universe.

But first, I had to get to where the backpack was folded up like some bizarre bird in a nest. My space suit fought my every move, and I needed both flexibility and mobility, the two things it did not have. It was blown up like a balloon figure in the Macy's Thanksgiving parade, and tried to hold that shape, no matter how I sought to bend it. Push in on a party balloon and it will resume its original shape when your finger pressure is removed. Same thing in outer space. A diamond-shaped web of material had been woven within the suit for additional strength, giving it all the flexibility of a rusty suit of armor. Just to bend my arm required exerting muscle strength to hold the new position. My heartbeat increased with the effort, and I was breathing hard, trying to find leverage. I was thankful for those long hours I had spent in a gym, building muscles and staying in shape.

The bell-shaped Gemini package was made of two sections. When the second-stage rockets tore away after launch, we were left with the reentry module, which was our living and working environment, and behind that was a larger section like a caboose on a train. Designed to connect the reentry module to the rocket, the aerodynamic "adapter section" contained things like fuel cells, oxygen tanks, and mechanical apparatus. When the booster rocket was kicked away, a recessed area was exposed at the bottom of the adapter section, and in the middle of that inward curving base was my rocket pack.

I worked my way hand-over-hand along a small railing, stopping periodically to hook the umbilical through small rings similar to the wire supports that hold a TV antenna cable stretched above a rooftop. By putting the umbilical through one of those "eyes," my line of life support would be steady and out of harm's way. Or so I thought until I found a nasty surprise waiting at the end of the adapter section. A jagged, sawtooth edge had been left all the way around when the Titan ripped away, something nobody had thought about when planning my spacewalk. With careful fingers, I positioned the supporting wires just above the razor-sharp metal to prevent it from slicing my lifeline or my suit. A space suit with a hole in it can quickly become the shroud of a corpse.

As I swung around the rear of the adapter and vanished from Tom's view in the mirror, the Sun blinked out and we entered darkness over South Africa. I unfolded the restraining bars alongside the backpack, and clicked on a pair of tiny lights for illumination. Only one lit up, providing less help than a candle. I raised my golden outer visor and grabbed the bars tightly.

Lord, I was tired. My heart was motoring at about 155 beats per minute, I was sweating like a pig, the pickle was a pest, and I had yet to begin my real work. I held on for dear life to those two thin metal bars as I was hauled through space at the incredible speed of some five miles per second.

Barbara had gotten up early that morning and, after some coffee, stood before her closet, planning what to wear. The women of America would be eyeing what Mrs. Astronaut wore when she stepped to the microphones to say how proud she was of her husband. She chose a pink sweater and pants, then swept her ash-blond hair into a pyramid of curls. Tracy was also dressed in pink, matching her mom, and they were camera-ready knockouts.

Many astronauts and cosmonauts had gone up in rockets, so a launch, even one as troublesome as *Gemini 9*, had become somewhat routine for the nation's huge audience of spaceophiles. Only two, however, had ever walked in space. I had coached Barbara as much as possible on what to expect, but since I really had no firm idea what it was going to be like, both of us had to accept the unknown. Roy Neal of NBC, an old friend, had come by for a visit and she confided, "I'm so scared." Roy took her by the hand and replied, "Let me tell you something, and never forget it. The more times they fly, the more they learn and the better chance they have of success."

When I opened the hatch, all she knew was that her 176-pound husband was out there seeing and feeling things about which mankind had only dreamed. Roger Chaffee spread out charts and briefing papers in the living room that morning, ready to explain every detail and answer any questions she might have, and the Mission Control squawk box relayed our conversations. Martha walked over with her husband to lend moral support, and slowly our living room filled with people. On television, the spacewalk explanations of anchormen were supplemented by dangling puppets that were supposed to represent me.

Tom could no longer see me preparing the backpack for the ride of a lifetime, but the communications link through the umbilical allowed me to explain that things weren't quite going as expected. "It's pretty much of a bear getting at this thing," I told him.

The single working light, not much more than a flashlight bulb, was totally inadequate. I could barely see anything at all as I worked through the thirty-five different functions required to make the thing ready to fly, everything from pushing buttons and opening valves to connecting the oxygen supply. My exertions were taking a toll because what seemed simple during our Earth simulations was nearly impossible in true zero gravity. I had done this exercise a hundred times aboard an Air Force cargo plane that could fly a maneuver to create weightlessness for about twenty seconds. *The airplane said I can do this, so why isn't it working?* Sweat beaded on me and stung my eyes. The helmet prevented me from wiping them. Eventually I flipped the final switch and the backpack powered up. Almost time to fly.

An hour and thirty-seven minutes into my spacewalk, as I became the first human ever to circle the Earth outside a spacecraft and see the night on his own planet during a spacewalk, our old nemesis, the Gemini jinx, struck again.

I was having a hard time seeing things, but it took a while to realize that it wasn't just because of the darkness. I was working so hard that the artificial environment created by the space suit simply could not absorb all of the carbon dioxide and humidity I was pumping out. Vision through my helmet was as mottled as the inside of a windshield on a winter morning, and I told Tom, "This visor is sure fogging up." That's when the spacecraft commander became concerned, perhaps thinking about his little chat with Deke about what to do in the event I could not get back into the spacecraft.

Why is floating in space and turning a few dials so difficult? Let me give you a couple of tests. Connect two garden hoses and turn on the water. Now, using only one hand, try to unscrew them. Or, hold a bottle of soda or beer at arm's length, and using a single hand, remove the twist-off top. For extra reality, run a mile before you start so you're nice and tired, do it while wearing two pairs of extra-thick gloves and close your eyes to simulate being unable to see. Stand on your head while doing some of these things to resemble tumbling in space. You get the idea.

The major problem was my inability to purchase any leverage without the help of gravity. A couple of thin metal stirrups designed to hold my feet in place were entirely insufficient, and to get some stability, I slid my right foot beneath the loop and stood on it, hard, with the left. Like an old sailor who always kept one hand on a brace when aloft, I held tightly to the restraining bar with one hand while working with the other. Sheer arm and wrist strength was needed just to stay in place, and I was again thankful for the long hours that Charlie Bassett and I spent lifting weights to develop muscular forearms.

As soon as one end of me was stabilized, the other end tended to float away. The work was more than hard, and I was panting for breath as my heartbeat soared to 180 beats per minute. Since the visor was fogged on the inside, and I obviously couldn't remove the helmet to wipe it dry, my only choice was to rub my nose against the inside of the shield to make a hole through which I could see.

Then the backpack itself was a complex piece of machinery, loaded with valves and levers and dials, many tucked away, in hard-to-reach places, forcing me to rely on the reflection in a polished metal mirror on my wrist, and on the reduced sense of touch through bulky space gloves.

When I tried to turn one of the valves, Mr. Newton's laws of motion would go into effect, the valve would turn me equally as hard in the opposite direction, and there I would go again, drifting off into space. Without leverage, just turning a small knob was nearly impossible: *Aghhhh*, my body went the other way until I could snag a new hand-hold. Then my feet would flip free again. Weariness threatened to overcome me and my body screamed for a rest period, but I could not oblige, for I was in a race with the Sun. This was my only chance and I couldn't afford to quit. At dawn, I was supposed to be wearing this damned backpack, and, by God, I intended to do just that. If my body could hold out. I was sucking oxygen at a fearsome rate, and always at the edge of my mind was that sharp, sawtoothed metal ring around the adapter section, which threatened to prick my suit while I tumbled without direction.

For ease of stowage, the slick arms of the backpack were telescoped and folded, and trying to get them extended into place was akin to straightening wet spaghetti. I pulled, and the arms pulled back. I twisted them and they twisted me. Progress was measured in millimeters and rapid heartbeats. I eventually got them locked into place, turned, and slid my bottom onto the little saddle seat, and strapped in with a common seatbelt.

Although my mask was cold, my lower back was scalding hot. During the somersaults of daylight umbilical dynamics, I had ripped apart the rear seams on those seven inner layers of heavy insulation and the Sun had baked the exposed triangle of unprotected skin. Now I had a major sunburn and nothing could be done about it until I took off the suit, which would be at least another day. I had a lot bigger things to worry about at the moment, so I disregarded the fiery sensation.

Now I had to exchange the umbilical from the spacecraft for the oxygen and power contained in the backpack itself. More twisting and turning, but at least now, being buckled in, I had a bit of leverage, and could make the swap. It was the first time that a human had cut the secure lifeline to a spacecraft. I was now really out there on my own.

By doing so, I lost radio contact with Tom. The communications link that ran through the umbilical was gone, replaced by a little line-of-sight radio in the backpack. Since I was in the rear of the adapter section and Tom was in the spacecraft, the weak signal couldn't penetrate the steel between us. When I spoke, he heard mostly crackling garble and barely heard me report, "I can't see in front of my eyeballs."

He told the ground controllers, who could not hear me, that the workload was about four or five times more than what had been anticipated, that communications had degraded, and I couldn't see through my visor. "If the situation doesn't improve . . . call it a no go on the AMU. Let him stay there and rest a while." Although I knew he was only being prudent, I had hoped he would not say that, because it just gave Mission Control reason to scrub my flight with the backpack.

Prior to switching over from the umbilical, the medical teams on Earth had been able to read data from my body sensors. Now they could not, and being a rather hand-wringing lot by nature, the doctors grew alarmed. They had lost control! They knew I had been panting with exertion, although I had tried not to breathe heavily. The last thing I wanted was for important decisions to be reached because of pessimism around the flight surgeon's console, for I knew my situation much better than anyone on the ground.

Nevertheless, their most recent charts determined I was spending energy at a rate equivalent to running up a flight of 116 steps every minute. My normal heartbeat had almost tripled, and in their expert opinions, things had gone haywire and I was in a zone from which I might not return. Cernan, they declared, was in deep trouble.

I still wasn't ready to admit that, and gulped with a sense of disappointment at the realization of what must be going on in Mission Control. I had come so far and now this unique chance to accomplish something never done before might be snatched away from me. It was ridiculous, I thought, to have worked my ass off to get this far and not go all the way. If they were going to quit, they should have said so back when I was wrestling the snake. *I'm so close!* My determination not to fail could either lead to one of the greatest achievements in space exploration, or it could lead to my ultimate downfall and cost me my life. Tired as I was, I still wanted to go for it.

Sitting on my tiny throne, I rubbed my nose against the mask again to make a hole in the vaporous shield and peeked out. It was still night, and Australia was passing beneath me, lights sprinkling Perth in the west and Sydney in the east, on opposite coasts of that sprawling continent. I knew that on the other side of the world, where the Sun still shone, were my wife, our little daughter, everything that I loved and held dear. Space, for the first time, seemed hostile, as if I had finally met my match. I had to admit to myself that I was barely hanging on, but I still wanted to fly that damned backpack.

Wisdom prevailed on all of us as the Sun came up.

"Can you see out at all, Geno?" Tom's voice crackled, almost indecipherable. "Can you read me okay? Yes or no?" I shouted into my microphone but he could barely understand me, so we had a garbled, stilted discussion, and reached a disappointing decision.

"Okay," he said, "Your transmission is awfully garbled. Okay. Did you get the word? I say it's a no go . . . because you can't see it now. Switch back to the spacecraft electrical umbilical."

It was the correct decision, and Tom wasn't about to reconsider. He passed word to the ground. "Hawaii, *Gemini 9*."

The tracking station in Hawaii acknowledged.

"We called it quits with the AMU," said Tom. "We had no choice."

"Roger, we concur," came the reply.

"Gene said to pass along that he hated to do it, but he doesn't have any choice, and neither do I."

"Roger. We understand." And that was it for the nonflight of the rocket backpack.

With a sigh, I closed my eyes and turned my helmet to the new morning Sun so the warmth could defrost away some of the moisture on the visor. I had done all I could. I hadn't quit, and had been ready to romp if that had been the decision. Regretfully, the choice was taken out of my hands, and although I didn't particularly like leaving the job undone, I knew it was the right thing to do. It was time to go home.

Only two things left—getting out of the AMU and back into the spacecraft. Unstrapping, getting reconnected to the spacecraft umbilical and climbing out around the adapter section, carefully retrieving my lifeline as I went, was easier than going out, but time consuming. But I wasn't as gentle and precise this time. The AMU no longer had a mission on this flight and I didn't care about the damned thing any longer. Ten million dollars the Air Force had paid to build the gizmo and we were going to kick it into space and let it burn up in the atmosphere without a second thought.

Time sped by as I escaped the clutches of the backpack, and crawled and clawed my way back up the side of the spacecraft. The inflated space suit had lost none of its stiffness over the past two hours and the visor was clouded solid. My last reserves of energy were flowing out like a tide, and my problems were not over. In fact, one of the hardest parts of the mission was just at my fingertips.

The spacewalk had been on almost everyone's mind. Professional golfer Bert Yancey was so engrossed watching the television reports in his motel room that he forgot his tee time for the final round of the $100,000 Memphis Open. In Rome, Pope Paul VI offered a prayer for us during his address from the Apostolic Palace. At that point, I appreciated all the help I could get.

In Texas, worry had crept into our living room. Two hours into my spacewalk, Roger was concerned that what he was hearing didn't match the original mission plan. He left the room to talk privately on a special red telephone that was a direct link to Mission Control. When he returned, his face was tight, and he sat down with Barbara to examine the timeline again.

"Gene's got about twenty-five minutes before he hits the dark side again," he told her. "Without the Sun, it will be colder, and his face mask will fog up worse than ever." Then he raised a subject that few had thought about until that point. "That will make it difficult for him to get back into the spacecraft."

Barbara nodded. "How long will it take to get back in?" she asked.

Roger looked her in the eye. "About twenty minutes." A five-minute margin had never seemed so tiny.

Martha edged closer and put an arm around my wife. "Come on Gene," she whispered. "Get back in."

From Ed's experience, we knew that climbing back into the spacecraft was going to be a bitch. Instead of saying it was difficult, Ed should have said it was damned near impossible. If an astronaut was taller than five-foot-nine, he could not stretch out in the cramped cabin without bumping his head or feet. Even without the helmet, I was six feet tall, which meant I was going to have to scrunch down quite a bit to get back inside. I was also exhausted and wearing steel pants. But no Navy mission is finished until a pilot lands on the carrier, and in outer space, the job isn't done until the spacecraft hatch is closed and locked.

After I had left the hatch, we had closed it to about three inches to allow room for the snake to emerge but also to protect the interior of the craft from the direct rays of the broiling Sun. I groped blindly with my fingers to find the hatch. "I can't see," I told Tom, as I hunted for something familiar. My wandering gloves finally wrapped around the hatch and I lifted it open, turned and stuck my feet inside. Tom, who had reeled in the umbilical, now reached over and grabbed an ankle to anchor me and, at last, put an end to my weightless ballet.

But I kicked the Hasselblad camera that Tom had used to take pictures of my spacewalk. The camera floated out before my eyes and I made a grab for it, as if I were a first baseman going after a foul ball. The bulky glove hit it, and as I no longer had the strength to keep my fingers flexed enough to hold it tightly, the camera spun away. There went my still pictures, but I did retrieve the movie camera.

We were over the Atlantic when I began my eerie effort to squeeze into the spacecraft. Tom held my feet as the inflexible space suit fought like a live thing. Trying to bend it was like trying to fold an inflated life raft. Tom was unable to help any more than he was doing, and there was no one else around, so it was me against the suit and the spacecraft. I was panting hard with the effort, still taking care what I said, because the doctors were listening.

I inched lower and forced my legs to bend into a duckwalk position with Tom holding my feet on the L-shaped seat. If he let go so I could try and stick my legs into the well beyond the seat, I would just float away again, so I tried to crouch. Excruciating pain shot through my thighs as I pulled my body lower, pretzeling like a space limbo dancer, and managed to slide my toes, then my heels over the edge of the seat while pushing my knees beneath the instrument panel. My boots were now planted firmly against a steel plate that sealed the front side of the seat, toes pointed down, and my legs were bent in an awful V position as I pressed down even further on them. I had no choice but to ignore the painful cramps.

My goal was to get my butt flat in the seat and my spine against the backrest, but that was impossible because of the stiff, inflated suit. Effort turned to struggle, then to outright fight as I gained territory a sweaty millimeter at a time. My heart rate, which had calmed somewhat, shot up again as I squirmed about, and I was sucking air forty times a minute.

But this is what Mission Control heard. "Coming in, no problem," Tom said. "No problem," I agreed. No use telling the doctors more than they needed to know. They couldn't help anyway.

I got my fingers around the bottom of the instrument panel and pulled again. Another bit of movement as I wedged my knees beneath the panel so I could use them for even more leverage. That was a tight fit when the suit was soft, and almost impossible when inflated. Go like this, *unnhhh*. Like that, *arrghh*. Push and wiggle and push again, try to *ohhhh*, force the suit to bend. It was worse than trying to stuff a cork back into a champagne bottle.

Eventually, I was halfway in and halfway out the spacecraft, still using all my strength to shove my bulk down into the cabin. I forced my shoulders below the level of the hatch, scrunched down as hard as I could, bent my neck and head at an impossible angle, and pulled on the hatch. It hit the top of my helmet and wouldn't close. Sonofabitch! I still was not in far enough.

Tom reached over with his right hand and grabbed a broomsticklike handle with a chain on it that he could pull to lower my hatch further, and with a jolt, jammed it down another few inches. That caught the hatch on the first tooth of a closing ratchet, which was good, but made things worse than ever for me. I was compressed to a point where I had nothing left to bend and the damned door still wasn't secure. Another scrunch, and I was in awful pain. The body just wasn't built to fold like a piece of paper.

Finally, the latches engaged and I pumped the handle until the hatch closed enough so that it could not pop open. Pain clouded my eyes and I was frozen in place by the suit, unable to unfold my feet, which were still tight beneath me. I could not push my torso any lower, and my knees were immobile, pressed hard against the underside of the panel. We got another click. More work, more clicks from the closing ratchet as I ground my teeth. No bones had yet broken, although I don't know why. I'd never known such pain. I gave the handle a last twist, and the hatch finally locked tight.

I might admit that I was crying, but only Tom really knows. "Tom," I whispered on our private intercom, feeling mortally wounded. "If we can't pressurize the spacecraft in a hurry and I have to stay this way for the rest of the flight, I'll die!" I just couldn't remain trapped in that awful position. Air could not get to my lungs, spots danced before my eyes, and incredible agony lanced through me as I clung to the edge of consciousness.

Tom didn't waste a second, and the hiss of the incoming oxygen pressurizing the spacecraft was the most beautiful sound I had ever heard. As the pressure increased, the suit mercifully softened. When I could move my legs, I painfully unfolded my feet and straightened my body, finally able to fit back into the little seat.

I removed the helmet and inhaled sweet oxygen. My face was as red as a radish and Tom was shocked by the sight. One ironclad rule of our training was never, ever to spray water inside a spacecraft, because the floating bubbles might short out electrical circuits. Tom didn't hesitate. He grabbed the water nozzle, pointed it at me like a pistol and squirted streams of liquid coolness onto my burning skin. I closed my eyes with relief, feeling saved, resurrected, back from the near-dead.

I had spent two hours and nine minutes in space, and in that time had "walked" some 36,000 miles, making one complete circle of the world and more than one-third of the way around again. The job was done and I lived to tell the tale, although the memory still makes me tired.

When things calmed, we had the rest of the day to relax, which I was happy to do. I was as weary as I had ever been in my life and when I peeled off my gloves, my hands had swollen so much that the metal ring cuffs ripped the skin from them. At that point, I was so elated at just being alive that I didn't care about losing a few strips of flesh.

I was confident that no one could have fared any better on the spacewalk, for the unforeseen problems I encountered would have been the same for anyone. But the fact remained that I had been sent out to do a job and didn't get it done.

I wasn't worried so much about the whole world watching me, because most people wouldn't understand what had happened anyway. The audience that concerned me was my fellow astros, and there was a clear feeling in my own mind that, somehow, I had screwed up, that I had let them down. I had given it my all, and looking back over the years, I now know that the mission had been pretty damned ambitious from the start. But at that moment, I didn't know how to make the guys appreciate the problems. I knew they would never say anything to my face, but sly comments were sure to be made in a few private conversations around the office. *The rookie couldn't hack it. A real test pilot would have found some way to make the thing work.* Did that equate with failure on my part? So much had gone wrong with *Gemini 9*, would this be my one and only flight? Would anybody understand?

from High Adventure
by James Norman Hall

James Norman Hall (1887-1951) is best known for the novel Mutiny on the Bounty (written with Charles Nordhoff). Hall grew up in Iowa, but enlisted in the British army at the start of World War I. In 1916, he joined the Lafayette Flying Corps, a group of American volunteers who flew for France. One of his closest comrades was another young American, named Drew.

Drew and I, like most pilots during the first weeks of service at the front, were worth little to the Allied cause. We were warned often enough that the road to efficiency in military aviation is a long and dangerous one. We were given much excellent advice by aviators who knew what they were talking about. Much of this we solicited, in fact, and then proceeded to disregard it item by item. Eager to get results, we plunged into our work with the valor of ignorance, the result being that Drew was shot down in one of his first encounters, escaping with his life by one of those more than miracles for which there is no explanation. That I did not fare as badly or worse is due solely to the indulgence of that godfather of ours, already mentioned, who watched over my first flights while in a mood beneficently pro-Ally.

Drew's adventure followed soon after our first patrol, when he had the near combat with the two-seater. Luckily, on that occasion, both the German pilot and his machine-gunner were taken completely off their guard. Not only did he attack with the sun squarely in his face, but he went down in a long, gradual dive, in full view of the gunner, who could not have asked for a better target. But the man was asleep, and this gave J. B. a dangerous contempt for all gunners of enemy nationality.

Lieutenant Talbott cautioned him. "You have been lucky, but don't get it into your head that this sort of thing happens often. Now, I'm going to give you a standing order. You are not to attack again, neither of you are to think of attacking, during your first month here. As likely as not it would be your luck the next time to meet an old pilot. If you did, I wouldn't give much for your chances. He would outmaneuver you in a minute. You will go out on patrol with the others, of course; it's the only way to learn to fight. But if you get lost, go back to our balloons and stay there until it is time to go home."

Neither of us obeyed this order, and, as it happened, Drew was the one to suffer. A group of American officers visited the squadron one afternoon. In courtesy to our guests, it was decided to send out all the pilots for an additional patrol, to show them how the thing was done. Twelve machines were in readiness for the sortie, which was set for seven o'clock, the last one of the day. We were to meet at three thousand metres, and then to divide forces, one patrol to cover the east half of the sector and one the west.

We got away beautifully, with the exception of Drew, who had motor-trouble and was five minutes late in starting. With his permission I insert here his own account of the adventure—a letter written while he was in hospital.

No doubt you are wondering what happened, listening, meanwhile, to many I-told-you-so explanations from the others. This will be hard on you, but bear up, son. It might not be a bad plan to listen, with the understanding as well as with the ear, to some expert advice on how to bag the

Hun. To quote the prophetic Miller, "I'm telling you this for your own good."

I gave my name and the number of the escadrille to the medical officer at the *poste de secours*. He said he would 'phone the captain at once, so that you must know before this, that I have been amazingly lucky. I fell the greater part of two miles—count 'em, two!—before I actually regained control, only to lose it again. I fainted while still several hundred feet from the ground; but more of this later. Couldn't sleep last night. Had a fever and my brain went on a spree, taking advantage of my helplessness. I just lay in bed and watched it function. Besides, there was a great artillery racket all night long. It appeared to be coming from our sector, so you must have heard it as well. This hospital is not very far back and we get the full orchestral effect of heavy firing. The result is that I am dead tired to-day. I believe I can sleep for a week.

They have given me a bed in the officers' ward—me, a corporal. It is because I am an American, of course. Wish there was some way of showing one's appreciation for so much kindness. My neighbor on the left is a *chasseur* captain. A hand-grenade exploded in his face. He will go through life horribly disfigured. An old padre, with two machine-gun bullets in his hip, is on the other side. He is very patient, but sometimes the pain is a little too much for him. To a Frenchman, "Oh, là, là!" is an expression for every conceivable kind of emotion. In the future it will mean unbearable physical pain to me. Our orderlies are two *poilus*, long past military age. They are as gentle and thoughtful as the nurses themselves. One of them brought me lemonade all night long. Worthwhile getting wounded just to have something taste so good.

I meant to finish this letter a week ago, but haven't felt up to it. Quite perky this morning, so I'll go on with the tale of my "heroic combat." Only, first, tell me how that absurd account of it got into the "Herald"? I hope Talbott knows that I was not foolish enough to attack six Germans single-handed. If he doesn't, please enlighten him. His opinion of my common sense must be low enough, as it is.

We were to meet over S—— at three thousand metres, you remember, and to cover the sector at five thousand until dusk. I was late in getting away, and by the time I reached the rendezvous you had all gone. There wasn't a chasse machine in sight. I ought to have gone back to the balloons as Talbott advised, but thought it would be easy to pick you up later, so went on alone after I had got some height. Crossed the lines at thirty-five hundred metres, and finally got up to four thousand, which was the best I could do with my rebuilt engine. The Huns started shelling, but there were only a few of them that barked. I went down the lines for a quarter of an hour, meeting two Sepwiths and a Letord, but no Spads. You were almost certain to be higher than I, but my old packet was doing its best at four thousand, and getting overheated with the exertion. Had to throttle down and *pique* several times to cool off.

Then I saw you—at least I thought it was you—about four kilometres inside the German lines. I counted six machines, well grouped, one a good deal higher than the others and one several hundred metres below them. The pilot on top was doing beautiful *renversements* and an occasional barrel-turn, in Barry's manner. I was so certain it was our patrol that I started over at once, to join you. It was getting dusk and I lost sight of the machine lowest down for a few seconds. Without my knowing it, he was approaching at exactly my altitude. You know how difficult it is to see a machine in that position. Suddenly he loomed up in front of me like an express train, as you have seen them approach from the depths of a moving-picture screen, only ten times faster; and he was firing as he came. I realized my awful mistake, of course. His tracer bullets were going by on the left side, but he corrected his aim, and my motor seemed to be eating them up. I banked to the right, and was about to cut my motor and dive, when I felt a smashing blow in the left shoulder. A sickening sensation and a very peculiar one, not at all what I thought it might feel like to be hit with a bullet. I believed that it came from the German in front of me. But it couldn't have, for he was still approaching when I was hit, and I have learned here that the bullet entered from behind.

This is the history of less than a minute I'm giving you. It seemed much longer than that, but I don't suppose it was. I tried to shut down the motor, but couldn't manage it because my left arm was gone. I really believed that it had been blown off into space until I glanced down and saw that it was still there. But for any service it was to me, I might just as well have lost it. There was a vacant period of ten or fifteen seconds which I can't fill in. After that I knew that I was falling, with my motor going full speed. It was a helpless realization. My brain refused to act. I could do nothing. Finally, I did have one clear thought, "Am I on fire?" This cut right through the fog, brought me up broad awake. I was falling almost vertically, in a sort of half *vrille*. No machine but a Spad could have stood the strain. The Huns were following me and were not far away, judging by the sound of their guns. I fully expected to feel another bullet or two boring its way through. One did cut the skin of my right leg, although I didn't know this until I reached the hospital. Perhaps it was well that I did fall out of control, for the firing soon stopped, the Germans thinking, and with reason, that they had bagged me. Some proud Boche airman is wearing an iron cross on my account. Perhaps the whole crew of dare-devils has been decorated. However, no unseemly sarcasm. We would pounce on a lonely Hun just as quickly. There is no chivalry in war in these modern days.

I pulled out of the spin, got the broomstick between my knees, reached over, and shut down the motor with my right hand. The propeller stopped dead. I didn't much care, being very drowsy and tired. The worst of it was that I couldn't get my breath. I was gasping as though I had been hit in the pit of the stomach. Then I lost control again and started falling. It was awful! I was almost ready to give up. I believe that I said, out loud, "I'm going to be killed. This is my last sortie." At any rate, I thought it. Made one last effort and came out in *ligne de vol*, as nearly as I could judge, about one hundred and fifty metres from the ground. It was an ugly-looking place for landing, trenches and shell-holes everywhere. I was wondering in a vague way whether they were French or German, when I fell into the most restful sleep I've ever had in my life.

I have no recollection of the crash, not the slightest. I might have fallen as gently as a leaf. That is one thing to be thankful for among a good many others. When I came to, it was at once, completely. I knew that I was on a stretcher and remembered immediately exactly what had happened. My heart was going pit-a-pat, pit-a-pat, and I could hardly breathe, but I had no sensation of pain except in my chest. This made me think that I had broken every bone in my body. I tried moving first one leg, then the other, then my arms, my head, my body. No trouble at all, except with my left arm and side.

I accepted the miracle without attempting to explain it, for I had something more important to wonder about: who had the handles of my stretcher? The first thing I did was to open my eyes, but I was bleeding from a scratch on the forehead and saw only a red blur. I wiped them dry with my sleeve and looked again. The broad back in front of me was covered with mud. Impossible to distinguish the color of the tunic. But the shrapnel helmet above it was—French! I was in French hands. If ever I live long enough in one place, so that I may gather a few possessions and make a home for myself, on one wall of my living-room I will have a bust length portrait, rear view, of a French *brancardier*, mud-covered back and battered tin hat.

Do you remember our walk with Ménault in the rain, and the *déjeuner* at the restaurant where they made such wonderful omelettes? I am sure that you will recall the occasion, although you may have forgotten the conversation. I have not forgotten one remark of Ménault's apropos of talk about risks. If a man were willing, he said, to stake everything for it, he would accumulate an experience of fifteen or twenty minutes which would compensate him, a thousand times over, for all the hazard. "And if you live to be old," he said quaintly, "you can never be bored with life. You will have something, always, very pleasant to think about." I mention this in connection with my discovery that I was not in German hands. I have had five minutes of perfect happiness without any background—no thought of yesterday or to-morrow—to spoil it.

I said, "Bonjour, messieurs," in a gurgling voice. The man in front turned his head sidewise and said,—

"Tiens! Ça va, monsieur l'aviateur?"

The other one said, "Ah, mon vieux!" You know the inflection they give this expression, particularly when it means, "This is something wonderful!" He added that they had seen the combat and my fall, and little expected to find the pilot living, to say nothing of speaking. I hoped that they would go on talking, but I was being carried along a trench; they had to lift me shoulder-high at every turn, and needed all their energy. The Germans were shelling the lines. Several fell fairly close, and they brought me down a long flight of wooden steps into a dugout to wait until the worst of it should be over. While waiting, they told me that I had fallen just within the first-line trenches, at a spot where a slight rise in ground hid me from sight of the enemy. Otherwise, they might have had a bad time rescuing me. My Spad was completely wrecked. It fell squarely into a trench, the wings breaking the force of the fall. Before reaching the ground, I turned, they said, and was making straight for Germany. Fifty metres higher, and I would have come down in No Man's Land.

For a long time we listened in silence to the subdued *crr-ump, crr-ump*, of the shells. Sometimes showers of earth pattered down the stairway, and we would hear the high-pitched, droning *V-z-z-z* of pieces of shell-casing as they whizzed over the opening. One of them would say, "Not far, that one"; or, "He's looking for some one, that fellow," in a voice without a hint of emotion. Then, long silences and other deep, earth-shaking rumbles.

They asked me, several times, if I was suffering, and offered to go on to the *poste de secours* if I wanted them to. It was not heavy bombardment, but it would be safer to wait for a little while. I told them that I was ready to go on at any time, but not to hurry on my account; I was quite comfortable.

The light glimmering down the stairway faded out and we were in complete darkness. My brain was amazingly clear. It registered every trifling impression. I wish it might always be so intensely awake and active. There seemed to be four of us in the dugout; the two *brancardiers*, and this second self of mine, as curious as an eavesdropper at a key-hole, listening intently to everything, and then turning to whisper to me. The *brancardiers* repeated the same comments after every explosion. I thought: "They have been saying this to each other for over three years. It has become automatic. They will never be able to stop." I was feverish, perhaps. If it was fever, it burned away any illusions I may have had of modern warfare from the infantryman's viewpoint. I know that there is no glamour in it for them; that it has long since become a deadly monotony, an endless repetition of the same kinds of horror and suffering, a boredom more terrible than death itself, which is repeating itself in the same ways, day after day and month after month. It isn't often that an aviator has the chance I've had. It would be a good thing if they were to send us into the trenches for twenty-four hours, every few months. It would make us keener fighters, more eager to do our utmost to bring the war to an end for the sake of those *poilus*.

The dressing-station was in a very deep dugout, lighted by candles. At a table in the center of the room the medical officer was working over a man with a terribly crushed leg. Several others were sitting or lying along the wall, awaiting their turn. They watched every movement he made in an apprehensive, animal way, and so did I. They put me on the table next, although it was not my turn. I protested, but the doctor paid no attention. "Aviateur américain," again. It's a pity that Frenchmen can't treat us Americans as though we belong here.

As soon as the doctor had finished with me, my stretcher was fastened to a two-wheeled carrier and we started down a cobbled road to the ambulance station. I was light-headed and don't remember much of that part of the journey. Had to take refuge in another dugout when the Huns dropped a shell on an ammunition-dump in a village through which we were to pass. There was a deafening banging and booming for a long time, and when we did go through the town it was on the run. The whole place was in flames and small-arms ammunition still exploding. I remember seeing a long column of soldiers going at the double in the opposite direction, and they were in full marching order.

Well, this is the end of the tale; all of it, at any rate, in which you would be interested. It was one o'clock in the morning before I got between cool, clean sheets, and I was wounded about a quarter past eight. I have been tired ever since.

There is another aviator here, a Frenchman, who broke his jaw and both legs in a fall while returning from a night bombardment. His bed is across the aisle from mine; he has a formidable-looking apparatus fastened on his head and under his chin, to hold his jaw firm until the bones knit. He is forbidden to talk, but breaks the rule whenever the nurse leaves the ward. He speaks a little English and has told me a delightful story about the origin of aerial combat. A French pilot, a friend of his, he says, attached to a certain army group during August and September, 1914, often met a German aviator during his reconnaissance patrols. In those Arcadian days, fighting in the air was a development for the future, and these two pilots exchanged greetings, not cordially, perhaps, but courteously: a wave of the hand, as much as to say, "We are enemies, but we need not forget the civilities." Then they both went about their work of spotting batteries, watching for movements of troops, etc. One morning the German failed to return the salute. The Frenchman thought little of this, and greeted him in the customary manner at their next meeting. To his surprise, the Boche shook his fist at him in the most blustering and caddish way. There was no mistaking the insult. They had passed not fifty metres from each other, and the Frenchman distinctly saw the closed fist. He was saddened by the incident, for he had hoped that some of the ancient courtesies of war would survive in the aerial branch of the service, at least. It angered him too; therefore, on his next reconnaissance, he ignored the German. Evidently the Boche air-squadrons were being Prussianized. The enemy pilot approached very closely and threw a missile at him. He could not be sure what it was, as the object went wide of the mark; but he was so incensed that he made a *virage*, and drawing a small flask from his pocket, hurled it at his boorish antagonist. The flask contained some excellent port, he said, but he was repaid for the loss in seeing it crash on the exhaust-pipe of the enemy machine.

This marked the end of courtesy and the beginning of active hostilities in the air. They were soon shooting at each other with rifles, automatic pistols, and at last with machine guns. Later developments we know about. The night bombarder has been telling me this yarn in serial form. When the nurse is present, he illustrates the last chapter by means of gestures. I am ready to believe everything but the incident about the port. That doesn't sound plausible. A Frenchman would have thrown his watch before making such a sacrifice!

A little more than a year after our first meeting in the Paris restaurant which has so many pleasant memories for us, Drew completed his first one hundred hours of flight over the lines, an event in the life of an airman which calls for a celebration of some sort. Therefore, having been granted leave for the afternoon, the two of us came into the old French town of Bar-le-Duc, by the toy train which wanders down from the Verdun sector. We had dinner in one of those homelike little places where the food is served by the proprietor himself. On this occasion it was served hurriedly, and the bill presented promptly at eight o'clock. Our host was very sorry, but "les sales Boches, vous savez, messieurs?" They had come the night before: a dozen houses destroyed, women and children killed and maimed. With a full moon to guide them, they would be sure to return to-night. "Ah, cette guerre! Quand sera-t-elle finie?" He offered us a refuge until our train should leave. Usually, he said, he played solitaire while waiting for the Germans, but with houses tumbling about one's ears, he much preferred company. "And my wife and I are old people. She is very deaf, heureusement. She hears nothing."

J. B. declined the invitation. "A brave way that would be to finish our evening!" he said as we walked down the silent street. "I wanted to say, 'Monsieur, I have just finished my first one hundred hours of flight at the front.' But he wouldn't have known what that means."

I said, "No, he wouldn't have known." Then we had no further talk for about two hours. A few soldiers, late arrivals, were prowling about in the shadow of the houses, searching for food and a warm kitchen where they might eat it. Some insistent ones pounded on the door of a restaurant far in the distance.

"Dites donc, patron! Nous avons faim, nom de Dieu! Est-ce-que tout le monde est mort ici?"

> "Only a host of phantom listeners,
> That dwelt in the lone house then,
> Stood listening in the quiet of the moonlight
> To that voice from the world of men."

It was that kind of silence, profound, tense, ghostlike. We walked through street after street, from one end of the town to the other, and saw only one light, a faint glimmer which came from a slit of a cellar window almost on the level of the pavement. We were curious, no doubt. At any rate, we looked in. A woman was sitting on a cot bed with her arms around two little children. They were snuggled up against her and both fast asleep; but she was sitting very erect, in a strained, listening attitude, staring straight before her. Since that night we have believed, both of us, that if wars can be won only by haphazard night bombardments of towns where there are women and children, then they had far better be lost.

But I am writing a journal of high adventure of a cleaner kind, in which all the resources in skill and cleverness of one set of men are pitted against those of another set. We have no bomb-dropping to do, and there are but few women and children living in the territory over which we fly. One hundred hours is not a great while as time is measured on the ground, but in terms of combat patrols, the one hundredth part of it has held more of adventure in the true meaning of the word than we have had during the whole of our lives previously.

At first we were far too busy learning the rudiments of combat to keep an accurate record of flying time. We thought our aeroplane clocks convenient pieces of equipment rather than necessary ones. I remember coming down from my first air battle and the breathless account I gave of it at the bureau, breathless and vague. Lieutenant Talbott listened quietly, making out the *compte rendu* as I talked. When I had finished, he emphasized the haziness of my answers to his questions by quoting them: "Region: 'You know, that big wood!' Time: 'This morning, of course!' Rounds fired: 'Oh, a lot!' " etc.

Not until we had been flying for a month or more did we learn how to make the right use of our clocks and of our eyes while in the air. We listened with amazement to after-patrol talk at the mess. We learned more of what actually happened on our sorties, after they were over than while they were in progress. All of the older pilots missed seeing nothing which there was to see. They reported the numbers of the enemy planes encountered, the types, where seen and when. They spotted batteries, trains in stations back of the enemy lines, gave the hour precisely, reported any activity on the roads. In moments of exasperation Drew would say, "I think they are stringing us! This is all a put-up job!" Certainly this did appear to be the case at first. For we were air-blind. We saw little of the activity all around us, and details on the ground had no significance. How were we to take thought of time and place and altitude, note the peculiarities of enemy machines, count their numbers, and store all this information away in memory at the moment of combat? This was a great problem.

"What I need," J. B. used to say, "is a traveling private secretary. I'll do the fighting and he can keep the diary."

I needed one, too, a man air-wise and battle-wise, who could calmly take note of my clock, altimeter, temperature and pressure dials, identify exactly the locality on my map, count the numbers of the enemy, estimate their approximate altitude,—all this when the air was crisscrossed with streamers of smoke from machine-gun tracer bullets, and opposing aircraft were maneuvering for position, diving and firing at each other, spiraling, nose-spinning, wing-slipping, climbing, in a confusing intermingling of tricolor cocards and black crosses.

We made gradual progress, the result being that our patrols became a hundred-fold more fascinating, sometimes, in fact, too much so. It was important that we should be able to read the ground, but more important still to remember that what was happening there was only of secondary concern to us. Often we became absorbed in watching what was taking place below us, to the exclusion of any thought of aerial activity, our chances for attack or of being attacked. The view, from the air, of a heavy bombardment, or of an infantry attack under cover of barrage fires, is a truly terrible spectacle, and in the air one has a feeling of detachment which is not easily overcome.

Yet it must be overcome, as I have said, and cannot say too many times for the benefit of any young airman who may read this journal. During an offensive the air swarms with planes. They are at all altitudes, from the lowest artillery *réglage* machines at a few hundreds of metres, to the highest *avions de chasse* at six thousand meters and above. *Réglage*, photographic, and reconnaissance planes have their particular work to do. They defend themselves as best they can, but almost never attack. Combat *avions*, on the other hand, are always looking for victims. They are the ones chiefly dangerous to the unwary pursuit pilot.

Drew's first official victory came as the result of a one-sided battle with an Albatross single-seater, whose pilot evidently did not know there was an enemy within miles of him. No more did J. B. for that matter. "It was pure accident," he told me afterward. He had gone from Rheims to the Argonne forest without meeting a single German. "And I didn't want to meet one; for it was Thanksgiving Day. It has associations for me, you know. I'm a New Englander." It is not possible to convince him that it has any real significance for men who were not born on the North Atlantic seaboard. Well, all the way he had been humming

"Over the river and through the wood
To grandfather's house we go,"

to himself. It is easy to understand why he didn't want to meet a German. He must have been in a curiously mixed frame of mind. He covered the sector again and passed over Rheims, going northeast. Then he saw the Albatross; "and if you had been standing on one of the towers of the cathedral you would have seen a very unequal battle." The German was about two kilometres inside his own lines, and at least a thousand metres below. Drew had every advantage.

"He did n't see me until I opened fire, and then, as it happened, it was too late. My gun didn't jam!"

The German started falling out of control, Drew following him down until he lost sight of him in making a *virage*.

I leaned against the canvas wall of a hangar, registering incredulity. Three times out of seven, to make a conservative estimate, we fight inconclusive battles because of faulty machine guns or defective ammunition. The ammunition, most of it that is bad, comes from America.

While Drew was giving me the details, an orderly from the bureau brought word that an enemy machine had just been reported shot down on our sector. It was Drew's Albatross, but he nearly lost official credit for having destroyed it, because he did not know exactly the hour when the combat occurred. His watch was broken and he had neglected asking for another before starting. He judged the time of the attack, approximately, as two-thirty, and the infantry observers, reporting the result, gave it as twenty minutes to three. The region in both cases coincided exactly, however, and, fortunately, Drew's was the only combat which had taken place in that vicinity during the afternoon.

For an hour after his return he was very happy. He had won his first victory, always the hardest to gain, and had been complimented by the commandant, by Lieutenant Nungesser, the *Roides Aces*, and by other French and American pilots. There is no petty jealousy among airmen, and in our group the *esprit de corps* is unusually fine. Rivalry is keen, but each squadron takes almost as much pride in the work of the other squadrons as it does in its own.

The details of the result were horrible. The Albatross broke up two thousand metres from the ground, one wing falling within the French lines. Drew knew what it meant to be wounded and falling out of control. But his Spad held together. He had a chance for his life. Supposing the German to have been merely wounded—An airman's joy in victory is a short-lived one.

Nevertheless, a curious change takes place in his attitude toward his work, as the months pass. I can best describe it in terms of Drew's experience and my own. We came to the front feeling deeply sorry for ourselves, and for all airmen of whatever nationality, whose lives were to be snuffed out in their promising beginnings. I used to play "The Minstrel Boy to the War Has Gone" on a tin flute, and Drew wrote poetry. While we were waiting for our first machine, he composed "The Airman's Rendezvous," written in the manner of Alan Seeger's poem.

> "And I in the wide fields of air
> Must keep with him my rendezvous.
> It may be I shall meet him there
> When clouds, like sheep, move slowly through
> The pathless meadows of the sky
> And their cool shadows go beneath,—
> I have a rendezvous with Death
> Some summer noon of white and blue."

There is more of it, in the same manner, all of which he read me in a husky voice. I, too, was ready to weep at our untimely fate. The strange thing is that his prophecy came so very near being true. He had the first draft of the poem in his breast-pocket when wounded, and has kept the gory relic to remind him—not that he needs reminding—of the airy manner in which he canceled what ought to have been a *bona-fide* appointment.

I do not mean to reflect in any way upon Alan Seeger's beautiful poem. Who can doubt that it is a sincere, as well as a perfect, expression of a mood common to all young soldiers? Drew was just as sincere in writing his verses, and I put all the feeling I could into my tin-whistle interpretation of "The Minstrel Boy." What I want to make clear is, that a soldier's moods of self-pity are fleeting ones, and if he lives, he outgrows them.

Imagination is an especial curse to an airman, particularly if it takes a gloomy or morbid turn. We used to write "To whom it may concern" letters before going out on patrol, in which we left directions for the notification of our relatives and the disposal of our personal effects in case of death. Then we would climb into our machines thinking, "This may be our last sortie. We may be dead in an hour, in half an hour, in twenty minutes." We planned splendidly spectacular ways in which we were to be brought down, always omitting one, however, the most horrible as well as the most common,—in flames. Thank Fortune, we have outgrown this second and belated period of adolescence and can now take a healthy interest in our work.

Now, an inevitable part of the daily routine is to be shelled, persistently, methodically, and often accurately shelled. Our interest in this may, I suppose, be called healthy, inasmuch as it would be decidedly unhealthy to become indifferent to the activities of the German anti-aircraft gunners. It would be far-fetched to say that any airman ever looks forward zestfully to the business of being shot at with one hundred and fives; and seventy-fives, if they are well placed, are unpleasant enough. After one hundred hours of it, we have learned to assume that attitude of contemptuous toleration which is the manner common to all *pilotes de chasse*. We know that the chances of a direct hit are almost negligible, and that we have all the blue dome of the heavens in which to maneuver.

Furthermore, we have learned many little tricks by means of which we can keep the gunners guessing. By way of illustration, we are patrolling, let us say, at thirty-five hundred metres, crossing and recrossing the lines, following the patrol leader, who has his motor throttled down so that we may keep well in formation. The guns may be silent for the moment, but we know well enough what the gunners are doing. We know exactly where some of the batteries are, and the approximate location of all of them along the sector; and we know, from earlier experience, when we come within range of each individual battery. Presently one of them begins firing in bursts of four shells. If their first estimate of our range has been an accurate one, if they place them uncomfortably close, so that we can hear, all too well, above the roar of our motors, the rending *Gr-r-rOW, Gr-r-rOW*, of the shells as they explode, we sail calmly—to all outward appearances—on, maneuvering very little. The gunners, seeing that we are not disturbed, will alter their ranges, four times out of five, which is exactly what we want them to do.

The next bursts will be hundreds of metres below or above us, whereupon we show signs of great uneasiness, and the gunners, thinking they have our altitude, begin to fire like demons. We employ our well-earned immunity in preparing for the next series of batteries, or in thinking of the cost to Germany, at one hundred francs a shot, of all this futile shelling. Drew, in particular, loves this cost-accounting business, and I must admit that much pleasure may be had in it, after patrol. They rarely fire less than fifty shells at us during a two-hour patrol. Making a low general average, the number is nearer one hundred and fifty. On our present front, where aerial activity is fairly brisk and the sector is a large one, three or four hundred shells are wasted upon us often before we have been out an hour.

We have memories of all the good batteries from Flanders to the Vosges Mountains. Battery after battery, we make their acquaintance along the entire sector, wherever we go. Many of them, of course, are mobile, so that we never lose the sport of searching for them. Only a few days ago we located one of this kind which came into action in the open by the side of a road. First we saw the flashes and then the shell-bursts in the same cadence. We tipped up and fired at him in bursts of twenty to thirty rounds, which is the only way airmen have of passing the time of day with their friends, the enemy anti-aircraft gunners, who ignore the art of *camouflage*.

But we can converse with them, after a fashion, even though we do not know their exact position. It will be long before this chapter of my journal is in print. Having given no indication of the date of writing, I may say, without indiscretion, that we are again on the Champagne front. We have a wholesome respect for one battery here, a respect it has justly earned by shooting which is really remarkable. We talk of this battery, which is east of Rheims and not far distant from Nogent l'Abbesse, and take professional pride in keeping its gunners in ignorance of their fine marksmanship. We signal them their bad shots—which are better than the good ones of most of the batteries on the sector—by doing stunts, a barrel turn, a loop, two or three turns of a *vrille*.

As for their good shots, they are often so very good that we are forced into acrobacy of a wholly individual kind. Our *avions* have received many scars from their shells. Between forty-five hundred and five thousand metres, their bursts have been so close under us that we have been lifted by the concussions and set down violently again at the bottom of the vacuum; and this on a clear day when a *chasse* machine is almost invisible at that height, and despite its speed of two hundred kilometres an hour. On a gray day, when we are flying between twenty-five hundred and three thousand metres beneath a film of cloud, they repay the honor we do them by our acrobatic turns. They bracket us, put barrages between us and our own lines, give us more trouble than all the other batteries on the sector combined.

For this reason it is all the more humiliating to be forced to land with motor trouble, just at the moment when they are paying off some old scores. This happened to Drew while I have been writing up my journal. Coming out of a tonneau in answer to three *coups* from the battery, his propeller stopped dead. By planing flatly (the wind was dead ahead, and the area back of the first lines there is a wide one, crossed by many intersecting lines of trenches) he got well over them and chose a field as level as a billiard table for landing-ground. In the very center of it, however, there was one post, a small worm-eaten thing, of the color of the dead grass around it. He hit it, just as he was setting his Spad on the ground, the only post in a field acres wide, and it tore a piece of fabric from one of his lower wings. No doubt the crack battery has been given credit for disabling an enemy plane. The honor, such as it is, belongs to our aerial godfather, among whose lesser vices may be included that of practical joking.

The remnants of the post were immediately confiscated for fire-wood by some *poilus* who were living in a dugout near by.

The French attack which has been in preparation for the past month is to begin at dawn tomorrow. It has been hard, waiting, but it must have been a great deal worse for the infantrymen who are billeted in all of the surrounding villages. They are moving up to-night to the first lines, for these are the shock troops who are to lead the attack. They are chiefly regiments of Chasseurs—small men in stature, but clean, hard, well-knit—splendid types. They talk of the attack confidently. It is an inspiration to listen to them. Hundreds of them have visited our aerodome during the past week, mainly, I think, for a glimpse of Whiskey and Soda, our lions, who are known to French soldiers from one end of the line to the other. Whiskey is almost full-grown, and Soda about the size of a wild cat. They have the freedom of the camp and run about everywhere.

The guns are thundering at a terrific rate, the concussions shaking our barracks and rattling the dishes on the table. In the messroom the gramophone is playing, "I'm going 'way back home and have a wonderful time." Music at the front is sometimes a doubtful blessing.

We are keyed up, some of us, rather nervous in anticipation of tomorrow. Porter is trying to give Irving a light from his own cigarette. Irving, who doesn't know the meaning of nerves, asks him who in hell he is waving at. Poor old Porter! His usefulness as a combat pilot has long past, but he hangs on, doing the best he can. He should have been sent to the rear months ago.

The first phase of the battle is over. The French have taken eleven thousand prisoners, and have driven the enemy from all the hills, down to the low ground along the canal. For the most part, we have been too high above them to see the infantry actions; but knowing the plans and the objectives beforehand, we have been able to follow, quite closely, the progress of the battle.

It opened on a wet morning with the clouds very low. We were to have gone on patrol immediately the attack commenced, but this was impossible. About nine o'clock the rain stopped, and Rodman and Davis were sent out to learn weather conditions over the lines. They came back with the report that flying was possible at two hundred metres. This was too low an altitude to serve any useful purpose, and the commandant gave us orders to stand by.

About noon the clouds began to break up, and both high and low patrols prepared to leave the ground. Drew, Dunham, and I were on high patrol, with Lieutenant Barry leading. Our orders were to go up through the clouds, using them as cover for making surprise attacks upon enemy *réglage* machines. We were also to attack any enemy formations sighted within three kilometres of their old first lines. The clouds soon disappeared and so we climbed to forty-five hundred metres and lay in wait for combat patrols.

Barry sighted one and signaled. Before I had placed it, he dived, almost full motor, I believe, for he dropped like a stone. We went down on his tail and saw him attack the topmost of three Albatross single-seaters. The other two dived at once, far into their own lines. Dunham, Drew, and I took long shots at them, but they were far outside effective range. The topmost German made a feeble effort to maneuver for position. Barry made a *renversement* with the utmost nicety of judgment and came out of it about thirty metres behind and above the Albatross. He fired about twenty shots, when the German began falling out of control, spinning round and round, then diving straight, then past the vertical, so that we could see the silver under-surface of his wings and tail, spinning again until we lost sight of him.[*]

Lieutenant Talbott joined us as we were taking our height again. He took command of the patrol and Barry went off hunting by himself, as he likes best to do. There were planes everywhere, of both nationalities. Mounting to four thousand metres within our own lines, we crossed over again, and at that moment I saw a Letord, a three-passenger *réglage* machine, burst into flames and fall. There was no time either to watch or to think of this horrible sight. We encountered a patrol of five Albatross planes almost on our level. Talbott dived at once. I was behind him and picked a German who was spiraling either upward or downward, for a few seconds I was not sure which. It was upward. He was climbing to offer combat. This was disconcerting. It always is to a green pilot. If your foe is running, you may be sure he is at least as badly rattled as you are. If he is a single-seater and climbing, you may be equally certain that he is not a novice, and that he has plenty of sand. Otherwise he would not accept battle at a disadvantage in the hope of having his inning next.

I was foolish enough to begin firing while still about three hundred metres distant. My opponent ungraciously offered the poorest kind of a target, getting out of the range of my sights by some very skillful maneuvering. I didn't want him to think that he had an inexperienced pilot to deal with. Therefore, judging my distance very carefully, I did a *renversement* in the Lieutenant Barry fashion. But it was not so well done. Instead of coming out of it above and behind the German, when I pulled up in *ligne de vol* I was under him!

I don't know exactly what happened then, but the next moment I was falling in a *vrille* (spinning nose dive) and heard the well-known

---

[*] This combat was seen from the ground, and Barry's victory was confirmed before we returned to the field.

crackling sound of machine-gun fire. I kept on falling in a *vrille*, thinking this would give the German the poorest possible target.[*]

Pulling up in *ligne de vol* I looked over my shoulder again. The German had lost sight of me for a moment in the swiftness of his dive, but evidently he saw me just before I pulled out of the *vrille*. He was turning up for another shot, in exactly the same position in which I had last seen him. And he was very close, not more than fifty metres distant.

I believed, of course, that I was lost; and why that German didn't bag me remains a mystery. Heaven knows I gave him opportunity enough! In the end, by the merciful intervention of Chance, our godfather, I escaped. I have said that the sky had cleared. But there was one strand of cloud left, not very broad, not very long; but a refuge,—oh! what a welcome refuge! It was right in my path and I tumbled into it, literally, head over heels. I came skidding out, but pulled up, put on my motor, and climbed back at once; and I kept turning round and round in it for several minutes. If the German had waited, he must have seen me raveling it out like a cat tangled in a ball of cotton. I thought that he was waiting. I even expected him to come nosing into it, in search of me. In that case there would have been a glorious smash, for there wasn't room for two of us. I almost hoped that he would try this. If I couldn't bag a German with my gun, the next best thing was to run into him and so be gathered to my fathers while he was being gathered to his. There was no crash, and taking sudden resolution, I dived vertically out of the cloud, head over shoulder, expecting to see my relentless foe. He was nowhere in sight.

In that wild tumble, and while chasing my tail in the cloud, I lost my bearings. The compass, which was mounted on a swinging holder, had been tilted upside down. It stuck in that position. I could not get it loose. I had fallen to six hundred metres, so that I could not get a

[*] A mistake which many new pilots make. In a *vrille*, the machine spins pretty nearly on its own axis, and although it is turning, a skillful pilot above it can keep it fairly well within the line of his sights.

large view of the landscape. Under the continuous bombardment the air was filled with smoke, and through it nothing looked familiar. I knew the direction of our lines by the position of the sun, but I was in a suspicious mood. My motor, which I had praised to the heavens to the other pilots, had let me down at a critical moment. The sun might be ready to play some fantastic trick. I had to steer by it, although I was uneasy until I came within sight of our observation balloons. I identified them as French by sailing close to one of them so that I could see the tricolor pennant floating out from a cord on the bag.

Then, being safe, I put my old Spad through every antic we two had ever done together. The observers in the balloons must have thought me crazy, a pilot running amuck from aerial shell shock. I had discovered a new meaning for that "grand and glorious feeling" which is so often the subject of Briggs's cartoons.

Looking at my watch I received the same old start of surprise upon learning how much of wisdom one may accumulate in a half-hour of aerial adventure. I had still an hour and a half to get through with before I could go home with a clear conscience. Therefore, taking height again, I went cautiously, gingerly, watchfully, toward the lines.

The "grand and glorious feeling" is one of the finest compensations for this uncertain life in the air. One has it every time he turns from the lines toward—home! It comes in richer glow, if hazardous work has been done, after moments of strain, uncertainty, when the result of a combat sways back and forth; and it gushes up like a fountain, when, after making a forced landing in what appears to be enemy territory, you find yourself among friends.

Late this afternoon we started, four of us, with Davis as leader, to make the usual two-hour sortie over the lines. No Germans were sighted, and after an uneventful half-hour, Davis, who is always springing these surprises, decided to stalk them in their lairs. The clouds were at the right altitude for this, and there were gaps in them over which we could hover, examining roads, railroads, villages, can-tonments. The danger of attack was negligible. We could easily escape any large hostile patrol by dodging into the clouds. But the wind was unfavorable for such a reconnaissance. It was blowing into Germany. We would have it dead against us on the journey home.

We played about for a half-hour, blown by a strong wind farther into Germany than we knew. We walked down the main street of a vil-lage where we saw a large crowd of German soldiers, spraying bullets among them, then climbed into the clouds before a shot could be fired at us. Later we nearly attacked a hospital, mistaking it for an aviation field. It was housed in *bessonneau* hangars, and had none of the marks of a hospital excepting a large red cross in the middle of the field. For-tunately we saw this before any of us had fired, and passed on over it at a low altitude to attack a train. There is a good deal of excitement in an expedition of this kind, and soldiers themselves say that surprise sorties from the air have a demoralizing effect upon troops. But as a form of sport, there is little to be said for it. It is too unfair. For this reason, among others, I was glad when Davis turned homeward.

While coming back I climbed to five thousand metres, far above the others, and lagged a long way behind them. This was a direct violation of patrol discipline, and the result was, that while cruising leisurely along, with motor throttled down, watching the swift changes of light over a wide expanse of cloud, I lost sight of the group. Then came the inevitable feeling of loneliness, and the swift realization that it was growing late and that I was still far within enemy country.

I held a southerly course, estimating, as I flew, the velocity of the wind which had carried us into Germany, and judging from this esti-mate the length of time I should need to reach our lines. When satis-fied that I had gone far enough, I started down. Below the clouds it was almost night, so dark that I could not be sure of my location. In the distance I saw a large building, brilliantly lighted. This was evidence enough that I was a good way from the lines. Unshielded windows were never to be seen near the front. I spiraled slowly down over this building, examining, as well as I could, the ground behind it, and decided to risk a landing. A blind chance and blind luck attended it. In broad day, Drew hit the only post in a field five hundred metres wide. At night, a very dark night, I missed colliding with an enormous factory chimney (a matter of inches), glided over a line of telegraph wires, passed at a few metres' height over a field littered with huge piles of sugar beets, and settled, *comme une fleur*, in a little cleared space which I could never have judged accurately had I known what I was doing.

Shadowy figures came running toward me. Forgetting, in the joy of so fortunate a landing, my anxiety of a moment before, I shouted out, "Bonsoir, messieurs!" Then I heard some one say, "Ich glaube—" losing the rest of it in the sound of tramping feet and an undercurrent of low, guttural murmurs. In a moment my Spad was surrounded by a widening circle of round hats, German infantrymen's hats.

Here was the ignoble end to my career as an airman. I was a prisoner, a prisoner because of my own folly, because I had dallied along like a silly girl, to "look at the pretty clouds." I saw in front of me a long captivity embittered by this thought. Not only this: my Spad was intact. The German authorities would examine it, use it. Some German pilot might fly with it over the lines, attack other French machines with my gun, my ammunition!

Not if I could help it! They stood there, those soldiers, gaping, muttering among themselves, waiting, I thought, for an officer to tell them what to do. I took off my leather gloves, then my silk ones under them, and these I washed about in the oil under my feet. Then, as quietly as possible, I reached for my box of matches.

"Qu'est-ce-que vous faites là? Allez! Vite!"

A tramping of feet again, and a sea of round hats bobbing up and down and vanishing in the gloom. Then I heard a cheery "Ça va, monsieur? Pas de mal?" By way of answer I lighted a match and held it out, torch fashion. The light glistened on a round, red face and a long French bayonet. Finally I said, "Vous êtes Français, monsieur?" in a weak, watery voice.

"Mais oui, mon vieux! Mais oui!" this rather testily. He didn't understand at first that I thought myself in Germany. "Do I look like a Boche?"

Then I explained, and I have never heard a Frenchman laugh more heartily. Then he explained and I laughed, not so heartily, a great deal more foolishly.

I may not give my location precisely. But I shall be disclosing no military secrets in saying that I am not in Germany. I am not even in the French war-zone. I am closer to Paris than I am to the enemy first-line trenches. In a little while the sergeant with the round red face and the long French bayonet, whose guest I am for the night, will join me here. If he were an American, to the manner born and bred, and if he knew the cartoons of that man Briggs, he might greet me in this fashion:—

"When you have been on patrol a long way behind the enemy lines, shooting up towns and camps and railway trains like a pack of aerial cowboys; when, on your way home, you have deliberately disobeyed orders and loafed a long way behind the other members of your group in order to watch the pretty sunset, and, as a punishment for this aesthetic indulgence, have been overtaken by darkness and compelled to land in strange country, only to have your machine immediately surrounded by German soldiers; then, having taken the desperate resolve that they shall not have possession of your old battle-scarred *avion* as well as of your person, when you are about to touch a match to it, if the light glistens on a long French bayonet and you learn that the German soldiers have been prisoners since the battle of the Somme, and have just finished their day's work at harvesting beets to be used in making sugar for French *poilus*—Oh, BOY! Ain't it a GRAND AND GLORYUS FEELING?"

To which I would reply in his own memorable words,—

"Mais oui, mon vieux! Mais Oui!"

from Fighting the Flying Circus
by Eddie Rickenbacker

Eddie Rickenbacker (1890–1973) shot down 22 enemy planes during World War I, making him America's top ace. He joined the 94th Aero Pursuit Squadron on the French front in March, 1918.

September 25th, 1918, was my first day as Captain of 94 Squadron. Early that forenoon I started for the lines alone, flew over Verdun and Fort Douaumont, then turned east towards Etain. Almost immediately I picked up a pair of L. V. G. two-seater machines below me. They were coming out of Germany and were certainly bent upon an expedition over our lines. Five Fokker machines were above them and somewhat behind, acting as protection for the photographers until the lines were reached.

Climbing for the sun for all I was worth, I soon had the satisfaction of realizing that I had escaped their notice and was now well in their rear. I shut down my motor, put down my head and made a bee line for the nearest Fokker.

I was not observed by the enemy until it was too late for him to escape. I had him exactly in my sights when I pulled both triggers for a long burst. He made a sudden attempt to pull away, but my bullets were already ripping through his fusilage and he must have been killed instantly. His machine fell wildly away and crashed just south of Etain.

It had been my intention to zoom violently upwards and protect myself against the expected attack from the four remaining Fokkers as soon as I had finished the first man. But when I saw the effect of my attack upon the four dumbfounded Boches I instantly changed my tactics and plunged straight on through their formation to attack the photographing L. V. G's ahead. For the Heinies were so surprised by finding a Spad in their midst and seeing one of their number suddenly drop that the remaining three viraged to right and left. Their one idea was to escape and save their own skins. Though they did not actually pique for home, they cleared a space large enough for me to slip through and continue my dive upon the two-seaters before they could recover their formation.

The two-seaters had seen my attack and had already put down their heads to escape. I plunged along after them, getting the rear machine in my sights as I drew nearer to him. A glance back over my shoulder showed me that the four Fokkers had not yet reformed their line and were even now circling about with the purpose of again solidifying their formation. I had a few seconds yet before they could begin their attack.

The two L. V. G. machines began to draw apart. Both observers in the rear seats were firing at me, although the range was still too long for accurate shooting. I dove more steeply, passed out of the gunner's view under the nearest machine and zoomed quickly up at him from below. But the victory was not to be an easy one. The pilot suddenly kicked his tail around, giving the gunner another good aim at me. I had to postpone shooting until I had more time for my own aiming. And in the meantime the second photographing machine had stolen up behind me and I saw tracer bullets go whizzing and streaking past my face. I zoomed up diagonally out of range, made a renversement and came directly back at my first target.

Several times we repeated these maneuvers, the four Fokkers still wrangling among themselves about their formation. And all the time we were getting farther and farther back into Germany. I decided upon one bold attack and if this failed I would get back to my own lines before it was too late.

Watching my two adversaries closely, I suddenly found an opening between them. They were flying parallel to each other and not fifty yards apart. Dropping down in a sideslip until I had one machine between me and the other I straightened out smartly, leveled my Spad and began firing. The nearest Boche passed directly through my line of fire and just as I ceased firing I had the infinite satisfaction of seeing him gush forth flames. Turning over and over as he fell the L. V. G. started a blazing path to earth just as the Fokker escort came tearing up to the rescue. I put on the gas and piqued for my own lines.

Pleased as I was over this double-header, the effect it might have upon my pilots was far more gratifying to me.

Arriving at the aerodrome at 9:30 I immediately jumped into a motorcar, called to Lieutenant Chambers to come with me and we set off at once to get official confirmation for this double victory. We took the main road to Verdun, passed through the town and gained the hills beyond the Mouse, towards Etain. Taking the road up to Fort de Tavannes we passed over that bloody battlefield of 1916 where so many thousand German troops fell before French fire in the memorable Battle for Verdun. At the very crest of the hill we were halted by a French poilu, who told us the rest of the road was in full view of the Germans and that we must go no farther.

We asked him as to whether he had seen my combat overhead this morning. He replied in the affirmative and added that the officers in the adjacent fort too had witnessed the whole fight through their field glasses. We thanked him and leaving our car under his care took our way on foot to the Fort.

Two or three hundred yards of shell-holes sprinkled the ground between us and the Fort. We made our way through them, gained admittance to the interior of the Fort and in our best Pidgin French stated our errand to M. le Commandant. He immediately wrote out full particulars of the combat I had had with the L. V. G., signed it and congratulated me upon my victory with a warm shake of the hand. Having no further business at this place, we made our adieus and hastened back to our car.

Plunging through the shallowest shell-holes we had traversed about half the distance to our car, which stood boldly out on the top of the road, when a shrill whining noise made us pause and listen. The next instant a heavy explosion announced that a shell had landed about fifty yards short of us. Simultaneously with the shower of gravel and dirt which headed our way we dropped unceremoniously on our faces in the bottom of the deepest shell-hole in our vicinity.

The Huns had spotted our car and were actually trying to get its range!

Two or three times we crawled out of our hole, only to duck back at the signal of the next coming shell. After six or eight shots the Boche gunners evidently considered their target too small, for they ceased firing long enough for us to make a bolt across the intervening holes and throw ourselves into the waiting automobile. I most fervently wished that I had turned the car around before leaving it, and I shall never forget the frightful length of time it took me to get our car backed around and headed in the right direction. We lost no time in getting down that hill.

Next day was to be an important one for us and for the whole American Army. Officially it was designated as "D" day and the "Zero hour," by the same code, was set for four o'clock in the morning. At that moment the artillery barrage would begin and forty thousand doughboys who were posted along the front line trenches from the Meuse to the Argonne Forest would go over the top. It was the 26th day of September, 1918.

Precisely at four o'clock I was awakened by my orderly who informed me that the weather was good. Hastily getting out of doors, I looked over the dark sky, wondering as I did so how many of our boys it would claim before this day's work was done! For we had an important part to play in this day's operations. Headquarters had sent us orders to attack all the enemy observation balloons along that entire front this morning and to continue the attacks until the infantry's operations were completed. Accordingly every fighting squadron had been assigned certain of these balloons for attack and it was our duty to see that they were destroyed. The safety of thousands of our attacking soldiers depended upon our success in eliminating these all-watching eyes of the enemy. Incidentally, it was the first balloon strafing party that 94 Squadron had been given since I had been made its leader and I desired to make a good showing on this first expedition.

Just here it may be well to point out the difficulties of balloon strafing, which make this undertaking so unattractive to the new pilot.

German "Archy" is terrifying at first acquaintance. Pilots affect a scorn for it, and indeed at high altitudes the probabilities of a hit are small. But when attacking a balloon which hangs only 1,500 feet above the guns (and this altitude is of course known precisely to the anti-aircraft gunner) Archy becomes far more dangerous.

So when a pilot begins his first balloon attacking expeditions, he knows that he runs a gauntlet of fire that may be very deadly. His natural impulse is to make a nervous plunge into the zone of danger, fire his bullets, and get away. Few victories are won with this method of attack.

The experienced balloon strafers, particularly such daring airmen as Coolidge and Luke, do not consider the risks or terrors about them. They proceed in the attack as calmly as though they were sailing through a stormless sky. Regardless of flaming missiles from the ground, they pass through the defensive barrage of fire, and often return again and again, to attack the target, until it finally bursts into flame from their incendiary bullets.

The office charts informed me that day would break this morning at six o'clock. Consequently we must be ready to leave the ground in our machines at 5:20, permitting us thirty minutes in which to reach our objectives, and ten minutes in which to locate our individual balloons. For it is essential to strike at these well defended targets just at the edge of dawn. Then the balloons are just starting aloft, and our attacking aeroplanes are but scantily visible from below. Moreover enemy aero-planes are not apt to be about so early in the morning, unless the enemy has some inkling of what is going on.

I routed out five of my best pilots, Lieutenants Cook, Chambers, Taylor, Coolidge and Palmer; and as we gathered together for an early breakfast, we went over again all the details of our pre-arranged plans. We had two balloons assigned to our Squadron, and three of us were delegated to each balloon. Both lay along the Meuse between Brabant and Dun. Every one of us had noted down the exact location of his target on the evening before. It would be difficult perhaps to find them before daylight if they were still in their nests, but we were to hang about the vicinity until we did find them, if it took all day. With every man fully posted on his course and objective, we put on our coats and walked over to the hangars.

I was the last to leave the field, getting off the ground at exactly 5:20. It was still dark and we had to have the searchlights turned onto the field for a moment to see the ground while we took off. As soon as we lifted into the darkness the lights were extinguished. And then I saw the most marvelous sight that my eyes have ever seen.

A terrific barrage of artillery fire was going on ahead of me. Through the darkness the whole western horizon was illumined with one mass of sudden flashes. The big guns were belching out their shells with such rapidity that there appeared to be millions of them shooting at the same time. Looking back I saw the same scene in my rear. From Luneville on the east to Rheims on the west there was not one spot of darkness along the whole front. The French were attacking along both our flanks at the same time with us in order to help demoralize the weakening Boche. The picture made me think of a giant switchboard which emitted thousands of electric flashes as invisible hands manip-ulated the plugs.

So fascinated did I become over this extraordinary fireworks display that I was startled upon peering over the side of my machine to discover the city of Verdun below my aeroplane's wings. Fastening my course above the dim outline of the Meuse River I followed its windings down stream, occasionally cutting across little peninsulas which I recognized along the way. Every inch of this route was as familiar to me as was the path around the corner of my old home. I knew exactly the point in the Meuse Valley where I would leave the river and turn left to strike the spot where my balloon lay last night. I did not know what course the other pilots had taken. Perhaps they had already—

Just as these thoughts were going through my mind I saw directly ahead of me the long snaky flashes of enemy tracer bullets from the ground piercing the sky. There was the location of my balloon and either Cook or Chambers was already attacking it. The enemy had discovered them and were putting up the usual hail of flaming projectiles around the balloon site. But even as the flaming bullets continued streaming upwards I saw a gigantic flame burst out in their midst! One of the boys had destroyed his gas-bag!

Even before the glare of the first had died I saw our second enemy balloon go up in flames. My pilots had succeeded beyond my fondest expectations. Undoubtedly the enemy would soon be swinging new balloons up in their places, but we must wait awhile for that. I resolved to divert my course and fly further to the north where I knew of the nest of another German observation balloon near Damvillers.

Dawn was just breaking as I headed more to the east and tried to pick out the location of Damvillers. I was piercing the gloom with my eyes when again—straight in front of my revolving propeller I saw another gush of flame which announced the doom of another enemy balloon—the very one I had determined to attack. While I was still jubilating over the extraordinary good luck that had attended us in this morning's expedition, I glanced off to my right and was almost startled out of my senses to discover that a German Fokker was flying alongside me not a hundred yards away! Not expecting any of the enemy aeroplanes to be abroad at this early hour, I was naturally upset for the moment. The next instant I saw that he had headed for me and was coming straight at my machine. We both began firing at the same time. It was still so dark that our four streams of flaming bullets cut brilliant lines of fire through the air. For a moment it looked as though our two machines were tied together with four ropes of fire. All my ammunition was of the incendiary variety for use against gas-bags. The Hun's ammunition was part tracer, part incendiary and part regular chunks of lead.

As we drew nearer and nearer I began to wonder whether this was to be a collision or whether he would get out of my way. He settled the question by tipping down his head to dive under me. I instantly made a renversement which put me close behind him and in a most favorable position for careful aim. Training my sights into the center of his fusilage I pulled both triggers. With one long burst the fight was over. The Fokker fell over onto one wing and dropped aimlessly to earth. It was too dark to see the crash, and moreover I had all thoughts of my victory dissipated by a sudden ugly jerk to my motor which immediately developed into a violent vibration. As I turned back towards Verdun, which was the nearest point to our lines, I had recurring visions of crashing down into Germany to find myself a prisoner. This would be a nice ending to our glorious balloon expedition!

Throttling down to reduce the pounding I was able just to maintain headway. If my motor failed completely I was most certainly doomed, for I was less than a thousand feet above ground and could glide but a few hundred yards without power. Providence was again with me, for I cleared the lines and made our Verdun aerodrome where one flight of the 27th Squadron was housed. I landed without damage and hastily climbed out of my machine to investigate the cause of my trouble.

Imagine my surprise when I discovered that one blade of my propeller had been shot in two by my late adversary! He had evidently put several holes through it when he made his head-on-attack. And utterly unconscious of the damage I had received, I had reversed my direction and shot him down before the weakened blade gave way! The heavy jolting of my engine was now clear to me-only half of the propeller caught the air.

Lieutenant Jerry Vasconcelles of Denver, Colorado, was in charge of the Verdun field on which I had landed. He soon came out and joined me as I was staring at my broken propeller. And then I learned that he had just landed himself from a balloon expedition. A few questions followed and then we shook hands spontaneously. He had shot down the Darnvillers balloon himself—the same one for which I had been headed. And as he was returning he had seen me shoot down my Fokker! This was extremely lucky for both of us, for we were able each to verify the other's victory for him, although of course corroboration from ground witnesses was necessary to make these victories official.

His mechanics placed a new propeller on my Spad, and none the worse for its recent rough usage the little bus took me rapidly home. I landed at 8:30 on my own field. And there I heard great news. Our Group had that morning shot down ten German balloons! My victory over the Fokker made it eleven victories to be credited us for this hour's work. And we had not lost a single pilot!

As the jubilant and famished pilots crowded into the mess hall one could not hear a word through all the excited chatter. Each one had some strange and fearful adventure to relate about his morning's experiences. But the tale which aroused howls of laughter was the droll story told by Lieutenant White of the 147th Squadron.

White had searched long and earnestly for the balloon that he desired to attack. He thought himself hopelessly lost in the darkness, when off to one side he distinguished the dark outline of what he thought was his balloon. Immediately redressing his machine he tipped downwards and began plugging furious streams of flaming bullets into his target. He made a miscalculation in his distance and before he could swerve away from the dark mass ahead of him his machine had plunged straight through it!

And then he discovered that he had been piquing upon a round puff of black smoke that had just been made by a German Archy!

from A Man on the Moon
by Andrew Chaikin

The first manned Apollo mission scheduled for mid-February, 1976. Andrew Chaikin's (born 1956) history of the Apollo program begins with a description of what should have been a routine training exercise for that mission.

When the moon rises beyond the Atlantic shore of Florida, full and luminous, it seems so close that you could just row out to the end of the water and touch it. In January 1967, the moon seemed to draw nearer by the day to the hard, flat beaches of Cape Kennedy. Seen from there it was no longer the governess of the tides, the lovers' beacon, the celebrated mistress of song; it was a target, a Cold War beachhead in the sky. It was NASA's moon.

Almost six years had passed since John Kennedy's challenge for a lunar landing by decade's end. The moon program had grown into an effort whose size and complexity dwarfed even the Manhattan Project. At aerospace contractors around the country, 400,000 people were hard at work on the moonships for Project Apollo. Meanwhile, Project Gemini had just come to a spectacular finale. These two manned missions had bridged the gap between the pioneering Mercury flights and the challenge of the lunar landing. For the first time in the race to the moon, the United States appeared to have pulled ahead of the Soviet Union. With the first manned, earth-orbit Apollo flight scheduled for mid-February, all seemed on target to make Kennedy's vision a reality. But one evening late in January, that soaring optimism suddenly, terribly fell to earth.

January 27, 1967
Merritt Island Launch Area, Kennedy Space Center
Cape Kennedy, Florida

"How are we going to get to the moon if we can't talk between three buildings?"

Gus Grissom's voice was low and calm, but with an unmistakable edge of irritation. A senior astronaut, veteran of two space missions, Grissom was the commander of the first manned Apollo flight set for February 1967. On this warm January afternoon Grissom and his crew, veteran astronaut Ed White and a rookie named Roger Chaffee, were participating in a simulated countdown, the kind of routine test that preceded every mission. They were sealed inside the cone-shaped Apollo 1 command module, high atop a huge Saturn IB booster rocket at Pad 34, one of dozens of launch complexes that lined the beach at Cape Kennedy. A few hundred yards away, inside the concrete bunker called the Saturn blockhouse, some two hundred members of the launch team heard Grissom's words. At the Capsule Communicator, or "Stony," console, a young rookie astronaut named Stuart Roosa tried in vain to answer.

"Apollo 1, this is Stony; how do you read?"

In 1967 there were so many astronauts that Grissom and Roosa hardly knew each other, but the younger man could hear the barely contained exasperation in Grissom's voice:

"I can't hear a thing you're saying. Jesus Christ . . . I said, how are we going to get to the moon if we can't talk between two or three buildings?"

No one who knew Gus Grissom took him lightly. Small and powerful, he was known as a fierce competitor. When Grissom was a young air force fighter pilot in the Korean War, the fliers would ride an old school bus from the hangar to the flight line. Only those who had been in air-to-air combat could sit down; the uninitiated pilots had to stand. Grissom stood only once. He brought the same hard-driving determination to his spaceflight career, as one of the Mercury astronauts, known as the Original 7. Even among these most elite fliers, the Seven had a status approaching royalty. Despite their rivalries they had a unique bond that came from being the first Americans to venture into the heavens. Everything the Original 7 did was energized with competition, from flying airplanes to their impromptu drag races on straight Florida roads to their adventures in the nightspots of Cocoa Beach, and Grissom was always a zealous participant. But even to other astronauts, Grissom was not an easy man to know; he was a loner among loners.

In 1967 Gus Grissom stood at the top of the active roster of astronauts, but he had started out as something of an underdog. His first spaceflight, a suborbital Mercury mission in 1961, ended in near-disaster when the hatch of his tiny spacecraft *Liberty Bell 7* blew off prematurely after splashdown in the Atlantic. *Liberty Bell* sank; Grissom narrowly escaped drowning. He maintained it had been a malfunction, that the hatch had blown off by itself, but somehow there had been a lingering skepticism—in the press, at NASA, even among other astronauts. The doubts infuriated him. He fought to make up for that image. In 1965, after helping to design the two-man Gemini spacecraft, he commanded its successful first flight. Now, at age forty, after more than a year immersed in the development and testing of the Apollo command module, he would fly its maiden voyage in earth orbit. Commanding the first flight of any new craft was always a prize assignment, but Grissom's ambitions didn't end there. He had his sights on the most coveted mission of all, the lunar landing. More than anything, Grissom wanted to be the first man on the moon.

But on January 27, the moon seemed a long way off. For several months now, Grissom had worked to help ready his spacecraft for its mission, and he had become more and more displeased with the way things were going. When engineering problems came up, he pushed for better solutions using his experience from Mercury and Gemini, but no one seemed to be listening. It made him so mad, he confided to an interviewer, he couldn't see straight. By the time the Apollo 1 command module left the factory in Downey, California, last August, it still had dozens of separate discrepancies, some of them serious. To make matters worse, the command module simulator here at the Cape was a constant source of difficulty. Just a few days ago, to show his frustration, he'd hung a big Texas lemon on it. Today, his patience was being strained once again by a trouble-plagued test. Despite all the frustrations, Grissom was pushing to get Apollo 1 into space on schedule, not because he was reckless—Grissom hadn't lived this long by being reckless—but because problems were to be expected in any new flight program, whether a new airplane or, especially, a moonship.

Today's simulated countdown was nothing new; it wasn't considered dangerous—the Saturn booster was not fueled—or even difficult. But there was trouble almost from the time Grissom and his crew climbed into the command module cabin, around 1 p.m. First there was an unidentified odor in the breathing oxygen that reminded Grissom of sour milk; that alone had held up the test for an hour. Finally the problem was solved, and at 2:45 p.m. the pad crews installed the command module's heavy, two-piece hatch and sealed it shut. The spacecraft was pressurized with pure oxygen, just as it would be on launch day. Then came the communications trouble. By late afternoon Roosa was able to converse with the men inside the sealed spacecraft, but there were problems with the voice link to the Manned Spaceflight Operations building 5½ miles away. In the blockhouse, controllers weighed the decision of whether to abort the test. They decided to continue.

In the blockhouse, seated next to Roosa at the Stony console, Deke Slayton listened as technicians tried to fix the faulty communications. Slayton was forty-three years old. He had been a civilian for several years now, but he still carried himself with the quiet, serious demeanor he'd had as a young air force fighter pilot. Another member of the Original 7, Slayton was one of Gus Grissom's best friends, but their fortunes could not have been more different. Grissom was now a veteran of two space missions, while Slayton had been grounded since 1962 for a minor heart irregularity and was still waiting for his first chance to fly in space. Now, as chief of the Manned Spacecraft Center's Flight Crew Operations Directorate, Slayton's role included following astronauts through tests like this one.

Slayton knew only too well that Grissom wasn't happy with the way things were going. He'd had breakfast with Grissom, White, and Chaffee this morning, along with Joe Shea, the hard-driving NASA manager in charge of the command module effort, and they were all running through the litany of troubles with Grissom's spacecraft: Malfunctions in the environmental control system. Coolant leaks. Faulty wiring. Grissom bemoaned the communications trouble that plagued almost every test. "If you don't believe it," Grissom told Shea, "you ought to get in there with us."

Shea declined, largely because there was some question about whether technicians would be able to rig up an extra communications headset for him in time. But Slayton gave the matter some thought. There would be space for him to sit, in shirtsleeves, in the command module's lower equipment bay beneath the footrests. He was still weighing the idea around midday as Grissom, White, and Chaffee suited up. Slayton rode with them in the transfer van to Pad 34, and by the time they arrived he had made his decision. He would be better off in the blockhouse, he told Grissom, where he could keep a close eye on the test. Years later, he would still wonder whether or not he made the right choice.

By evening, as dusk settled onto the marshlands, technicians continued to troubleshoot the faulty communications. Searchlights came on, bathing the giant Saturn rocket in white light. Meanwhile other events in the countdown continued. Apollo I was on its own electrical power now, just as it would be in the final minutes before liftoff. But the communications troubles were still unsolved, and at T minus 10 minutes, the test director called a hold in the count.

At 6:31 p.m., eleven minutes into the hold, Slayton was looking over the test schedule when he heard a brief, clipped transmission from Apollo 1. It sounded like "Fire."

On the other side of the country, at the North American Aviation plant in Downey, California, veteran astronauts Tom Stafford, John Young, and Gene Cernan were sealed inside the second Apollo command module in their own spacecraft test. Besides being the most experienced space crew yet assembled—Cernan had flown once before on Gemini, while Stafford and Young each had two missions under their belts—they had a camaraderie seldom matched on a space crew. Now the three men were assigned as the backup team for the second manned Apollo mission.

This command module, like Grissom's, was a prototype called Block I. It was never built to go to the moon, but was instead designed only to fly in earth orbit, on the first Apollo flights. An improved version, called Block II, was already being developed for the lunar missions, and last month, NASA had decided that there would be only one Block I mission, Apollo 1. Stafford and his crew were here at North American, the prime contractor for the command module, to help provide engineering support for the activities at the Cape.

The work on Block I had been frustrating, in part because of the atmosphere here at Downey. North American had some very competent people, but they had never built a manned spacecraft before. Bundles of wire on the command module floor were unprotected, making them susceptible to damage. There were so many changes made within the cabin that the workmen could barely keep track of them all. Wires were constantly being rerouted, black boxes replaced. And lately, astronauts had felt a strain in their relationship with the North American engineers, who had begun to resist their suggestions.

It had been different during Gemini. That spacecraft, like Mercury, was the product of the McDonnell Aircraft Corporation in St. Louis, which had forged a harmonious relationship with NASA. The astronauts who visited the factory had no trouble making inputs into the design process. And if they had a problem, they could always take it to "Mr. Mac" himself, and he would get results. But Apollo wasn't like Gemini. The intimacy was gone now. There was no single boss who could respond to the astronauts' concerns; now there were bosses scattered throughout this massive operation.

Even within NASA, there was a disturbing lack of coordination. In Houston, some of the engineers in the Apollo program office acted as if Gemini had never existed. They had an arrogance that seemed to say, *We know this business better than you do.* Experience from Gemini— Stafford's or anyone else's—seemed to make no impression on them. They rolled their eyes at "those Apollo astronauts and their Gemini war stories." Trying to get through to them was like talking to the wall.

All of them knew of the trouble with Block I, but in the back of everyone's mind was the end-of-the-decade deadline for the lunar landing. However dissatisfied they were, Stafford and the other astronauts had been willing to put up with Block I for the first couple of flights in order to stay on schedule. Their feeling was, "Just get us airborne; we'll fly it."

But on this day, Stafford wasn't so sure. Their test, too, was in trouble: Leaking coolant lines. Short-circuits. At one point the hatch fell on Cernan's foot.

"Go to the moon?" Stafford growled, "This son of a bitch won't even make it into earth orbit."

Finally Stafford stopped the test. When he climbed out of the spacecraft, an emergency call from the Cape was waiting for him.

When Deke Slayton heard the report of fire from Apollo 1, his gaze shot to a nearby closed-circuit television monitor. It showed the picture from a camera pointed at the command module's hatch window. The window was filled with bright flame.

Suddenly there was another message from the spacecraft, this time quite clear, in a voice of contained urgency: "We've got a fire in the cockpit!"

Slayton recognized the voice as Roger Chaffee's. Chaffee was on the right side of the spacecraft, where the radio controls were. It was his job, in an emergency, to maintain contact with the blockhouse.

On the television monitor Slayton could see Ed White's arms reaching back over his head, trying to undo the bolts that held the side hatch shut. Neither Slayton nor anyone else in the blockhouse fully understood what was happening; Slayton would say later that his main concern was not fire, but smoke. But now Slayton heard another voice, clearly frantic:

"We've got a bad fire. . . . We're burning up!"

At first Slayton thought it was Pad Leader Don Babbitt, stationed next to the spacecraft, calling for help. Later, on the tapes, listeners identified the voice as Chaffee's. Seconds later—less than half a minute after the first report of fire—Slayton and the horrified controllers heard the last transmission from Apollo 1. It was a brief cry of pain.

Long seconds passed. Now the communications loop surged with activity as technicians struggled to get the hatch open. "It's too hot," you could hear them say. On the television monitor, through dense smoke, Slayton could see the pad crews approach the hatch only to be driven back by the intense heat. Roosa tried several times to reestablish contact with the crew, with no response. Several long minutes elapsed before the hatch was finally opened, and a short time after that the pad leader came on the communications loop with a terse and ominous transmission: "I'd better not describe what I see."

Physicians Fred Kelly and Alan Harter were in the blockhouse, and Slayton instructed them to go to the pad. Then he put in a call to the Manned Spacecraft Center in Houston, to set up a command center and get word to the families in case things were as bad as he feared. After several minutes the call came from the doctors, confirming what everyone had dreaded. Slayton made another call to Houston; then he and Roosa left the blockhouse and headed to Pad 34.

It was a slow Friday afternoon in the Astronaut Office at the Manned Spacecraft Center. Here, twenty-five miles from downtown Houston, built on a flat, coastal prairie that had once been owned by a Texas oilman, was a collection of modern buildings, all dark glass and white stone, set among neatly manicured lawns and artificial duck ponds. Here and there a windowless training facility or a laboratory with massive cryogenic storage tanks, hinted at the true nature of this place, but for the most part it looked more like the campus of a community college than a place where engineers, scientists, and astronauts were waging an all-out assault on the moon.

The Astronaut Office was located on the top floor of the three-story structure called Building 4. On this Friday afternoon it was nearly deserted. Most of the astronauts were out of town, chasing down some piece of the Apollo effort at contractors' plants around the country. But a young rookie named Alan Bean was here. Although he had been an astronaut since 1963—like Roger Chaffee, he was a member of the third astronaut group—Bean was still waiting for his first chance to fly in space. A few months ago, Deke Slayton had named him as the Astronaut Office representative on the manned space station project that was planned for the early 1970s. Bean didn't always hear about the details of what was going on in Apollo, but he knew Grissom, White, and Chaffee were at the Cape, getting ready for their mission.

Sometime before 6 p.m. the phone rang. It was one of the support people at the Cape. What he said sounded so strange that Bean did not at first understand:

"We've lost the crew."

The man's voice was quiet. Bean heard no anguish in it. He had to stop and think about the words. "The crew" was surely Grissom's; were the people at the Cape having trouble finding them? *Lost the crew*?

Bean answered, "Where do you think they've gone?"

The voice stumbled over more words that didn't make sense; he just didn't seem to want to tell Bean what had really happened. It took a long time for him to say it: Grissom, White, and Chaffee were dead.

Bean had barely hung up the phone when it rang again; this time it was Mike Collins, in Deke Slayton's office up in the administration building. Collins, acting as the Astronaut Office representative for the

Friday afternoon staff meeting, had just heard the same news. Now there was no miscommunication, for it was one pilot talking to another and both knew what needed to be done. They agreed that Bean would coordinate astronauts and wives to go to the homes of the dead pilots. Bean called his wife, Sue, and sent her to the home of Martha Chaffee until Collins could get there. Wally Schirra's wife, Jo, and Chuck Berry, the space center's chief physician, would go to Betty Grissom's. Neil Armstrong's wife, Jan, would go to her next-door neighbor Pat White's, and Bill Anders, another member of the third group, and like Bean, a rookie, would follow.

El Lago was one of a handful of planned communities that had sprung up around the space center, scattered with ranch houses and criss-crossed with tidy streets winding through the greenery. Here was the space community's own suburb: astronauts and NASA engineers and managers all lived next door to each other. And aside from the tourists who occasionally came by looking for some sign of an astronaut as if they were on a tour bus in Beverly Hills, and the mobs of reporters who, during missions, stood watch on an astronaut's lawn as if the Fischer quintuplets had just been born inside, there was nothing remarkable about the way it felt to live here. That was precisely the point: the residents of El Lago, and of nearby Nassau Bay, and Timber Cove, and Clear Lake, clung to normalcy in the midst of the most extraordinary enterprise of the twentieth century.

It was already dark when Bill Anders arrived at the ranch house belonging to Ed and Pat White. Normally there wouldn't have been any reason for Anders to know White very well; the two had never been on a crew together, and they belonged to different astronaut groups, White a Gemini veteran from the second group, Anders a rookie from the third. Anders and his wife, Valerie, had gotten to know Ed and Pat White mostly because they lived one street apart.

Even among the astronauts, Ed White had always stood out; a strapping six-footer who had barely missed becoming an Olympic hurdler, he was known as one of the finest physical specimens in the

Astronaut Office. And perhaps more than any astronaut except John Glenn, White subscribed to their all-American image. In 1965, after he became the first American to walk in space, White easily wore the mantle of a national hero. There appeared to be no limit to how far he might go. Ed and Pat seemed perfectly matched. Few women were so devoted to their husbands. Now, Bill Anders would have to tell Pat White that her husband was dead.

Bill Anders had lived with death for most of his adult life, first as an air force fighter pilot, then as an astronaut. He had been to his share of funerals. And it was at funerals that Anders had noticed something about himself that made him feel different from other people He did not shed tears. While he felt sadness for the family, he did not grieve for the man who was killed. When he'd decided to become a fighter pilot, he'd accepted deadly risk as part of the bargain. And he knew the dead pilot would have felt the same way: "Sure, it's a shame to lose a good man—but he knew what he was getting into. He flipped a coin, and he lost."

By 1967 death had become a part of the astronaut life. Just last year Charlie Bassett and Elliot See had been killed in a plane crash, and two years before that, it was Ted Freeman who perished the same way. And none of this had made Anders hesitate to climb into the cockpit of a supersonic jet fighter, or trust his life to a pressure suit in the vacuum of a test chamber. It didn't blunt his desire to ride a moon rocket. Like all the astronauts, Anders accepted the risks of the job, and it wasn't difficult for him to do that. What was difficult—the hardest thing Anders would ever do—was to go to the house of this attractive woman in her thirties who was raising two children, bearing bad news. A short while ago Pat had picked up her daughter from a ballet lesson. When she arrived home her neighbor Jan Armstrong was waiting silently for her. She must have been surprised, then confused—after all, Ed was at the Cape, he wasn't flying tonight—and then she must have filled with dread. But it wasn't up to one astronaut wife to tell another that her darkest nightmare had come true. That task most often fell to another astronaut. Anders rang the doorbell.

• • •

When Slayton and Roosa arrived at Pad 34 ambulances waited in vain at the base of the huge launch tower, their rotating beacons flashing in the night. Entering the steel gridwork of the gantry, the two men boarded a small elevator and rode it to Adjustable Level A-8, 218 feet up, and headed across the swing arm to the small enclosure at the other end, called the White Room. Even before they arrived they were assaulted by the stench of burned electrical insulation and incinerated plastics. At last, reaching the end of the swing arm, they could see it: the command module's square hatchway, flush against the side of the White Room. Something was hanging from the open hatch; it was an arm, clad in a white spacesuit. Kelly and Harter, the two doctors, were here; they told Slayton the dead men were still inside, snared in a web of melted nylon netting that had once hung within the cabin. The doctors had been unable to remove them.

Slayton gripped the coil just above the hatchway and leaned into the cabin of Apollo 1. He could see the familiar configuration of the command module cabin: three couches, side by side; the broad center instrument panel, amid a forest of switches, knobs, and controls. Warning lights still glowed amber on the blackened panel. Much of the once spotless cabin was covered with soot. On the right side of the cabin Slayton could see Chaffee, his space-suited form motionlessz in his couch, still strapped in. The other two couches were empty. Slayton looked down, below the edge of the hatchway, and spotted two helmeted heads, both with clear faceplates still closed. Right below the hatch were a pair of legs, doubled up, from which the layers of space suit material had been burned off. It was impossible to tell who was Grissom and who was White.

Slayton told Kelly and Harter not to do anything more until photographs could be taken. Then he and Roosa turned away from the blackened cabin of Apollo 1, carrying the smell of fire and death with them. For the rest of their lives, even after the terrible images had faded in memory, they would remember that smell.

• • •

The astronauts had always known it was only a matter of time. Gemini had had its share of close calls, none worse than when Gemini 8 began tumbling out of control: Neil Armstrong and Dave Scott had narrowly escaped with their lives. And the Gemini pilots had taken some calculated risks. For example, everyone knew that the Gemini ejection seat and parachute that served as the only means of escape in a launch emergency was effective only under very limited conditions. And there were other risks, not only on Gemini but on the comparatively primitive Mercury flights. Looking back, it was not only superb hardware and outstanding people, in space and on the ground, that had averted tragedy, it was also luck. But the lunar missions were even more complex, and among the astronauts there was an unspoken feeling that it was only a matter of time before their luck ran out.

Gus Grissom had known that. Sometime during Gemini, he had told his wife, "If there's ever a serious accident in the program, it's probably going to be me." And a few weeks ago, at a press conference, he had said, "if we die, we want people to accept it. We're in a risky business. . . ." But he was talking about dying in space. If Grissom, White, and Chaffee had burned up in reentry, if they had perished in the fireball of an exploding booster, if their parachutes hadn't opened and they had plummeted into the ocean—any of those fates would have been easier to accept. The terrible shock of this January night, and the irony, was that they died while their spacecraft was sitting on the pad, with technicians all around them, safety just on the other side of the hatch. And yet, no one had been able to save them.

What went wrong? Even years after investigators began to sift through the wreckage of Apollo 1 piece by piece, no one could say exactly. But within weeks, the general picture became clear; the fire was a disaster waiting to happen. During the test, the command module was pressurized with pure oxygen at 16.7 pounds per square inch, slightly above sea-level atmospheric pressure. Pure oxygen can be a fire hazard even at low pressure, but at 16.7 psi, the danger grows to frightening proportions. And yet, the practice of pressurizing with oxygen on the pad had been used dozens of times during Mercury and Gemini, without mishap.

NASA had chosen pure oxygen for Apollo for the same reasons it had been used in Mercury and Gemini: it eliminated the weight and complexity that would have been required for an oxygen/nitrogen mixture. Pure oxygen was essential while in orbit, when the cabin pressure was only 5 psi. Somehow, no one had absorbed the realization that on the pad, the pressure was kept slightly above sea-level conditions. And if oxygen carried a fire risk, the command module's designers thought they had removed all possible sources of ignition from the command module cabin.

But they were wrong. Shortly after 6:31 p.m. on January 27, the review board concluded, there was a spark inside Apollo 1, probably in the vicinity of some damaged wires in the lower equipment bay at the foot of Grissom's couch. Perhaps aided by flammable fumes leaking from a nearby coolant pipe, the spark ignited some nylon netting that had been installed underneath the couches to catch dropped equipment, and the fire spread quickly. Other flammable items, including foam pads that were there to protect the interior finish during the test, fueled the blaze. Even materials normally considered flame-resistant burned as if they had been doused in kerosene. On the walls Velcro fasteners, a favorite means of securing loose gear in weightlessness, exploded in a shower of fireballs. In seconds, as the temperature soared to 2,500 degrees Fahrenheit, the command module became an incinerator, and Grissom, White, and Chaffee never had a hope of escape—because the hatch had become impossible to open.

The command module's side hatch was one of the inevitable design compromises. It was a two-piece affair, with an outer hatch and an inner hatch that opened inward, into the cabin. Some NASA engineers and astronauts, and even engineers at North American, had questioned the design, calling for a one-piece hatch that could be swung open, like the one used in Gemini. But the Apollo managers, and Joe

Shea in particular, always had sound reasons for vetoing the change. Mostly it was a matter of weight: Each pound of payload cost many times its own weight in propellant to haul it off the surface of the earth and send it to the moon. The two-piece hatch was not only the most lightweight design, it was also the simplest. And to anyone concerned about air leaks during a two-week trip to the moon and back, an inward-opening hatch solved the problem: cabin pressure would keep it tightly sealed. But even under the best conditions it was very difficult to open. The inner hatch was a heavy, cumbersome metal plate secured by a set of bolts. The man in the center couch had to reach back over his head, undo the bolts using a special tool, and then lower it out of the way. Ed White had been in Apollo 1's center couch, and no astronaut surpassed him for sheer physical strength. For exercise, White and his backup, Dave Scott, used to practice opening the hatch; it was like pressing a couple of hundred pounds at the gym. But only seconds after the fire started neither Ed White nor any other human being would have been strong enough to open it. As the fire progressed the buildup of hot gases sealed the hatch shut with thousands of pounds of force. As it was, White never had a chance even to undo the bolts.

The blaze would undoubtedly have consumed the three men had it continued, but within fifteen seconds after the first report of fire, the pressure in the cabin soared to nearly twice sea-level atmospheric pressure—high enough to rupture the command module's hull. Hot gases rushed through the breach with a loud whoosh that startled the pad crews, leaving the cabin enveloped in thick smoke. But by then, the horror of being trapped in an inferno was nearly over for Grissom's crew. Seconds later their oxygen hoses burned through and carbon monoxide forced its way into their space suits. Fifteen to 30 seconds after that, the medical examiners estimated, the men lost consciousness. Within four minutes there was no hope of reviving them. Grissom, White, and Chaffee did not burn to death; they were asphyxiated.

The greatest irony was that Gus Grissom, who had almost drowned after his Mercury mission because of a hatch that opened prematurely, was claimed by a hatch that could not be opened at all.

• • •

Even the astronauts who did not see the charred spacecraft or smell its acrid odor in the Florida night were stunned by the news from the Cape that Friday evening. They were appalled to realize how much they had overlooked. They had talked about what they would do if a fire broke out while they were in space, how the flames might propagate in zero gravity. But none of them had even considered a fire on the pad. Like so many things about this disaster, it was almost beyond comprehension.

In hindsight, there was enough blame to go around. Some astronauts, in anger, singled out North American, saying its engineers, yielding to schedule pressure, had taken shortcuts. And as the investigation of the fire progressed, there were charges of mismanagement and shoddy workmanship. Nor was NASA without fault: All of this had happened under the agency's supervision.

But there was another, more forgiving view. True, North American wasn't like McDonnell. But no one had ever tried to assemble a moonship before. The Apollo command module was the most complex flying machine ever devised, an intricate package crammed full of state-of-the-art equipment. It would have been naive not to expect all kinds of things to go wrong the first time they put one together. And no one, at NASA or North American, had knowingly compromised the astronauts' safety.

And in the next weeks the astronauts came to admit what Stafford, Young, and Cernan did over a few drinks one night, that there was a hidden blessing in this disaster: the wreckage of Apollo 1 was there for the accident board to examine, not a silent tomb circling the earth or drifting in the translunar void. Although three men had died, three or perhaps six more lives had probably been saved.

On the cold, wet January day when they buried Grissom, White, and Chaffee, most of the astronauts put the tragedy of the fire behind them with an acceptance that was difficult for outsiders to understand. Ultimately, when Grissom had spoken of accepting death in a dangerous, critical undertaking, he had been speaking for all of them. Their

biggest concern now was making Apollo fly. The immediate causes of
the fire had to be fixed—and now there was a much needed chance to
correct the long list of other inadequacies. It would take time, but they
had to recover and move on. Before them was the most extraordinary
goal of the twentieth century, and it came with a deadline.

Heart of the Delta

by Donovan Webster

Crop dusting sounds like a tame business compared to some other airborne pursuits. Writer Donovan Webster spent a month with Arkansas crop dusters, and discovered that these pilots encounter more than their share of difficulty and danger.

To understand just why crop dusting is necessary to agriculture in the Mississippi River Delta, it helps to have planted a bean there. On July 4, 1989, I planted a single scarlet-runner-bean seed at the edge of a farm road outside Clarksdale, Mississippi. Seventeen days later, without my ever watering or fertilizing that seed, it had produced a bright-green vine eight feet nine inches long. Then, on the twentieth day, tragedy struck: bugs discovered my vine. The insects (they were aphids, I later learned) were tiny, the size of pencil dots on a sheet of paper, and there were thousands of them. By the evening of that day, July 24th, the vine was so covered with little bugs that it had become a pulsing, gray-white strand running along the ground. Two days after that—only three weeks after I planted my seed—the vine was dead: a brown, wizened strand that no longer attracted any bugs. My vine, as impressive as its sweet youth had been, had died before producing a single bean.

Were it not for crop dusting, the story of agriculture in the Delta would mirror the sad, speedy history of my bean. There is so much farmland there, and so much of it is swampy or (in the case of the rice fields) totally submerged, that the only way to tend it is from the air. If agricultural aviation should suddenly disappear from the Delta, here's what would happen: Most of the United States rice crop would be destroyed by insects and fungi. Forty per cent of our national cotton harvest would be ruined by bollworm and boll weevil. Roughly a quarter of our national soybean yield would never make it to the silo. The cotton gins would stop, the area's grain elevators would empty, and the farmers of the Delta would have almost no new produce to sell. Rice would have to be imported, the price of domestic cotton would skyrocket, and the spiralling cost of soybeans (used in everything from Hamburger Helper to automobile tires and pharmaceuticals) would make the price of being an everyday American rise appreciably.

The Mississippi River Delta is a roughly triangular floodplain that stretches away—east and west—from each bank of the mighty brown river itself. Though the state of Mississippi has claimed the Delta as its own, the region's topographic and agricultural character actually extends to Cairo, Illinois, where the Ohio River joins the Mississippi. From there, the Delta traces a constantly broadening path south, always keeping the river roughly at its center. Through the bootheel of Missouri, across western Tennessee, past Memphis and into the Cotton Belt, the Delta encompasses much of the western half of the state of Mississippi, the eastern half of Arkansas, and most of Louisiana as it makes its cross-bayou splay for the Gulf of Mexico.

Through the millennia, as the Mississippi has moved south, it has also etched a switchback east-west course over hundreds of miles—an apparently random path that has widened its floodplain considerably and has left behind a layer of fertile topsoil sediment, which, in some places, is more than forty feet thick. At its widest, the Delta spans more than five hundred ballroom-floor-flat miles (its topographic influences can be seen as far west as Houston), and over its entire length it contains nearly three hundred thousand square miles of Delta-grade silt, a loosely packed dirt as rich as any potting soil you could buy at the local garden nursery.

If you take the time to drive across the Delta in winter, its sky and earth and seemingly abandoned shotgun shacks all assume the same shade of gray. It's a world of three-hundred-and-sixty-degree horizon— a damp, windy, desolate place, where daytime temperatures hover just above freezing, and where dormant fields stretch away forever, snagged only occasionally by a brake of cypress trees, a planter's shack, or a boxy, whitewashed, single-story Baptist church. In the cold months, wintering red-tailed hawks rest on top of telephone poles and fence posts, and stringy trails of cotton blow across the farm roads. Road-killed armadillos and hounds lie along the highways like mile markers. And, all season long, there are vast flocks of ducks and geese overhead, moving south and, later, back north along the Mississippi River flyway. The birds often stop to rest, and they can be seen by the million in the flooded river bottoms, gorging themselves in the drained rice fields. They are a squawking, honking, cacophonous lot, and their noise is the soundtrack of Delta winters.

Then comes the explosion of spring and summer: the verdant pastels of young rice fields, the deep green of cotton plants, the thick growths of soybeans. And above it all lies the flat and pale-blue sky, where monstrous thunderheads form every afternoon at about three-thirty. During the hot months, weeds sprout in every sidewalk crack, and the air is thick with the smell of flowers and drying mud and dirt-road dust. The sun crushes down at midday, washing the color from everything and adding its own shimmery silver patina. And then there's the animal life: the deer hiding in the swamp brakes; the snakes crossing the two-lanes like dark, slippery lengths of rope; the buzzards riding afternoon thermals in the sky; and, of course, the flying insects, which swarm there in infuriating, mind-numbing density. You drive through the Mississippi River Delta during summer, and, day or night, insects clatter constantly against your car's windshield.

• • •

One afternoon in mid-July, the usual thunderstorm crouches on the horizon just southwest of West Helena, Arkansas, and in the offices of Planter's Ag, one of the local crop-dusting outfits, Jim Lawhon and Gus Rogers are worrying. Lawhon, a tall, beefy man of forty-five, with a handsome pug face and with legs that make him appear to have grown up on horseback, paces up and back in the planked, three-room shack that Planter's Ag calls home. "Looks like rain again," he says. "Rain. Rain. Every day, rain. How the *hell* do I get caught up when it keeps raining?"

He strolls to his desk, a gray pressed-steel affair in a corner. On one wall above the desk is a Presidential portrait of Ronald Reagan; on the other is a cheesecake calendar (nearly clothed women posed on commuter-aircraft noses). It's a little after three o'clock, and Lawhon has been flying non-stop since sunup, his most recent chore having been to sift white granulated fertilizer onto flooded rice fields around West Helena. "It's amazing I'm still in business," Lawhon says, sitting down in his desk chair. "God-*damned* amazing." He rubs his face with a broad, suntanned hand.

Lawhon decides to find some lunch, and gets up and walks into the back room, which functions as a kitchen. In a minute, he returns, with a Coke Classic and a Winston cigarette. "Nothing to eat in this whole place," he says. "God, I'll tell you, between the E.P.A., the F.A.A., OSHA, my overhead, and this *God-damned* weather, I should be out of business or dead. These fields have to be sprayed today, *right now,* or the farmers' yields will fall off. And it's rained every afternoon now for twenty-two days, and I can't fly in all this rain." He shakes his head. "This farming-from-the-air stuff, shit. If I could make this kind of money managing a shoe store, I'd do it in a heartbeat."

He paces to the shack's west-facing window and inspects his airplane, a single-engine, red-white-and-blue, pilot-only model, whose wings are placed low along its fuselage. The plane, a Turbo-thrush, has the aggressive, I'll-do-this-myself look of Second World War fighter aircraft as it sits on the black asphalt strip of the Planter's Ag runway, just beyond the window. Now that the day's rice-fertilizing orders have been filled, it's on to the next job, which is to apply insecticide to a cotton field two miles away.

Lawhon walks to the front of the shack, which faces north. He stares through the screen door for a moment, shaking his head at the thunderclouds on the horizon.

Gus Rogers, a roostery man of fifty-four who's always wearing a billed cap, is Lawhon's partner and the manager of Planter's Ag. Rogers is seated at the other desk in the shack, and, as is almost always the case, he has a telephone cradled on his left shoulder; he's taking a farmer's order, writing it down on a carboned ticket. Still, he looks up from his order-taking and glances at Lawhon. "Aw, Jimmy," he says. "It's just a little *rain*, man. And anyway"—he pauses for a drag on his cigarette—"you couldn't quit. You'd miss the flying."

The rains have now descended on Planter's Ag from the southwest, and Jim Lawhon is airborne, somewhere inside the storm. The sky is charcoal gray, and is growing darker and more ominous by the minute. Thunder booms, and the rain falls horizontally and in sheets. Leafy branches—torn from trees somewhere upwind—tumble along the road that the shack fronts on. Inside the Planter's Ag office, Gus Rogers, at his desk, listens to the spitting hiss of the two-way radio. Jim Lawhon's signal spills weakly through the radio's squeals. "It's storming on our cotton," Lawhon says. "Can't get home, neither. I'm gonna look for another place to set down, or maybe I'll dodge around till this stuff passes through."

Rogers lifts the office microphone and depresses the send key on the mike's stand. "O.K., Jimmy," he says.

"Flying north by east," Lawhon says. "I'll see how the airport looks. Maybe I can land there. If not, come looking."

The radio screeches and squalls again. Then it is silent. Rain beats against the shack's walls and windows. Wind whips at its corners. I ask Rogers why he doesn't radio the storm's movements to Lawhon.

"He knows where the storm is," Rogers says. "He's in it. And, anyway, Jimmy's got better things to do right now than listen to me."

In twenty minutes the storm has passed through. In another five minutes, the sky overhead is pale blue again; the clouds have moved to the northwest, their hulking gray shapes dragging tentacles of rain toward the horizon. A minute later, Lawhon's plane can be seen moving out of the northwest—a low-winged silhouette coming in just above a line of trees. At half a mile out, the humming sound of the plane's turbine engine becomes audible. Thirty seconds later, Lawhon is on the ground at the runway's far end, the plane tipping and bucking on the asphalt.

The Turbo-thrush hurtles up the runway, going far too fast. It hops and teeters on its landing-gear struts; its tires squeal against the asphalt surface. Lawhon feathers the propeller, and the plane speeds toward the shack, bouncing and pitching from side to side. Finally, at fifty yards, it begins to brake, yet it's still going too fast, seemingly out of control. At the last possible moment, Lawhon cranks down the wing flaps and kicks the rudder to the left. The aircraft turns a hundred and eighty degrees in a spin that stops it dead. Lawhon shuts off the engine, and its turbine whine dies out across the nearby cotton fields. He removes his white crash helmet and hangs it on the rudder stick. He shakes his head vigorously and rubs his face with his right hand.

After a moment, he lifts the cockpit door and gets out—stepping heavily onto the wing, then down to the ground. He is smiling broadly. "God, God. Thank you, *God*," he says. He throws his hands into the air, fluttering them theatrically; he keeps walking toward the shack. "I couldn't hardly fly that thing with the hopper full of pesticide," he continues. "I thought for *God-damned sure* I was going to hit the house. God knows, I couldn't just open the gate and dump that poison. I'd be buying dead crops from now till Christmas."

I'm standing on the porch watching Lawhon walk toward the shack; he passes the porch steps, moving toward the bed of his white Chevrolet pickup truck. "Did you *see* that?" he says. "Did you notice? That plane, it's not made to land with four thousand pounds sitting in the hopper. Man, it was *slug*-gish. That plane—*God love it*—it was slooow!" He opens the lid of a cooler in the bed of his truck. It's empty. He looks over to me. "Hey," he says. "You got any beer in that jeep of yours?"

It happens that on my way to Planter's Ag (and hoping for this exact question) I stopped to buy a twelve-pack of Budweiser and a six-pack of 7UP at a convenience store.

I walk out to my jeep (which is actually an aging Toyota Land Cruiser), swing open the back doors, and grab two cans of Bud from my cooler. I walk over to Lawhon's truck and hand him one.

"Sir," Lawhon says, "you are obviously a man of fine breeding." He drains the can in a single, lengthy pull, then turns his gaze back to me. "Got another?" he says.

I fetch him another. He pops it and drinks this one more slowly.

"With this rain we can't spray anymore today," he says. "I only hope that liquid fertilizer I sprayed on those beans first thing this morning dried before the rain hit. If it didn't, the chemicals in that fertilizer will mix with the rainwater and burn the plants' leaves. Boy, that'll be more hell to pay." Lawhon leans against his truck and examines the sky. "We're done for today," he says. "What you say we jump in my truck, get some beer, and I'll show you around *be-yew-ti-ful* West Helena?"

"Like every other complicated thing in life, agricultural aviation seems easy on the surface," Lawhon says, steering his truck along a deserted Arkansas two-lane. "I mean, you just fly your plane a foot or two above some crops at a hundred-some miles per hour, and you distribute your load by pushing forward on a lever. And, hey"—he tosses up a hand— "that's it."

The truck rolls on, windows down, tires humming on the pavement. We pass a crawfish/catfish farm on the right, a stand of swamp-tupelo trees on the left; the sky is pale blue, the air is thick with humidity. "It really does seem easy," Lawhon goes on. "I mean, you just carry liquid insecticide or granular fertilizer in the hopper of your aircraft, and at the right time you push this little cockpit lever forward, and that opens a gate on the hopper's bottom. Air-pressure differentials and gravity pull your load through that opened gate, and it's distributed onto the fields through the spreader. To quit, you just pull that lever back, and the hopper gate shuts. There's a little math to it—you have to figure distribution amounts of the materials you're spraying—but it's relatively simple, especially if you have a pocket calculator handy."

He pauses to light a Winston, then scans the fields on both sides of the highway. "But ag aviation is also the toughest job there is," he says. "There's all this stuff ag pilots have to be watching for. Like whether your aircraft is flying right, and whether *you're flying* it right. And there's always trees. I've hit some in my time. And high-tension wires. Always wires. And silos and barns. And then there's other aircraft, too. A few years back, two boys north of here got killed when they collided in midair. They were working fields on different sides of a strip of trees. Both of 'em came over those trees at the same time and *bammo!*" He bangs on the steering wheel with the butt of his right hand. "They hit head on. Yep, there's always something to be watching for, to be careful of."

Lawhon looks out over the farmland some more; he is given to regular breaks in his monologue, moments when—like all agricultural people—he is no doubt remarking silently on crop conditions in different fields. "As an ag pilot, you've always got to be mindful of the toxicity of what you're laying out," he says. "Whether you're applying your load evenly, making even swaths. Because if you aren't, you won't be in business long. If you spray too heavily, or if the wind blows some of what you're spraying onto Farmer Brown's crops, where it doesn't belong, there's a state examiner who comes out and verifies Farmer Brown's claim. And, man, if you screwed up you just bought some useless plants. Most ag aircraft have this little button inside the cockpit. When you mash it, it puts out a string of smoke, so that you can gauge the wind and figure the drift. And the edges of some of the fields around here are flagged with white posts or white pennants, or such. We pilots use those flags to know where our last swath went in. You've got to be extremely careful with chemicals these days.

"That stuff sitting in my hopper, it's called methyl parathion," he continues, "and it's mixed together with some other stuff. And it's bad.

If you get sloppy and lay a little of that stuff onto a creek or a catfish farmer's pond, it kills the fish. All of 'em. That stuff's so noxious that if some gets sprayed on your car it'll eat the paint right off. Or if, for some stupid reason, somebody's out sunbathing in a cotton field and gets misted, that stuff will burn on their skin like a bicycle trip to the Devil. You got to shower—and *really* scrub with soap—to get it off."

The truck is approaching the edge of West Helena, and the warehouselike corrugated-steel rectangles of some cotton gins come into view. "If I'd have wrecked my aircraft this afternoon?" Lawhon says. "With all that poison in it? That poison would have run out into the ground, and nothing—nothing at all—would grow within twenty yards of there for years. I mean, you get a drop of that undiluted methyl parathion into an open cut on your hand, and, man, you die. You get no appeals. You get no lucky breaks. Your story is over."

Lawhon turns onto a larger road, and begins talking about how he got into agricultural aviation. "When I was eighteen, I wanted to learn to fly," he says. "I'd done pretty well in school, so I sold my water-ski boat for three hundred and fifty dollars and used that money for tuition at Memphis State. I was studying a little of everything, but I was especially interested in engineering, because I wanted to fly for the military. Well, I did well at college. I got some A's. But when the next year came around I didn't have another ski boat to sell, so I dropped out and joined the Marines. This was in 1966. And in the Marines in 1966, even if the recruiter said you could become eligible to be an aviator you were still an enlisted man. You got placed in the infantry, and you ended up in Vietnam."

Without substantial prodding, this is all Jim Lawhon will say about his time in Vietnam. He does not say that after two years he rose to become a Marine platoon commander. He does not say that he was severely wounded at Camlo by mortar fire, and was hospitalized for eighteen months. Instead, he cuts right to his return to West Helena, where he matriculated at the local ag-flying school, which was then housed at West Helena's local airfield.

Lawhon has been flying commercially since 1973, and that makes him one of the longer-lived ag pilots going. Though actuarial estimates on the longevity of agricultural pilots vary, ag flying tends to be a young man's profession. When I ask Lawhon about this, he says, "Yes, yes, that's true. But after you've wrecked a few planes you get smart. If you're lucky enough to live through your first few crashes, then your odds of staying alive rise significantly."

I ask him about his plane wrecks.

"You want to hear stories about wrecking aircraft?" Lawhon says, stopping the truck at a Kwik-Stop supermarket at the edge of West Helena. "You're gonna *love* the boys at the airfield."

A SHORT HISTORY OF AGRICULTURAL AVIATION, PART 1: If you were an American aviator returning from the First World War, and you wanted to fly for a living, your prospects for eating regularly were pretty grim. The Army Air Service was releasing most of its aviators, and there were precious few commercial outlets for civilian pilots. If you had a little money (or a soul to sell), you could possibly obtain one of the ragged training biplanes that the government was unloading and become a barnstormer, but the demand for such entertainers was lean. If you didn't have any money, you simply went back to the farm or the neighborhood and tried to wangle getting re-upped in the Air Service.

The Army Air Service was where things were happening for pilots in 1919 and 1920. The military paid regularly, they gave you a place to live, and, best of all, they had opened airfields around the country where they were busy testing ways to make the airplane more militarily useful. If you could become an Army test pilot, you were sent up daily to risk your tail on the cutting edge of aviation, and for a First World War pilot—a guy used to dogfights and strafing runs—that made dirt farming or bond-selling look pretty dull.

Meanwhile, electric lights were spreading their friendly glow to even the farthest-flung parts of America, and the upstart fad of telephoning (instead of walking up the street to talk) had seized the national consciousness. Both these technological wonders required wires for their transmission, and stringing wires required poles. Poles were made from trees, and some of the best trees for making poles were northern catalpas—fast-growing hardwoods from the Eastern forests which were prized for their straight trunks. But northern catalpas had recently been laid siege to by the larvae of the catalpa sphinx moth—an inchworm that could infest a catalpa tree and sometimes kill it in a matter of weeks.

One day in 1921, at the Air Service's McCook Field, near Dayton, Ohio, C. R. Neillie, a state entomologist, stopped by with a question: Was there any way an airplane could apply insecticide to the catalpa trees? If you could drop insecticide from the air, Neillie said, you would be working with gravity instead of against it, and the trees would have a much better chance of being fully covered. The authorities at McCook were interested in the challenge, and put one of their most resourceful engineers, a Frenchman named Étienne Darmoy, on the job. Darmoy fashioned a metal hopper, which was then bolted to the left side of an old biplane, a Curtiss Jenny, and filled with lead arsenate, the only hundred-per-cent-lethal insecticide of the time.

On the afternoon of August 31, 1921, Lieutenant John Macready took the Jenny up and flew low over a catalpa grove near Troy, Ohio. Darmoy sat in the aircraft's passenger seat, distributing the lead arsenate by opening and closing the sliding gate that separated the hopper's cargo area from its spreader. The plane flew swaths back and forth above the grove for fifty-four seconds. When the flight was over, Macready and Darmoy landed in a nearby field and were greeted by three breathless state agriculturalists. The trees were perfectly covered, the scientists said. There was an evenly sifted layer of lead arsenate over the entire catalpa grove. The crop, they said, had been dusted.

The sun is setting gold and warm across the flat Arkansas cropland, and at Thompson-Robbins Airfield, in West Helena, eight men have gathered around the bed of Jim Lawhon's pickup. It's sometime after seven o'clock, and everyone is telling plane-wreck stories. Besides Lawhon, the group includes four crop-duster pilots, their mechanic (a former crop duster), their gas-and-parts supplier (also a former crop duster), and a seventeen-year-old worshipper. All of them except the seventeen-year-old are licensed to fly airplanes (and the seventeen-year-old will have his license in less than a week). All of them—the seventeen-year-old again excluded—are drinking beer. All are dressed similarly: bluejeans, short-sleeved madras shirts, sunglasses. Most are in their late thirties or early forties. A few are going bald, and a few are wearing caps; most are smoking cigarettes.

Lawhon's pickup sits just outside the opened sliding door of the airfield's largest hangar. The sunlight falls through the doorway, leaving a dusty rhomboid footprint on the oil-blackened concrete of the hangar floor. In the past ninety minutes, the group around the truck has systematically drained the cases of beer that Lawhon bought at the Kwik-Stop. One by one, the empty cans are tossed into the bed of the truck with a clank. The white-enamelled steel of the truck bed, once fully visible, has become obscured by a stratum of empty Budweisers.

The men around the truck bed tell their crash stories in order—in a hierarchy that honors those who are oldest and those who have wrecked the worst. Bruce Hayes, the mechanic, is acknowledged by all to have had a "real bad" wreck. "I ran out of intelligence just a second before I ran out of airspeed," Hayes says. "I was on my last certification flight to become an ag pilot, and the guy who was certifying me couldn't show up at the last minute. So I said, 'Hell, I'll just fly one for fun,' and I filled the plane's hopper with water to simulate the weight of a real load." Hayes stops and smiles. "I was doing great," he says. "Really flying well, moving low and smooth over the rice fields. It was beautiful. But then I started playing around, coming down too steep, and I couldn't pull out. I didn't have any altitude, and the plane went in—and it went in *hard*. Hell, it just goes to show I had a lot to learn. I'd been going way too fast, and the aircraft hit the deck of that rice field, and, man, it was like *death*. The aircraft tore through five dikes in that rice field before it stopped. Hell, as you guys all know, I broke my neck."

Mike Akin, the airfield's gas-and-parts supplier, says, "You were so scared you got up out of the cockpit and walked off!" The crowd around the truck chuckles.

"That plane," Hayes says. "It was sitting up on its nose out in that field. The propeller was all bent back, and the plane was just sitting vertical out there, as quiet and pretty as can be." He pauses, then says, "It was in that rice field, gentlemen, right then and there, that I decided I'd rather fix ag planes than fly them. Boys, right then and there my ag-piloting days were over."

"It was those old helmets," another pilot says. "They were so heavy."

"It's not like now," Hayes says. "These days, we've got those light-weight, seven-hundred-dollar helmets like the F-14 pilots wear. Those old heavy things, if you were to wreck, they played crack-the-whip with you. The unluckiest pilots flipped upside down when they wrecked. Those old heavy helmets would keep going forward with inertia while the pilot's body was strapped into the seat. With those old helmets, sometimes a wrecked pilot's neck would stretch to two foot long." Hayes lifts his hands in the air and holds them about two feet apart; he regards the open space between his palms for a moment, then turns to Lawhon and smiles. "How 'bout your stories, Jimmy?" he says.

Lawhon shakes his head. "Man," he says, taking a drag from his cigarette, "I've never wrecked."

"Let's see," Hayes says, still smiling. "Let's see. The first one, Jimmy, to refresh your memory, was in the summer of 1973. You were showing off." Hayes turns to me, still talking. "Jimmy took off in an old Stearman. That's one of the old two-hole Second World War pilot trainers—they were biplanes converted for ag aviation—and he took off from here to play hard guy for some photographers who were visiting the airfield. He made a few low passes, then held the plane down for a second too long." Hayes laughs. "The aircraft's landing gear clipped a water tank, then went on to hit a levee, and then the plane came down onto a grass runway and ended up on its nose." Hayes laughs. Everyone around the truck bed begins laughing, too. "And Jimmy," Hayes says, "old handsome Jimmy, he just got out of that wrecked plane and walked away smiling."

The seventeen-year-old can't help himself. He's been hovering quietly around the truck now for two hours, listening to the stories, hearing the technical talk, and watching the swagger, and he looks about to burst with his knowledge of agricultural aviation. Finally, he asks, "What about Randy?"

"*Ohhhh*, Randy," Hayes says.

"Randy, Randy, Randy," Mike Akin adds.

"Oh, Randy," the others say.

Hayes points across the truck bed to a tall, tanned pilot of about thirty-five. "Our Randy Gibbons, over there," he says. "He's our finest achievement. Randy had *nine wrecks* in 1982 alone, two of them in the space of thirty days." Hayes hoots. "This boy probably had five per cent of America's commercial-aviation accidents that month."

"Roll-Over Randy," the others say in unison. "Roll-Over Randy."

"The boy can fly," Hayes says. "He's actually a really fine pilot. He showed up here from spraying tobacco in North Carolina, and he was the hottest stick-and-rudder man around. Then, like I say, in 1982 he got into the habit of flipping his plane over on the landings, and we took to calling him Roll-Over Randy. He went through aircraft like—"

Another pilot interrupts, "After he'd been here awhile, we were beginning to worry about the number of aircraft we had left, so we checked up on him."

"Turns out," Hayes goes on, "that back in North Carolina they used to call him Kilowatt Randy, because he kept hitting power lines."

"You boys know I'm a good pilot," Gibbons says, coming to his own defense. "I can fly as good as anybody."

Heads nod all around the truck.

"It's just that sometimes I have this trouble with my landings," he adds.

Everyone laughs again. This time, their faces are turned up, facing the deep blue of the Delta's nighttime sky. Their hoots roll out across the dark, flat concrete runways of the airfield, moving away through the darkness toward the cotton fields on the horizon.

Now it's the following morning. After the hangar's drinking crew broke up, Lawhon and I had some late dinner—or, to be more accurate, some 10 p.m. breakfast—at a local restaurant. (Lawhon devoured a dozen eggs, two orders of sausage, three orders of biscuits, an order of toast, three glasses of milk, and a vat of coffee.) Then, not feeling like driving me back to West Helena's Holiday Inn, he suggested that I sleep in the extra room at his house. He said we'd have to get up early, at five, because he had a big day of flying. It was the busiest time of the year for an ag pilot, he said, and he couldn't "wait around for some long-haired writer from New York to get his ass into gear."

I reminded Lawhon that I lived in Little Rock.

"You're still too goddam long-haired," he said. "You're probably a Communist, or something."

I said 5 a.m. would be fine.

I have spent the night in Lawhon's guest room, which contains only two things: a moldy-smelling bed and a quickly revolving ceiling fan. The bed is placed near a window, which, at four-fifty-six, affords a view of the blue air of pre-sunrise West Helena. Beyond the window screen, I discover, to my surprise, that Lawhon lives in a typical suburban neighborhood. Neat bungalows line a curbed street. There are green lawns and thick trimmed hedges. In Lawhon's driveway sits a string of three pickup trucks. In front of his Chevy 1500—the truck we were in last night—are two older, battered trucks. One is blue, the other pale green; the green one has very large dents all along the driver's side.

I get up and dress, then find the bathroom. I gulp cold water from the bathroom faucet, wet my face, and slick back my hair. I look around the house. The kitchen, the first room I encounter, is modern, and seemingly unused. The floor is that linoleum with small squares in varying shades of umber which was so popular in the early sixties. All the appliances—sink, range, refrigerator—are white. The ceiling is white acoustic tile. In a corner near the back door stands a monolith of red-and-white striped Kentucky Fried Chicken boxes (the three-piece-dinner size). I walk through the kitchen into the living room. It's empty except for a large-screen TV, a La-Z-Boy recliner, a metal folding chair, and a card table with a monstrously tall lamp on top of it. Also on the tabletop are plastic cigarette lighters (of various colors, including camouflage), a catalogue of airplane-engine parts, some more empty Kentucky Fried Chicken boxes, a handful of pocketknives, a few shotgun and rifle shells, empty packs of Winstons and Camels, a white plastic Arkansas Razorbacks ashtray, a couple of empty Big Gulp cups from the 7-Eleven, and several pairs of aviator sunglasses. I switch on the TV and quietly indulge in CNN for about thirty minutes, until—from virtually out of nowhere—a hungover moment sends me scrambling back to bed.

At six-thirty, the telephone rings and rings. Finally, far away, I hear Lawhon answer. "O.K., O.K.," he says from somewhere deep inside the house. "Awright then, Gus. O.K. Good. I'll be along before too long. Good. Yeah. Good. O.K. Bye."

A minute later, I can hear a shower hissing. Time to go to work.

We get in the truck, and roll out of West Helena's neighborhoods and onto deserted farm roads; a thick layer of morning mist floats across the fields. "God loves me," Lawhon says. "I don't know what I did to deserve this, but the Lord loves me. With this mist, there's no way I could have flown early this morning. Ag pilots work under laws known as V.F.R.—that's Visual Flight Rules. We don't use radios or navigational instrumentation to speak of, and if there are storms or mists in the air we're grounded. And, with what we did last night, I would have had to take a late start today anyway. There's a rule of thumb about drinking and flying. It goes 'Twelve hours from bottle to throttle,' and if you want to survive as a pilot you always try to remember it. Oh, God, thank you. I got lucky today."

I ask Lawhon about his plane wrecks.

"The last one was last November," he says. "I was spraying north of town, next to this national forest over there, and the engine on this Ag-Cat I had just quit. I'd just finished flying a swath, came up over the forest, and the engine failed. Man, below me there was nothing but trees. I was so low to the ground, and I was moving so fast, that I had this much time"—he snaps his fingers—"to decide how I'd crash. There was no place to land, so I decided to glide the plane onto the smoothest-looking patch of trees out there, because trees will sometimes soften your landing if you lay your aircraft in gently enough. I was going a hundred-some miles per hour, and I had about one second to decide what to do. You've only got two decisions to make at a time like that— which patch of trees you'll use for a runway, and whether you'll cover your face or your balls on impact. I didn't get a scratch on me." He reconsiders. "No, that's wrong," he says. "I did get a scratch. When I got down out of the aircraft, I began running away, because I thought the plane was on fire and might explode. While I was running and looking over my shoulder, I tripped over a stick, or something, and fell." He holds up his left hand and points to its palm with his right index finger. "I got a cut along here from a rock." He smiles. "The insurance from that wreck bought me a nice new Turbo-thrush."

We roll up to Planter's Ag, leave the truck, and head into the office. Gus Rogers says that Lawhon's plane has been washed, gassed, and reloaded with methyl parathion. Rogers and Lawhon discuss which fields Lawhon is to spray this morning, and I move toward the office coffee machine. In minutes Lawhon is in his aircraft, rolling down the runway toward another long, hot, lucrative day of work.

A SHORT HISTORY OF AGRICULTURAL AVIATION, PART 2: In the early nineteen-twenties, Cotton Belt farmers needed a way to kill the boll weevil. Throughout the region, the little downspout-nosed beetle was destroying millions of dollars' worth of cotton crops annually, and Delta farmers were just starting to try to control the weevil by broadcasting lead arsenate and, later, calcium arsenate over their crops from behind mule-drawn, hand-cranked carts. But this primitive method of applying insecticides was only marginally effective, and after a few months of such applications the insecticides often burned sections of hide completely off the mules. Then, in 1922, Dr. Bert R. Coad, a Department of Agriculture entomologist, heard of the crop-dusting experiments at Ohio's McCook Field, and, after lobbying Congress, he transported the Air Service crop dusters to the U.S.D.A.'s Delta Laboratory, in Tallulah, Louisiana. At the Delta Lab, Dr. Coad began experimenting on cotton fields with the spreader-equipped Curtiss Jennies; the results were immediate, and resoundingly positive.

While the Delta Lab was refining ways to combat the boll weevil from the air, the crop-dusting equipment was being modified. Instead of being bolted to the side of the aircraft, for instance, the calcium-arsenate hopper was moved to a spot inside the plane's fuselage just forward of the cockpit. Then, beneath the newly installed hopper, a gravity-fed conduit tube ran from the hopper's gate to an hourglass-bodied spreader, with a scoop mouth, that was bolted horizontally to the bottom of the aircraft. This newly designed spreader, with its narrowed throat, took advantage of the venturi principle and gave off a wider, more evenly sifted layer of insecticide dust. It, too, was an instant success. Within a few years, a crop-dusting apparatus almost identical to the one used today had been engineered, and Dr. Coad's successes with aerial pesticide application ballooned.

The Army Air Service pilots were also beginning to flourish during this time. Young, capable, and probably a little bored by the entertainments of Tallulah, the Air Service fliers established the code of fast living and technically perfect flying which persists today. After sifting their loads over the Delta Lab's cotton fields, Dr. Coad's pilots would often take airborne detours on their way back to the U.S.D.A. airstrip—sometimes rolling the wheels of their aircraft across the tin roofs of tenant shacks on the cotton plantations, or, in slightly less daring moods, simply buzzing automobiles, which had only recently arrived on the Delta's roads.

As the Delta Lab successes mounted, and crop dusting became an accepted cotton-farming practice, a permanent airfield, known as Scott Field, was built for the Delta Lab fliers, three miles east of Tallulah. From its runways, Air Service dusters flew demonstration flights to plantations in Louisiana, Mississippi, and southern Arkansas. In 1923, Huff, Daland & Company, of Ogdensburg, New York, saw the huge potential of crop dusting, and in a few months a fleet of new, powerful Huff, Daland biplanes was transported south. The planes were fitted with crop-dusting rigs and put to work in the surrounding croplands, thereby making Huff, Daland the first commercial ag-flying company ever. By the end of 1924, eighteen aircraft owned by Huff, Daland were working more than fifty thousand acres of cotton.

The following year, Huff, Daland Dusters applied insecticides to almost ninety thousand acres in Louisiana, Arkansas, and Mississippi. To attract new customers, Huff, Daland pilots made demonstration crop-dusting flights across the region, which quickly proved their worth and justified their catchy slogan: "It doesn't cost to dust—it costs not to dust." The company grew quickly, extending its reach across the Delta by establishing a series of well-situated auxiliary airstrips. Then, in November of 1928, a Huff, Daland vice-president named C. E. Woolman bought the company's dusting division, for forty thousand dollars, and, after renaming it the Delta Air Service, assembled the contracts and the equipment to transport passengers and parcels around the region. Six years later, in 1934, Delta carried nearly fifteen hundred passengers and countless canvas bags of "Air Mail" throughout the South. Woolman eventually weaned his company from its crop-dusting past, and today it is known as Delta Air Lines and is the third-largest passenger-transportation company in the world.

While the business of dusting cotton was expanding, in the mid-thirties, agricultural aviation was also branching out to other areas of farming. By 1937, the U.S.D.A. was experimenting with new poisons, like nicotine sulfate and calcium Cyanamid, which were broadening the variety of crops that could be tended by aircraft. Crop dusting was enjoying its honeymoon—a period that helped to raise the American farmer's cotton and produce yields by as much as twenty-five per cent. For the next thirty years, crop dusting was acknowledged to be an indisputable key to agricultural prosperity.

Since its inception, agricultural aviation has been a profitable yet costly business. Bruce Hayes' repair hangar at the West Helena airfield is testament to the cost of being a crop duster. Inside the hangar sit five bright-yellow crop-dusting planes, in varying states of repair. Their ribbon-thin metallic skins have been peeled off in sections and lean against the walls. In the more serious cases, the wings have been removed and stowed at the building's far end, fifty yards away. Up close, the planes seem like gigantic, highly elaborate toys; they can be snapped apart in minutes, and reassembled in the same amount of time. Hayes himself has just stepped out from under the skeletal steel body of a totally dismantled airframe to take a Coca-Cola break. He's wearing a short-sleeved navy-blue cotton shirt with an oval patch embroidered in white thread on the breast pocket. It reads:

HAYES AVIATION
BRUCE

On the back of the shirt, embroidered in two-inch-tall white script, is Hayes' professional title:

DUSTER DOCTOR

Outside the hangar, the sun burns down on the airfield, bleaching everything but the far-off cotton fields white. Hayes is talking in general terms about crop dusting. "It's greed," he says. "That's why ag flying has got so expensive. That's why crop dusters are a slowly dying breed. The aircraft-makers, they know they're necessary, so they jack up the prices of their planes. It makes it hard for young pilots to get started. Those young guys either have to work for someone else, a big dusting outfit, or they've got to shell out one blistering-ass bunch of cash for their own aircraft."

Hayes walks to what he calls his wrench table, an eight-foot-long, three-foot-wide red-enamelled rolling-steel monster from the Snap-On Tool Corporation. The table has eight tiers of drawers, and its top is littered with small motors and electric drills and tubes of grease. Eagle decals from Pratt & Whitney (the aircraft-engine maker) emblazon its sides, and a prominent skull-and-crossbones decal reading "YOU TOUCH, YOU DIE" has been applied to its backside.

Hayes picks up a bolt. "These little things," he says. "They mark them with a little insignia that identifies them as aircraft parts. And they charge us extra for these bolts, because of that little mark. We get shafted on this kind of stuff—and on the more complicated parts the cost grows plenty bigger. The new aircraft, the turbine-engined ones— they cost upward of four hundred thousand dollars, but I could assemble you a new one from scratch for two-thirds of that. And the older aircraft, the ones with the round, nine-cylinder engines, they still run about a hundred and fifty thousand dollars. And those old nine-bang numbers are becoming obsolete. Nowadays, you've got to buy reconditioned parts for them—they've been phased out of production. These days, I work on nothing but turbine aircraft. And there isn't an airframe in here right now that I'll bill less than ten thousand dollars on. Believe me, most of that cost is parts." He shakes his head. "Between the insurance and the overhead, ag aviation is one expensive way to make a living. The insurance, ultimately, is what kills the independents."

I ask about the insurance.

"The young, independent pilots can't even get it anymore," Hayes says. "There's a blanket no-go on new ag pilots. So the young guys work for flying services—the services get group insurance deals. The young guys establish a track record, and then they can get individually insured." He pauses to draw on his cigarette. "You know Lloyd's of London?" he goes on. "That company will insure you against ingrown toenails if you'll pay them the money for it. That company will insure *anything*. Or that's what everybody thinks. But until you're a second- or third-year ag pilot they won't touch you. The flying services are the only way we'll get young ag pilots. The good old days, they're over. Now the young guys show up with their helmets, fly for someone else, and pay their dues. The money, of course, isn't as good. A pilot working for a service will make—oh, maybe fifty thousand dollars a year. If you fly for yourself, you can make a lot more than that. You can net seventy to a hundred thousand dollars a year, maybe a hundred and fifty thousand, depending on how hard you want to work."

I remark that even at fifty thousand dollars a crop duster's salary is pretty favorable—especially in the Delta, where the cost of living is amazingly low.

"Yeah, man, that's true," Hayes says, smiling. "But then if you're working for yourself all it takes is one bad year, and you're done. The insurance man takes his twenty thousand dollars a year, and the note on the aircraft is about ninety thousand dollars a year. And then there's the cost of fixing the aircraft when you don't want to report the damage, and there's the plane's general upkeep, and the up-front cost of the chemicals you lay out, plus all the usual overhead of running a business. Man, it's just like all farming—you can get deep-tanked in the blink of an eye if you don't stay lucky. It's no wonder some of the boys look for other ways to make money."

I ask how they do that.

"Some of 'em—not too many, but some—they'll haul parcels," Hayes says.

"What kind of parcels?" I ask.

"Oh, about anything," Hayes says. "For the right price."

Hayes finishes his Coke and snuffs out his cigarette against the hangar floor. "There are boys around here, guys who're still flying ag aircraft, who make a couple extra hundred thousand dollars every year hauling packages," he says. Then he tells the story of Gary Betzner, an ag pilot from the Delta town of Hazen, Arkansas, who, in September, 1977, faked suicide by leaping off a bridge into the White River. On November 13, 1984, a man named Lucas Noel Harmony was arrested in Jacksonville, Florida, when he landed there in an airplane that contained seventeen duffelbags and two boxes full of cocaine. After a quick fingerprint check, Harmony proved to be Gary Betzner, and during Betzner's drug-trafficking trial—at the end of which he received a twenty-seven-year sentence—his tales of dirt air-strips in Central America, of gun-for-drug transactions, and of eluding United States Drug Enforcement Agency and Customs Department agents earned him a hearing before Senator John Kerry and his Iran-Contra subcommittee.

"Everybody who knew Gary Betzner also knew he wasn't dead," Hayes says. "A lot of pilots end up doing what Betzner did. It's just most of them don't get in as deep. I once saw an ag pilot who had a paper sack on his pickup truck's seat, and inside that sack was fifty thousand dollars in counted, stacked twenty-dollar bills." Hayes pauses, shakes his head, and grins. "Gary Betzner, though," he finally says, "he's gone. We haven't had word of him since he went to Washington, D.C., to testify at those Iran-Contra hearings. He's probably back in federal prison now."

Hayes shouts to Mike Akin, the gas-and-parts supplier, who sits in a parts-choked room connected to the hangar, "Hey, Mike! What's up with Gary Betzner?"

Akin, a medium-sized man with astonishingly blue eyes, strolls out of his office. He lights a cigarette as he advances across the huge, dark floor of the hangar. "Last I heard, he was guest-starring for the government," Akin says. "But that was more than a year ago. Man, that boy is one fine pilot gone wrong." Akin arrives at the wrench table. "What's going on?" he says. "You guys talking free-lance?"

I say yes. Hayes nods.

"You know," Akin says to Hayes, "Don, here, should go out and talk to Melvin."

"Man," Hayes says, "Don couldn't get out there right now—the river's too high. With all this rain, he couldn't get out there till Christmas."

"Boy, Don," Akin says to me, "you could learn—I mean *learn*—any number of things from Melvin, ag flying included. He was a Second World War bomber pilot. He was a thirty-year crop duster. Man, he knows *all*."

I ask who Melvin is.

"He's my dad," Hayes says. "And if there's a guy who knows this industry it's him. But he lives down in the bottoms, back in there where the Arkansas and White and Mississippi Rivers all run together. This time of year, he's up on a high knoll somewhere catching fish and living without electricity or running water. The bugs and snakes are awful. If you had a month, you likely couldn't find him. And even if you *did* find him it would be because he let you." Hayes pauses. Then, as if to warn me further, he says, "Word has it those woods hold some Claymore anti-personnel mines, too. And if you did go out there and find him he probably wouldn't talk. He's not a big talker."

"Unless you took along some liquor," Akin says. "You might get him talking then."

"Just sit on down there," Melvin Hayes says. "Make yourself at home." He motions toward a green five-gallon bucket turned bottom up. The bucket is next to a smoldering fire. It's early January now, a Saturday afternoon, and I've finally found Melvin. His camp is a scene from a Hollywoodized survivalist movie. Scattered concentrically farther and farther away from the fire are a pair of rusting metal deck chairs, a few flat-bottomed johnboats, some rusted iron skillets, two orange-and-white plastic coolers, a yellow school bus up on blocks, and a prodigious, five-foot-tall mound of empty, crushed, slowly corroding Budweiser cans. Farther away is Hayes' shack, a plywood box on ten-foot stilts. The shack sits on the highest knoll in the swamp, a last-ditch position against flooding.

We are in the deepest of all Arkansas forests—miles from the nearest road (paved or not)—and monstrous dormant trees, mostly cypress and water oak, create a dense screen above and around us. Somewhere a few miles east of where we sit, the deep-brown Mississippi River rushes toward the Gulf of Mexico. The wind blows through the swamp, whipping the acrid smoke into whorls and cutting through our insulated coveralls like a razor. The ground is paved with fallen leaves; they're brown and gold, curling and mist-sodden in the growing darkness. A pack of at least twenty hounds swarms near the fire. They're all Hayes' coonhounds and squirrel hounds—and they have names like Moon, Troubles, Tom, and Tom-Two.

"Crop dusting," Hayes says. "Crop dusting." He hobbles toward one of the chairs. His limp is a reminder that he broke his ankle and leg back in October, when he wrecked a three-wheeled all-terrain vehicle and was pinned beneath it. He managed to pull himself free from the accident, but since he lives alone in the bottoms—easily a day from the nearest hospital—he set the leg himself, by tying a half-inch-thick nylon rope to the ankle, knotting the rope's other end to the ladder of his shack, and "jerking the bones straight." His home remedy may have spared him gangrene, but it has left him with a blackened, six-inch-wide gnarl of an ankle and a permanent gimp. "Crop dusting," he says again. "Have you talked to anyone else about this?"

I mention half a dozen pilots.

"*Those* guys," Hayes says. "They're not dusters. Those guys are *ag pilots*." He shakes his head. "Have you talked to any *old*-timers? Guys like me, who laid out cyanide, black annie, DDT—stuff like that?"

I say no.

Melvin Hayes is sixty-nine years old. He is compact and lean; he has a scraggly white beard that conceals his mouth. When he tilts his head back to laugh (as he does often), you get a view of rotted, splintered, tobacco-stained stumps that were formerly his teeth. Despite his mountain-man looks, his manners are direct from Amy Vanderbilt. He has offered food. He has offered drink. He has given me a tour of his miles of surrounding bayou, stopping to explain each time I showed interest in a fish weir or a deer stand or some of his other means of gathering food from the forest.

"I've flown over cotton, rice, beans," he says. "I've dusted tomatoes and onions. Tomatoes and onions are what I worked right after the war. Then, in 1951, I came back to Arkansas and started flying for old Nathan Jones, in DeWitt. Jones was a good man. He'd been a flight instructor in the military. I flew for Jones for four years, then went to work for myself in Gillette, Arkansas, flying an old Stearman."

For most of ag aviation's history, Stearman aircraft have been the industry's standard airframe. During the Second World War, the Stearman biplane—made by Boeing in its Wichita factory—was the G.I. pilot-training aircraft. Then, after the war, with a vast surplus of Stearman pilot trainers, the government liquidated the planes, and the ag pilots and flying services bought all that were available. In the late nineteen-forties, two hundred dollars could buy a pilot an almost new Stearman. They were top-heavy and sometimes uncontrollable on the ground, but in the air they were as forgiving as any plane that has ever flown. A pilot in a Stearman could go into a flat spin—the most dangerous of all crash attitudes, because the plane rotates horizontally—and as often as not the Stearman could correct itself and get out of trouble. Not that the Stearmans were perfect in the air; they were light and underpowered. Compared with today's ag aircraft, the Stearmans were mosquitoes. The production models had two-hundred-and-twenty-horse-power engines, which seem rubber-band-powered next to today's standard seven-hundred-horse turbine models. But the Stearmans had two special advantages—they were plentiful, and they were inexpensive.

"I was taught to fly by the Army Air Corps," Hayes goes on. "When I first went into the military, at the start of the Second World War, they didn't have any pilots. I went to mechanics' school in Wichita Falls, then I went to a mechanics' specialty school at Santa Monica, California. I worked my way up to staff sergeant. Then, one day, this guy came out to the airfield where I was working, and he said, 'Hayes, if you can pass the entry tests, you can go to flying school.' They needed pilots. So I went down and passed that little old test. There wasn't nothing to it. You had to put a square peg into a square hole. I learned to fly, got bounced around to a number of different training grounds, then I went overseas as a co-pilot on a B-17. My pilot was moved to another aircraft, and I was made a full pilot. I flew lots of missions—I was the high man in the twelve-aircraft bombing formation. After the war, I wanted to stay in the Army, but, with the reduction in forces and a few other things, I was placed off active duty. I'd got married by that time, so I had to make some regular money. I met an old boy named Jack Barnes down in Laredo, Texas, and he's who I flew ag for first. Dusting tomatoes and onions. I went from flying a five-thousand-horsepower bomber to a sixty-five-horse J-3 Cub. We were putting out sulfur dust. That sulfur dust was highly explosive, and the planes were rigged with their exhaust going up over the wings, because when that dust ignited in the exhaust wash you'd look back and see a string of fire coming up from behind you, and all you could do was close the hopper gate as tight as you could, pull up to the right, and pray that you'd get away from the fire—else you'd burn up in that airplane. It was dangerous. Then I went into official crop dusting. Cotton. I worked in Winnsboro, Louisiana; Clarksdale, Mississippi; Gin City, Arkansas; and a couple places outside Lubbock, Texas. I sprayed a lot of cotton. We used sulfur dust mixed with DDT and benzene hexachloride. Those old cockpits weren't sealed too good, and that stuff would come back and burn you like crazy. It would get caked on your face. Your gullet would get full of it, and tears would start running out your eyes. And the more the tears ran down, the more that stuff burned. But I managed to survive it."

Hayes shakes his head. He lifts his right hand from the chair arm and points a finger my way. "Then Miss Rachel Carson came along, and in 1962 she wrote a little book called *Silent Spring,* " he says. "And because of it they outlawed DDT. Said DDT was bad for the planet. That was the beginning of the end—that was when Congress got involved in crop dusting. I laid out tons of DDT, and I don't know that it ever hurt me any. I've eaten more DDT than about anybody, and my son was born fine. He came to earth bald and naked. I've never been sick a day in my life. I've never been to a doctor, except when I had my Army physicals. Never had a cold, or anything. There's a cult of medicine these days, and people look to those doctors like priests. People who need to take better care of themselves, they use doctors to get out of things. Hell, I busted my leg in two places, and I still haven't been to a doctor. Though I must say I didn't set my ankle exactly right. Never been to a dentist, either. But you can probably tell that.

"I got into rice growing—fertilizing and seeding fields from the air. Then we started spraying hormonal herbicides. The original one was something called 2,4-D, and it worked well. It killed weeds and some of the bugs. Then, at just about that same time, this really fine herbicide came along. It was called 2,4,5-T, and it was what that Agent Orange stuff they used in Vietnam was. Hormonal herbicides make weeds grow themselves to death. When those weeds get sprayed, their growth speeds up considerably, and they don't have reserve food, so they start eating themselves to keep growing. It kills 'em.

"I sprayed those supposedly bad chemicals for most of my adult life, and the only health effect they ever gave me was that one day I spilled some DDT on my boot and it cured my athlete's foot. I'd had athlete's foot real bad, and two days later it was gone. So I spilled some onto my other boot, and I ain't never had athlete's foot from that day forward. And, far as I know, that's the only thing it'll do to a human being. Here I am, sixty-nine years old and still moving. I can still run a chain saw all day long. I can haul heavy stuff. I can break my ankle. I could still fly an airplane if I wanted. But at a certain age your reflexes aren't as good as they used to be. I'd guess that if you gave me an airplane today and thirty minutes to learn it I could keep up with the hottest pilot there is. But after a couple of days of flying I'd give out. It's the day-to-day concentration that gets you. You get older and your reflexes aren't as sturdy. I might still be flying, except my son tore up my last old Stearman. He went out and broke his neck in it. Literally broke his neck. Tore the aircraft all to pieces. Then I decided I'd had enough, and I moved down here to the bottoms. I was gonna quit flying altogether, but I didn't.

"One day in 1976, Bruce, my son, came down and told me that there was somebody who needed a pilot to take an aircraft from the Atlantic Ocean to the Pacific Ocean and not get lost. And I said, 'I'm your man.' I did that job, then got into ferrying aircraft. Spent the next five years just moving airplanes around the country. All because I didn't get lost. In 1978, I visited every state in the Lower Forty-eight ferrying airplanes. I never had time to do my laundry. They trusted me. I didn't get lost. You've probably heard the stories: an old boy somewhere, he picks up an airplane in New York State and ferries it to the Delta by way of Miami. This old boy wasn't doing anything but ferrying a plane. He wasn't flying contraband. He just got lost."

There's a long pause, and then Hayes says, "You get offers to fly contraband all the time, everybody does. All those boys you've been talking to get offers all the time, but they'll never tell you about it. Yep, no matter what our President says, drugs are still America's biggest growth industry. I tell you, though, I've ferried a lot of aircraft, from New York to California to North Carolina, and I've never had a federal inspector look in the hopper of the aircraft. Not once. They may have checked in the hopper at night, when I was gone up to the motel or something, but I've never seen it. I did lots of ferrying, too. I was a soldier of fortune. I did a little bit of everything."

Hayes sits quietly in his chair; a half dozen of his hounds lie piled around his legs. The wind blows the fire smoke around.

"Soldier of fortune?" I say.

"Yeah," Hayes says. He looks down at my tape recorder, which is placed on the wet dirt between us. "Back when old John F. Kennedy was President," he finally says, "there was this military operation called the Bay of Pigs. I was hired to fly. A lot of the old military pilots from the Delta were re-upped. It was good money, fine money. Then, when Bay of Pigs came apart, we got those boys out of Cuba and the government kept me on. It became my job to get political prisoners out of Cuba. I flew twin-engine aircraft down there and landed on dirt roads at night. I flew Piper Aztecs and Aero Commanders, anything fast and small. It was crazy back then. The C.I.A. would sanction one side, then the Customs or Treasury agents would come roust you when you got back home. The government worked both sides. That way, they were covered. Immokalee, Florida—that was usually my base. I'd be home in Arkansas, and I'd get a telephone call from somebody with a fake name and a Miami phone number. Then I'd head out to Immokalee, rent an aircraft, and fly out. Some nights, going down to Cuba, we hauled firebombs. Naphtha and phosphorus. You'd slipknot them to the underside of your aircraft's wings, then you'd just pull the strings when you felt like bombing Cuba. We'd bomb sugarcane fields or the edges of towns, just to piss Castro off. And when those bombs would hit the ground, man, they'd start burning. One of them once hit on some big wheel's patio. Or that was the report we got back. A lot of stuff went on like that. I ran guns down to Cuba, too, for an old Australian out of the Dominican Republic. He had the money, and I had the time. In those days, it was wide open."

The darkness of Saturday night is gently folding down on the bottoms now. The fire is smoldering lower, and the dogs are swarming nearer its warmth. Though Melvin Hayes is only a few feet from me, I can barely see him. "The ag fliers are always gonna be contraband fliers," he says. "It's fun for them. That's why the drug and gun suppliers come to us. We fly low to the ground, so the Customs people and the D.E.A. have to follow along behind us in planes. They can't track us on radar—we fly too low. So they tail along behind. And when we hit land—we dip down below the trees, into the Spanish moss, and, man, those D.E.A. pilots give up. To those D.E.A. guys, flying is just a job. That kind of dangerous flying ain't worth getting killed over. To the ag pilots, though, that kind of flying is fun. After a while, flying ag isn't interesting enough anymore, so you got to find other ways to have fun. Eventually, though, they catch up with you. That's what happened to me. They sent the tax man after me. That's where you get into trouble. I didn't have too much hassle with the tax guys, but I don't do hauling anymore, because they watch my bank accounts and tax returns."

Hayes looks up and around, staring out at the tangle of tree limbs and brown water in the darkness. He inhales a deep breath through his nose. "It ain't really bad out here," he says. "I have more money than I'll ever need. And there's an old boy who delivers cases of beer, and ice, and radio batteries to me. That's all I need from the outside world. I don't have big needs anymore. All I need is my cold beer and the radio. I love that Randy Travis. And George Jones. And those Paul Harvey newscasts. Red Neck, White Socks, and Blue Ribbon Beer, that's me. Here in the bottoms, I can do what I want. I don't have any neighbors. I know where the deer are. I know where the fish are. I've counted fifty-one different kinds of ants down here. Some people would say this is a little spare, but it's comfortable."

Rain again. It's yet another July afternoon cloudburst, and Jim Lawhon, Gus Rogers, and I are holed up inside the Planter's Ag office, waiting out the storm. "Look at me," Lawhon is saying, again and again. He's smoking cigarettes and pacing. Every once in a while, he stops at one of the windows and stares into the rain.

Ten minutes ago, Lawhon was out working, fertilizing a flooded rice field west of town. Not wanting to repeat his dicey flying of a few days back, he outpaced today's storm, beating it home to the Planter's Ag runway, where he has tethered the aircraft to the asphalt with steel cables. The relative safety of the Planter's Ag shack has not lifted his mood. He looks out at the Turbo-thrush, which hops on the pavement, fighting the tether lines, as gusts of wind get beneath its wings. He walks to his desk and lights up another Winston. He begins pacing again. "You know what *else* you see when you look at me?" he says, turning to face me. "You see the last of a type, the last generation of independent ag pilots."

"Aw, *Jesus*, Jimmy," Rogers pipes up. "It's just *rain*, man."

"No, really," Lawhon says to Rogers. "And, Gus, you know this is true. There are only a few guys younger than me that're flying independently. And I'm forty-five. I'm no young man. There just aren't new, young pilots coming up, like there used to be."

Rogers nods. "That's true," he says.

I ask Lawhon what will replace ag flying in the future.

"Oh, no," Lawhon says. "You're getting this wrong. There'll always be ag fliers. The farmers need us. But there won't be any *independent* guys left. It's just getting too expensive. The young pilots today, they're gonna fly for the big services. Some will even contract out to fly solely for the largest agri-corporations. That's the way American agriculture is going—it's become a volume business. Us small independents, the ag pilots and farmers, we're being forced out by the marketplace. The equipment costs too much, the materials are too expensive, and then"—Lawhon sweeps his arm broadly toward the rain outside—"when the weather turns bad, we independents can't make enough money to feed our dogs, much less run a business."

It's an hour later, the rain is still falling, and Lawhon decides that the day's flying is over. He and I walk out of the Planter's Ag office and head for his truck. He has suggested that we "go find a couple of beers, not too many, but a couple," and bring them back to the shack, where Rogers has started organizing the month's carboned job invoices. On the ride into town, I learn more of Lawhon's history. He grew up in the area, and has never married. Shortly after undergoing rehabilitation for his war injuries, in 1972, he returned home and learned to fly commercially. Then, late that year, he met Captain Al Verrico, who ran a salvage-diving operation in New Orleans, and Verrico persuaded Lawhon to give up flying and go to work underwater, raising towboats and river barges in the Crescent City's harbor. "My salary was a hundred dollars a day, in cash," Lawhon says. "It was good work, period: interesting and a little dangerous. And on dry land, man, in New Orleans, I had a big time. I about crapped money. But I also missed the flying. So at Thanksgiving of 1973, after a year or so of salvage diving, I came home and went to work full time as an ag pilot."

Until 1975, Lawhon and Rogers both worked for the McCarty Flying Service, at Thompson-Robbins Airfield. "Then, after a series of jobs, sometimes flying some real trash, Gus and I decided to go out on our own," Lawhon says. In 1981, Lawhon got some bank loans for his first ag aircraft (a Schweizer Ag-Cat biplane), rented the Planter's Ag shack, laid down an airstrip, and went to work for himself. "That's why I worry so much now," Lawhon explains. "That's why I'm getting this gray hair. I've got ten years of sweat and money invested in Planter's Ag. So when it rains like this, damn it, I worry about filling my orders. I worry about cash flow. I worry about"—he tosses up his hands— "everything."

Lawhon steers the truck into the parking lot of Alpe's Liquor Store, a corrugated-steel shack at the edge of town. The store's walls are lined with glass-fronted beer and soda coolers. Behind the cash-register counter, which faces the front wall, are bottles of liquor. The store seems deserted.

"I'm here to *rob* this place," Lawhon announces.

There's a shuffling noise from a back room, and two enormous figures step through a door behind the register counter. Both men are thickset and bearded; they're like bison. By my estimate, each is six feet four inches tall and weighs two hundred and seventy-five pounds.

"Lawhon!" one of the men says.

"Hey, Jimmy," says the other.

Introductions are made, and Lawhon and I follow the men into the back room. Just inside the doorway I notice a small table to the left. Two .45-calibre automatic pistols lie on the table, along with brass knuckles, a wooden cudgel with a leather wrist lanyard, and some clips of ammunition.

One of the men notices me staring at the coffee-table armory. "They're beautiful, aren't they?" he says of the pistols. "We used to get robbed pretty regularly. Then we bought those things and waved 'em around a little bit. We never have trouble anymore."

Lawhon unlatches the door of a large, walk-in refrigerator and disappears inside. He returns a minute later with two six-packs of Budweiser. We discuss the day's rain with the bison men for a moment, pay for the beer, and return to the truck.

On the ride back to Planter's Ag, windshield wipers slapping, I ask how ag pilots bill for their services.

"I'll tell you, I've been doing it now for more than fifteen years, and I still don't understand it," Lawhon says. "All I know for sure is that for me to pay for that nice new Turbo-thrush I have to gross between four hundred and five hundred dollars every hour I'm in the air. It's a formula. Each hour that I put on my plane's tachometer, I try to cover about three hundred acres. You've seen Gus taking job orders on those tickets back at the shack? Well, Gus logs in each job by the farmer, the chemicals sprayed, and the acres covered. Our fees start at about two and a half dollars an acre and go up to about four dollars, usually for putting herbicide on rice." Lawhon turns the truck onto the farm road leading to Planter's Ag. "Then, about once a month—and that's what we're doing today—Gus and I sit down," he says. "We separate out the invoices by farmer, tote up what we've sprayed where, and send the farmers their bills."

I ask whether the farmers ever feel they've been overcharged.

"Not often," Lawhon says. "Gus takes care of all that up front. He's got a great memory for prices and estimates, and, of course, we've got our records to help us. We're not here to rip anybody off. The slick ag pilots, the ones who come in overcharging or undercharging, they don't stay in business long. The farmers talk to one another, and if a pilot's charging too much for his services he won't get business for long. If a pilot's trying to lowball all the other pilots, undercharging the market, it'll eventually eat into his overhead. This isn't New York, it ain't about quick-buck scams. The farmers and ag fliers want to stay here. They know what they're buying and selling. They know what fair prices are. If some new pilot comes in offering too good a deal, everybody gets suspicious."

The rain is still falling as the truck pulls into the muddy parking area at Planter's Ag. I gather up the beer and follow Lawhon inside. As we step through the screen door, Rogers looks up from his desk. He's punching numbers into a calculator and riffling a stack of green-tinted invoices. He looks at Lawhon, then at me. With a tilt of his head, Rogers motions for Lawhon to look at his desk. On Lawhon's desk are more stacks of invoices, each stack bound by a thin, pale rubber band. Lawhon's face clouds.

"That's right, Jimmy," Rogers says. "No beer until we get this stuff added up."

Ninety minutes later, Rogers has finished tallying his half of the Planter's Ag tickets for July. He and I head through the screen door for the porch, leaving Lawhon inside, slaving away at his calculator. On the porch, we sit on planked benches beneath the sloped roof; the rain is still falling, and it rolls off the roof's lip like a watery curtain. "This is an amazing business," Rogers says. "Especially if you're an independent. You have to watch it constantly. It's like nurturing a plant. You're always tending it, keeping up with it. You're worried either about money or about equipment or about environmental laws. It's always something different, but it's always something."

I ask Rogers about the Environmental Protection Agency.

"The E.P.A.—they're not bad," he says. "They're pretty realistic about our work. They know that we're necessary to the economy here, and that we're careful with our chemicals. They know we're not screwing up the environment—killing fish, and things. There's this E.P.A. lady who came down here awhile back to look us over. I was loading certain chemicals into Jimmy's plane, and she told me to wear an India-rubber suit when I'm doing that. But she knows I won't wear that suit. It's ninety-seven degrees out, and I'm working in the sun on a black asphalt loading area. I ain't gonna wear no heavy rubber suit. Not ever. I won't even wear those elbow-length rubber gloves. But she has to say her warnings, because that's her job, and the E.P.A. laws say I have to hear her. The E.P.A.'s like that. They're not bad. They test all the new ag chemicals coming out. Not only for what they'll do to the environment but for what they'll do to the people who work with them. The E.P.A.—they're looking out for people as much as for the environment. They're realistic. It's the damned environmentalists, they're who'll drive you crazy.

"You ever see an environmentalist on the TV?" Rogers goes on. "While he's standing there saying don't use chemicals on cotton, what's he wearing? Is he wearing bluejeans and a shirt? Is he wearing a suit? Aren't all those things made of cotton? Where the hell does Mr. Environmental Protector think that cotton comes from?"

Rogers stares out into the rain. "Then Mr. Environmental Protector starts talking about how we need to use cotton diapers, because the plastic ones are bad for the environment," he says "In his next breath, he's arguing with himself. So what's he want? Plastic? Cotton? I'll tell you what he wants—he wants it all. And the dangerous part is, if that environmentalist can get people behind him from the TV exposure, then he can affect the laws. He can force tighter E.P.A. controls, he can work to outlaw certain chemicals. And those chemicals Mr. Environmentalist wants nixed, they're always the most effective ones—and they're usually the *least expensive* ones. The newer, synthetic chemicals, they're much more expensive, which only makes the price of bluejeans higher. So sooner or later Mr. Environmentalist will start bawling about the high price of bluejeans, too. He'll go complaining that folks less fortunate than him can't buy bluejeans anymore."

A minute later, Lawhon comes out onto the porch, the screen door clacking shut behind him. "O.K.," Lawhon says. "All done."

Rogers turns to look at his partner. "Good," he says.

"What are you guys talking about?" Lawhon asks.

"Environmentalists," Rogers says.

Lawhon slaps at the air. "In that case," he says, turning and walking toward his truck, "I'm tired. I'm going home."

Despite all the claims of ag people that "it's never hurt me," the application of agricultural chemicals remains a potentially dangerous matter. The effects of 2,4-D, for example, are currently under scrutiny by two government agencies—the National Cancer Institute and the E.P.A.—because of a Cancer Institute study that found a correlation between 2,4-D and elevated risks of non-Hodgkin's lymphoma among those who work with it. "The stumbling block to all these studies thus far is that it's impossible to identify concretely the specific link between certain forms of cancer and herbicides generally," says John Doull, the chairman of the toxicology committee for the National Academy of Sciences and a professor of toxicology at the University of Kansas Medical School. "There are too many other factors to consider. How often do these people use these chemicals? For how many years have they used them? What other carcinogens do they work with? All of these things have to be factored in. Any scientist who has studied these substances can show that people who work regularly with herbicides, especially 2,4-D, have an elevated risk of cancer, but nobody can present the exact cause-and-effect link. So while the heightened risk is almost universally agreed upon, without the specific link what we've got isn't good, solid science."

Yet, if the medical evidence on agri-chemicals is less than conclusive, there remains universal respect for the power of agri-dusts and liquids. No pilot in the Delta, however cavalier, goes out of his way to work with the chemicals that are applied there. After extensive E.P.A.

testing, the character of every pesticide, fungicide, herbicide, and plant treatment now used in the United States is recorded in the crop duster's bible—a 2,371-page handbook entitled "Crop Protection Chemical Reference." Five hundred and sixty-one substances are indexed there, and the handbook carries precautionary statements about risk to human, plant, or animal life from all of them.

Though farmers, fliers, and environmentalists will all readily admit that today's ag chemicals are less dangerous to man and planet than they were in the days of calcium arsenate, a growing number of environmentalists feel that pesticide and herbicide reform is still too slow in coming. "The denial that the aerial applicators use about how personally and environmentally dangerous these substances are is a self-defense mechanism," says Janet Hathaway, a senior attorney for the Natural Resources Defense Council. "The aerial applicators rightfully see tightening pesticide and herbicide laws as a threat to their livelihoods, but, while tragic from a career standpoint, those laws are a survival issue from human-health and environmental ones. We now have verifiable human data indicating that many herbicides, including 2,4-D, are carcinogenic. Years of tests have proved that to be true. The danger is no longer speculative. The *degree* of hazard arising from use of these chemicals—that remains debatable. But the hazard to human lives is established. Now, environmentalists—at least, the realistic ones—know that some chemical use is a fact of modern farming, but the fact remains that there is a very real human hazard in using many agricultural chemicals, and for the sake of both people and the environment changes need to be made."

As a preëmptive step in the escalating war against agri-chemicals, American farming has started to experiment with weed-and-pest-control techniques such as the Integrated Pest Management Plan—a program that monitors insect and weed populations in fields instead of simply dosing crops with chemicals on calendrical cycles. When a field's insect or weed density passes an established threshold, the farmer or ag pilot applies just enough pesticide or herbicide to constitute a lethal dose. This kind of management dramatically reduces the amount of poison spread on a field, and helps keep excess chemicals from running off into watersheds or leaching into the soil. Other anti-chemical reforms include the biotech movement, which is using genetic engineering to develop hardier, less vulnerable crops. And, in a still newer chemical-free agriculture, called alternative-use farming, a farmer with a real or anticipated insect problem introduces predators or competitors of that insect into his fields. Amazingly, the competition by "beneficial bugs" virtually keeps the insect populations in check, though the introduction of new insects into fields can have unpredictable results, such as the infestation of crops that haven't been targeted.

But it isn't simply these isolated, less chemically dependent farming techniques that presage changes for the ag fliers. The advent of liquid pesticides and herbicides has made it possible for farmers to use ground-based, rolling machinery to apply pressurized pesticide and herbicide liquids to trees and plants from nozzle-studded booms—an advance that has slowly made ag aviation obsolete for crops like apples and grapes. Though ground-based sprayers require hours to do what a boom-equipped aircraft can accomplish in minutes, they can spray pesticides and herbicides precisely onto apple trees, grapevines, and similar site-specific crops without coating the earth around them; thus, not only is the effectiveness of the chemicals far better utilized but far less damage is done to the surrounding environment. Certain croplands, such as flooded rice fields or swampy cotton or bean tracts, will always require tending from the air, and that means that, as Jim Lawhon notes, "there will always be ag fliers." But new farming and ag-chemical-application techniques may prove to be the leading edge of an industry-wide drop in demand for ag pilots. "There will always be some aerial applicators around," Janet Hathaway says. "Farming occasionally demands that agricultural chemicals be distributed from the air. But the market also demands more pesticide-free farming. Human-health concerns demand that we use fewer herbicides and pesticides on our crops. And a greater concern for the environment demands more chemical-free farming, too. It's a sad development for the agricultural-aviation industry, that's true, but it's a development that's coming nonetheless."

The Delta city of Helena, Arkansas—sister city to West Helena—is an old cotton town. In the eighteen-forties, it rivalled Memphis in size and economic force. It had its own cotton exchange, and, as the seat of Phillips County, it had a grand three-story county courthouse made of brick. It had large, ornate Victorian houses all along its river bluff, and rows of huge cotton warehouses lined its wharf. With the coming of the boll weevil, however, and with the growth of Memphis (whose larger, cobbled river landing could handle bigger shipments), Helena eventually found itself falling behind as a business center, and it began settling into the vaguely crumbling beauty of an Old South river city that it is today. These days, the fastest-growing thing in Helena is kudzu, a leguminous vine that was imported from Japan. It was used in the nineteen-thirties as a means of battling soil erosion, and since that time it has blanketed the entire region, growing faster than my scarlet runner bean could have hoped to grow. Kudzu is everywhere in Helena. It covers hillsides, trees, grain elevators, and house trailers like a soft green drift of snow. It engulfs newly erected telephone poles in a matter of months. If you go on vacation and leave your car parked near a growth of kudzu, when you return the bumpers and wheels will have been attacked.

Jerry Williams, the extension agent for Phillips County, understands kudzu. He understands every plant that grows in this part of the world. Ask Williams what he knows about cotton, rice, soybeans, winter wheat, milo, cantaloupes, peaches, plums, watermelon, or the control of broadleaf weeds, and he overflows with information.

Take cotton, for instance. Williams will tell you that it grows taller naturally than it does in the fields of the Delta. He'll tell you that these days cotton plants are purposely kept short by chemical means, to aid in the cotton harvest. "All stalky plants grow from knuckle to knuckle," he says. "And a farmer can control the length of stalk between those knuckles by applying a growth regulator called Pix, which has chemicals in it that inhibit the production of gibberellic acid, the hormone that makes the plants grow. The growth-regulated cotton probably has more bolls than the tall plants, and the bolls are concentrated in a smaller area. That way, the farmer can set his cotton picker for one height, and speed up the harvest. If you don't have any Pix around, you can also regulate cotton growth with sugar. The carbohydrates in the sugar get turned into proteins inside the cotton, and that slows the growth. But it's quite expensive to sift sugar over an entire cotton field."

The Phillips County Extension Service is on the first floor of the Phillips County Courthouse. From there, Wiliiams, with the help of three ag agents and two office staff people, works to educate local farmers in the most efficient ways to grow crops. "We're part of the University of Arkansas, and the state maintains one of these offices in every county," Williams says. "Phillips County is one of the larger counties in Arkansas, both in area and in the amount of crops we produce. So our office keeps busy. Before we go out and inspect a field, I'm waiting to see a draft of a letter I've written to Governor Clinton. I'm asking that Phillips County become eligible for federal disaster relief. With all this rain, especially in the southern end of the county, the crops are underwater, so we're asking for some of the flood-relief money that's being released right now."

Jerry Williams is a hybrid: one part farmer and one part botany professor. He's in his mid-forties, tall and solid. He has closely cropped hair, and wears checked shirts, Red Wing slip-on boots, and khaki trousers to the office. If you were to see him on the street, you'd think, There's a farmer. But when Williams talks he has the genteel, authoritative air of a Shakespeare professor. His office is a hybrid, too. A bronzed clump of peanuts still on their vine sits on his large desk, and the walls of the room are thick with charts tracking the idealized growth of rice and cotton and beans. There are also posters identifying different broadleaf weeds. And Williams' University of Arkansas diplomas hang on the wall behind his desk. Plant-husbandry and chemical books line long shelves around the office's lower walls. There is a computer in a corner, and a typewriter on a cart behind the desk.

"We're a clearing house for information to local farmers," Williams goes on. "Our office dispenses information on how farmers can grow their crops most efficiently. Then, when they get the plants in the ground and growing, we do field scouting. Some of the farmers hire private consultants for this kind of thing, but the state offers it free. We advise on fertilizer use, insect control, weed control, and pesticide use—and, we hope, not misuse. Then, in winter, we help to recertify farmers and aerial applicators for use of the chemicals the following year. The application of agricultural chemicals has become very closely regulated. Nowadays, everyone who uses them is certified."

Williams gets up, tidies his desk, and heads for the door. I follow. As we walk down the hall, he says, "What we're going to do now is go out and inspect a farmer's field. He called this afternoon and said that an aerial applicator had drifted some herbicide onto his bean field. He says his beans are dead, and he wants to make a claim to the State Plant Board. Before he can do that, though, I have to inspect the damage and decide if it's serious enough to warrant an investigation."

This is how plant-damage claims work: If a farmer believes that his crop has been killed by chemicals drifting onto the wrong field, Williams or his extension-service counterparts survey the extent of the damage and, if it is serious, call in the State Plant Board, a body that assesses the crop damage in monetary terms, to verify that the dead plants were killed by the poison drift. Then the board, after figuring out which field the poison drifted from and checking on which pilot recently sprayed that field, fines the pilot an appropriate damage cost.

"The Plant Board has got very good at knowing which damage is caused by drift and which isn't," Williams says. "The tough claims happen more with fish kills than with crop destruction. On catfish farms, for instance, where microorganisms or mechanical failure in the aeration can kill a bunch of catfish the same way that poison drift can, it's hard to know just how the fish died. Most plant-damage claims are easy to figure out. If the plants are dead in exact rows, then an aerial applicator didn't do it, because wind drift isn't that precise. Drifting poison kills plants unevenly, and you can usually see the difference immediately."

We go outside. When we reach Williams' navy-blue Chevrolet S-10 pickup, he opens both its doors, and we let the superheated air spill out before getting in. We drive southwest along the Mississippi River levee, along wide and blindingly sunlit streets. "We're having one of the worst years in history, in terms of trying to raise crops," Williams says. "At the experimental station up north in Lee County, we've already had fifty-three inches of rain this year, and it's only late July. We're supposed to get only forty-five inches of rain annually, and November, which is traditionally our rainy month, is still a long way off. The aerial applicators, though, are doing good business. They're spraying most of the fields this year—not just the rice. The ground around the county is too swampy for farmers to go in there with ground-based sprayers. But that's the way it is with farming. You just take it as it comes, and you try to think for the long haul. That's all you can do."

The Victorian houses of the town have given way to live-oak trees, shotgun shacks, and the flatness of Delta cropland. In the distance I can see the Mississippi River Bridge at Helena, a nearly parabolic arc that sails a mile and a half from levee to levee, hundreds of feet above the wide brown river's surface.

"Farming in the Delta is hard work," Williams says, turning south onto a farm road a quarter mile from the levee. "It's as complicated a job as there is. The ground is fertile, but the bugs and weeds and molds are impossible to contend with. The changing conditions through the year keep a farmer jumping. Take rice. You plant your rice in a dry field, then pass over it with fertilizer and with a chemical called propanil. That keeps the weeds down before the field is flooded. The weeds take hold so fast that farmers usually have to spray with propanil twice in the two weeks before the rice germinates and they can flood the fields. Rice has an enzyme that can break down propanil, but weeds don't. It's pretty sophisticated. Then, as the farmers flood the fields and the rice head starts growing, the aircraft come into play. The aerial applicators will fertilize the flooded fields and maybe apply herbicide a couple of times during the summer for maintenance, but, with rice, they very seldom have to lay out any insecticide. Once a rice field is flooded, it pretty much takes care of itself.

"With the growing and management of cotton, though, things are much more complicated. Cotton is a difficult crop even for the oldest hands at it. We have huge insect and weed problems with cotton, and the plant itself is very delicate. There are preemergence herbicides to control grass and broadleaf weeds. There are seed treatments to protect the seed before it has germinated. Then, the instant the cotton comes up, it's attacked by insects. And that's a long battle. Insecticides are hard on the plants, and they're hard on the environment. At least seventy per cent of all insecticides used in this region are applied on cotton, and in dry years they're mostly sprayed from ground-based equipment. It's best if you spray for pests up under the cotton leaves, so most years the aircraft aren't really needed. Then, after a lot of tending, the cotton gets ready to harvest, and the ag pilots spray a defoliant on it, which makes the leaves fall off so the cotton can be harvested. It also smells up the countryside something fierce. Still, the defoliant enables a farmer to harvest a field in one pass. It's very efficient."

Williams slows the truck and turns onto a muddy two-track. "The field damage is up here," he says. To our left is a cotton field. To our right is a healthy bean field. We roll a half mile up the two-track, with the truck's front tires chucking mud past the windows. On our right, a new planting of beans begins. The rows run parallel to the muddy road, and you can see immediately that something has killed them. The rows nearest the road are brown and only two inches tall. As the rows recede, they get taller—three inches, four inches, six inches, a foot, but they are all dead and brown. Finally, about a hundred yards away from the road, beginning with a single furrow line, the plants are tall and green again. Williams stops the truck, and even before getting out he says, "The farmer killed this field. An ag flier didn't do this."

As we step out of the truck, our feet sinking two inches into the road's mud, Williams lifts his right arm and swings it, pointing across the field. "See how the dead plants are on a tilt?" he says. "See how their tops make a plane that angles down toward this side?" He walks around the front of the truck and into the field, his boots tossing off clumps of mud. He squats near a row of small, dead plants and says, "I don't know what killed these beans, but they were dead just after emergence, so it must have been something pretty strong."

A white mongrel dog appears from the cotton field behind us; it trots over to Williams, and begins jumping on him as he stands up. He pets the dog, rubbing it behind the ears and saying, "Where'd you come from?" Finally, the dog gets down and sits at Williams' feet. As Williams slaps at the muddy paw prints on his trousers, he says, "Here's what I think happened to this field. Either the farmer got some bad beans, and out there where the healthy plants start is where he refilled the planter with untainted seeds, or—and this is what I *really* think happened—he didn't wash out the planter after he'd laid out some granular herbicide with it, and the residual chemicals in that planter killed the beans. That's why the beans nearest the road, where he began planting first, died the quickest. Whatever was in the planter grew less and less potent as the planting went on. By the time he got out there into the field, the planter was clean and the plants could grow up fine."

Williams returns to the truck, opens the door, and lifts one boot at a time, banging it against the truck's frame to get the mud off before stepping into the truck. I mimic him on the passenger side. "It's strange to see a field of beans dead," Williams says, starting the engine. "Beans are pretty resilient. Now, cotton—cotton plants die all the time. But beans? Not often. Soybeans can survive almost anything."

Williams turns the truck around, then drives back toward the paved farm road. The mongrel dog trots along behind us, falling steadily back and soon vanishing from sight. "We've got a whole bunch of soybean herbicides, for instance, but with cotton herbicides we're very limited," Williams says. "Cotton is just so delicate. Often you'll be driving along and you'll see a bunch of people with hoes out in a cotton field. They're chopping cotton—that means they're chopping the weeds out of that field, because, for one of many reasons, the cotton is too vulnerable for herbicides. Chopping cotton is hard work. It's a lot of hoeing and stooping. It's expensive, too. A farmer has to pay at least minimum wage to his choppers, which costs a lot more than spraying it himself or paying an ag pilot to fly over it. Chopping cotton is about the hardest, hottest work that I know of. And all for minimum wage."

We pull out onto the paved road and head north along the levee. "Cotton is just one hard crop to keep up," Williams says. "As I was saying before, it requires the most pesticides, because it attracts the most bugs. And the reason we can use all those pesticides is that we don't eat it. If cotton were a crop that we ate instead of one that we wore, the E.P.A. and the F.D.A. wouldn't allow us to spray it with some of the things we use."

I ask Williams about the environmental consequences of using pesticides and herbicides.

"The farmer, he's a conservationist," Williams says. "He's got more at stake than anybody when it comes to making sure his land is healthy. And farmland isn't just dirt. It's all that surrounds that dirt. You need clean water. You need bird and bat and animal populations to do their bit to control pests. I'm not saying that agricultural chemicals sometimes aren't abused—they are—but those instances are rare. Chemical engineering is a very specific science these days. It's not like it was thirty years ago, when one application of DDT or calcium arsenate would destroy all the unwanted plants and insects. These days, a farmer applies specific chemicals for specific things. For instance, we go after broadleaf weeds at one time and individual bug species at another. It's all very controlled. It's more like shooting a rifle than like shooting a shotgun, which is how it was in the old days. And now the chemical suppliers take their own precautions, which they didn't use to. These days, they design their products to break down quickly, which minimizes damage to the environment if there's some sort of accident."

As Williams drops me off back in Helena, he says, "The farmer doesn't want to mess up his land. He doesn't want to mess up the environment. That's his livelihood. And I can tell you, the farmers and the ag pilots are learning to read the bottle labels on the chemicals they're planning to apply. More and more, they're concerned with the chemicals they're using. Not because the E.P.A. laws say so, which they do, but because everybody knows they'd better. When a farmer uses a six-ounce bottle of concentrated herbicide, he'd better know how it works, because that little bottle costs fifty dollars. And he'd better employ it right, because if he doesn't he'll kill his crops, and that will ultimately cost him many thousands of dollars. Farmers can't afford not to know how to use agricultural chemicals. In no small way, farmers and environmentalists are coming together. It's like a big circle, and it all works together. That's farming: what you give out is what you get back."

A Short History of Agricultural Aviation, Part 3: In the nineteen-seventies, when ag aviation was at its peak, there were as many as ten thousand planes working crops across the country. Today, roughly six thousand ag planes, owned by two thousand different operators, are left in the United States. Through a combination of increased aircraft efficiency, the growing popularity of applying liquid pesticides and herbicides from ground-based spray rigs, and the hard-bitten economics of contemporary farming, the number of crop-dusting planes—and of pilots who fly them—is thinning. Arkansas has the most ag pilots, with about five hundred and fifty. Second in number of ag fliers is Texas, where about five hundred and thirty pilots double up, tending both the cotton fields of their own state and those of southern New Mexico. Next come the four hundred and fifty crop dusters of Louisiana, and their numbers are nearly equalled by the pilot populations of Nebraska and California. But slowly the fliers are disappearing. In response to this downturn in demand, the number of domestic ag-plane manufacturers has dwindled to just four, and which aircraft a pilot or a flying service selects these days is largely a question of available cash and brand loyalty. Given a choice, every ag pilot would prefer a turbine engine to a nine-cylinder radial one. The nine-cylinder rigs (the ag-flying standard since the nineteen-thirties, when they replaced automobile-style, on-line engines) churn out between four hundred and fifty and a thousand horsepower. They also take six seconds to go from idle to full throttle, and have a dangerous tendency to quit at unexpected times. The turbines, on the other hand, smoothly deliver between five hundred and twelve hundred horsepower, can go from idle to full power in three and a half seconds, and almost never have a mechanical failure. Bruce Hayes says, "If you see a wrecked ag plane with a turbine engine, you can be 99.44 per cent sure that the crash was caused by pilot error."

All of today's ag aircraft are designed to carry only one passenger: the pilot. And the dimensions of all ag planes are about the same: they have an over-all length of about twenty-eight feet and a wingspan of about forty-six. Prices for new aircraft run from a hundred and fifty thousand dollars, for a plane with a rebuilt nine-cylinder engine, to nearly six hundred thousand dollars, for a new turbine aircraft. For safety reasons, most ag planes are painted high-visibility yellow. Lawhon's red-white-and-blue model is an ag-flying anomaly. When he saw a red-white-and-blue Turbo-thrush at the Ayers Aviation factory, his patriotic stripe emerged strongly, and he demanded that his new aircraft be painted the same way. The folks at Ayers indulged their client, and now Lawhon has the most distinctive ag plane in the Delta.

These days, the only agricultural-aircraft manufacturer making biplanes is the Schweizer Aircraft Corporation, of Elmira, New York, and the Schweizer Ag-Cat is the industry's nod to the Stearman. The reason that Schweizer still makes biplanes, forty years after most of aviation has forgotten about them, is that a marketing study found that traditionalist pilots still preferred them to the low-winged monoplanes being rolled out by most ag-plane manufacturers. The Ag-Cat was once part of Grumman's famous Cat line of aircraft, which included the Second World War fighter the Hellcat, but Grumman, wanting to get out of the commercial-aircraft business, sold it to Schweizer in the nineteen-seventies. As for the domestic monoplane manufacturers, at one time there was no shortage of them—Curtiss, Piper, Cessna, Taylorcraft, Rockwell, Funk, Waco, and Rawdon, to name a few—and they all had production ag aircraft coming off their factory lines. These days, however, the only aircraft corporations still making ag planes are Ayers (of Albany, Georgia), Air Tractor (of Olney, Texas), and Weatherly (of Lincoln, California). All their aircraft come with a variety of engine options, and all the corporations offer production-line turbine engines. This year, a total of about a hundred and fifty new ag planes will be purchased by pilots across the United States—a figure that's down about ninety per cent from the nineteen-seventies, when more than thirteen hundred new planes a year were sold. For the roughly seven thousand American ag pilots still working, this is not an encouraging statistic.

"Isn't that article of yours done yet," Jim Lawhon says. Lawhon is sitting on the porch of Planter's Ag as I get out of my Land Cruiser. It's my last day in the Delta, and I'm driving around saying goodbye and thank you to those who have helped with my research. Lawhon is at the end of his lunch hour; he's resting in the shade, on one of the porch benches; he's enjoying a cigarette before going back to work. He's also, I notice, sweating through his red polo shirt.

"I'm just heading back to Little Rock now," I say. "You're my last stop."

"Well, you'd better ask me your questions quick, because I'm about to go back to flying," Lawhon says. "I'm gonna spray some cotton in Mississippi this afternoon."

I tell him that I don't have any more questions.

"In that case, I'm going back to work," he says, crushing out his cigarette. "It was nice to meet you, and come back anytime."

I tell him that I'll stop by when I can, and I thank him.

Lawhon heads for his aircraft, then stops short and turns to face me. "You know, you can't really understand this job in a month," he says. "You can't really understand this job in a year. Twenty years, maybe. Thirty years, probably. But not in a month."

I say I'll do my best.

Walking backward and facing me, Lawhon says, "Well, you'd better get us right. It'll make my life plenty difficult if you don't. I mean, I'll have to drive all the way to Little Rock just to shoot you." He laughs, waves good-bye, and walks toward his aircraft. He fires up the plane and is headed down the runway in seconds. A minute later, the Turbo-thrush has turned around in the sky and is flying right at me. I think of that scene from *North by Northwest,* the one where Cary Grant is being chased down and shot at by the crop-dusting plane. Lawhon, though, isn't shooting; he's just saying good-bye. He comes toward me thirty yards off the ground, dipping and wagging the aircraft's wings. As he draws near, he drops the left wing until the Turbo-thrush is almost vertical. The plane roars past, and Lawhon gives me a quick salute from inside the cockpit. He's smiling beneath his white crash helmet. Before I can lift my hand to salute back, the plane is headed for the horizon.

Remembering Don Sheldon
by David Roberts

Mountaineers and other adventurers who want to explore

Alaska's great ranges rely on bush pilots to fly them into

remote corners of the wilderness. Don Sheldon was one of

the greatest of those pilots. David Roberts (born 1943)

knew Sheldon and wrote this appreciation for Reader's

Digest *(August, 1982).*

It was just a milk run, the flight to drop off two fishermen at Otter Lake, but Don Sheldon was worried. For the last two days the fortunes of the eight U.S. Army Scouts had nagged away in the back of his mind. When the men had unloaded their fancy yellow twin-engine boat in Talkeetna, Alaska, Don had joined the crowd of curious onlookers. The scouts intended, it seemed, to use the boat to test the navigability of the Susitna River upstream from Talkeetna.

Don had been flying out of Talkeetna for seven years, and he knew that sixty miles up the Susitna lay a treacherous five-mile stretch of white water called Devil's Canyon. He had voiced his qualms, but the scouts had brushed them off. Within hours they had launched their fifty-foot boat and disappeared upriver.

Now, as Don flew up the Susitna, he kept an eye out for the boat. There was no sign of it—until the plane reached Devil's Canyon. To his horror, Don spotted pieces of bright yellow debris, unmistakably parts of the boat, bobbing through the rapids. He quickly reached Otter Lake, dropped off the fishermen, and headed back downriver. To search properly, he had to bring the plane down beneath the rim of the narrow canyon, where the air was characteristically turbulent. For three miles he saw no signs of life. Suddenly, he discovered seven men clinging to a shelf of rock on the shore. After several passes he could see that they were in very bad shape, with clothing torn off, life jackets in shreds. Don knew that, having been soaked and battered in the glacier-fed river, the scouts could succumb to hypothermia in a matter of hours. They were evidently powerless to save themselves.

The year was 1955. The possibilities of rescue seemed infinitesimal: there was no road within a hundred miles of Devil's Canyon, no spot anywhere nearby to land a helicopter. As Sheldon circled, he realized that unless he could perform a nearly superhuman feat, the seven men on the rock shelf were as good as dead.

A quarter-mile upstream from the shelf, Don spotted what he later described as "a slick, high-velocity stretch of river that looked like it might be big enough." Landing a float plane on a smooth river is tricky enough; landing in the middle of five miles of rapids verges on the suicidal. But this is what Sheldon did. He had read the river right: as the plane tore through the fast-moving water, it managed not to hit any rocks. Once the plane had slowed, Don held the throttle on low, so that the craft could float with the current yet keep its nose pointed upstream. It is a remarkable feat for a kayaker or canoeist to run rapids backwards, and here was Sheldon trying the stunt with an Aeronca Sedan that weighed 1400 pounds!

Don got through the quarter-mile unscathed, although the splashing water nearly conked out his engine. When he came even with the shelf, he put on just enough power to counteract the river's flow, while he sidled gently toward shore, mindful of the consequences of hitting the canyon wall with his wing tip. An incredulous G.I. clambered onto the plane's float and into the cabin.

Sheldon could not fight the current and take off upstream, so he rode backwards through another mile and a half of Devil's Canyon. Then he turned the plane around and made a downstream takeoff. On three subsequent trips he picked up the remaining men. To cap the extraordinary rescue, he searched farther downstream until he found the eighth man, who had floated an appalling eighteen miles out of control. "When I got to him," Don later told his biographer James Greiner, "he was a shock case and could barely crawl aboard. The water was about fifty-five degrees, and he was all skinned up and bruised but had no broken bones."

By the late 1950s Don Sheldon had become Alaska's most famous bush pilot. There were many who regarded him also as the Territory's best aviator, but others felt he took too many risks. Two of Sheldon's achievements were undeniable. He had perfected ski landings on the great glaciers around Mount McKinley, providing an access to the Alaska Range that would revolutionize mountaineering. And his rescues were the stuff of legend.

Bush flying came to Alaska in 1913. Because of the vast stretches of utter wilderness, the treacherous weather, and the scarcity of human outposts, aviation in the North quickly took on a heroic cast. The tradition grew during the same decades that saw flying become tame and systematized in the continental United States. The Alaskan bush pilot was a loner who "flew by the seat of his pants": he didn't bother with maps or instruments, relied on his knowledge of the country for navigation, knew how to fix his own plane after he had crash-landed it, and kept the whereabouts of all his clients in his head.

Two historians once compiled a list of the top one hundred bush pilots in Alaska history. Of those hundred, at least twenty-five had died in crashes. Between 1941 and 1974 Don Sheldon wore out some forty-five airplanes; at least four of them he totaled in forced landings. But his record with clients was unimpeachable. "The thing I'm proudest of," Sheldon used to say, "is I've never hurt a passenger."

Despite all the hazards of his flying life, it was not to be his destiny to die in an airplane. A lifelong teetotaler and non-smoker, Don contracted cancer in 1972. Fighting the pain and debilitation that attacked his body, he flew two of his heaviest seasons in 1973 and 1974. He would talk to virtually no one—at times, not even to his wife—about the disease. In January 1975 Don succumbed. He was only fifty-three, at the peak of his abilities.

I met Sheldon in 1963 on my first mountaineering expedition, when I joined six friends in an attempt on the north face of Mount McKinley. While two of our party hauled forty-eight boxes of food and gear to Talkeetna, five of us hiked in to Peters Glacier from Wonder Lake, where the road ends. Thus my first encounter with the famous pilot was a hasty one: he was thirty feet above my head in his Cessna 180, traveling at sixty miles an hour, delivering a classic Alaskan airdrop.

We had marked out on the glacier a long drop site a quarter-mile from camp. But the former World War II tail gunner disdained anything so imprecise: he put the first package within five feet of our tents. Sheldon made forty-eight passes, one to a box, yelping with delight out the open window after each accurate drop.

A bad airdrop results from a timid pilot, one who drops from too high or at too great a speed. Expeditions in Alaska have lost every last piece of gear and food; at least one has faced starvation as a result. From our forty-eight boxes, we lost, as I recall, only a bag of oatmeal and part of a can of strawberry jam.

Although it wasn't in the contract, Sheldon would check up on his parties each time he flew another group to McKinley. We had climbed most of the north face faster than expected, and by mid-July were stuck in a week-long storm at the 17,500-foot level. Unknown to us (we had no radio), Sheldon flew into the storm to look for signs of us. Finding that our tracks disappeared into the massive debris of an avalanche, he put out the alarm.

For three days half a dozen pilots searched for us. Fittingly, it was Sheldon who found us; acting on a hunch, he broke through the clouds at 17,500 exactly where we were digging out from the storm. We later paid some of the other pilots to help defray the costs of the search, but Don never asked for a penny.

Don grew up in rural Wyoming in the 1920s. He lost his father at age eight, his mother when he was eleven; the twin tragedies may explain why Sheldon was a loner. He drifted to Alaska in his teens, first arriving in Talkeetna in 1938. For three years he did odd jobs—cutting wood, sluicing for a miner, and building the very airstrip that would later be his front yard. Meanwhile he had been smitten with the urge to fly. He later told James Greiner his first impressions of the pilots of the day: "They looked to me like they came from Mars, and all I could ever think was how much better that kind of travel in this area of no roads was than beating yourself to death on a pair of snowshoes."

He delayed signing up for the war until he had flown enough to get his license. To his dismay, by the time he had enlisted, the Air Force needed tail gunners more than pilots. As a tail gunner, he flew twenty-six missions over Germany and survived two crash landings in England.

By 1948 Sheldon was back in Talkeetna. That year the Talkeetna Air Service was born; at twenty-seven, Sheldon had become a professional bush pilot. During the first years the business scraped along, flying hunters and fishermen and government workers.

In 1951 Sheldon met Bradford Washburn, then the leading Alaskan mountaineer. Needing a steady glacier pilot, Washburn took on Sheldon. The partnership changed the face of Alaskan mountaineering, as well as that of Talkeetna Air Service. By the 1960s Sheldon was flying mostly climbers, who were swarming to Talkeetna in ever growing numbers.

In 1965 I went back with three friends to try the west face of Mount Huntington, a much smaller mountain than McKinley, but a more difficult challenge. We had a long wait in Talkeetna while bad weather prevented flying. For the first time I got to see Sheldon at first hand.

He still seemed a remote being, a man of mythic proportions. There were a number of expeditions on hand, all frantic to get in to the glaciers; as the bad weather continued, the sense of jockeying for position intensified. Sheldon came and went, always on the move, utterly self-contained. A word of chat from him, a joke about the weather, thrilled us with the presumption that we stood out in his mind from the other loiterers. With McKinley socked in, there was still plenty of flying for him to do—groceries dropped off to remote homesteaders, local residents ferried to Anchorage. All of us watched his comings and goings with the avidity of groupies. Sheldon would roll down the pot-holed dirt strip as casually as a cab driver, then surge into the air just before the Susitna River cut off the runway. He landed just as casually, pulling the plane up next to his house the way a kid might park his tricycle.

The mystique was enhanced by Sheldon's battered old red hangar, in which he generously let waiting climbers camp. The place was, in effect, an international museum. We stumbled, awed, upon boxes of leftover French provisions—the remains, it was clear, of the crack French team led by the incomparable Lionel Terray. The Italian ice screws had to have belonged to the legendary Ricardo Cassin. The old field jackets had been Washburn's gear in 1951.

Sheldon himself cut a dashing figure. At forty-three he had a touch of silver in his straight brown hair; but the face, despite the rugged lines of a life outdoors, broke into expressive grimaces like a boy's. The vivid blue eyes stared right through you. A boy's, also, the exaggeratedly hearty inflections of Don's raspy voice. Just as he never drank or smoked, he never swore; yet he had concocted an idiosyncratic diction of his own, full of words like "huckledebuck" and "bimbo" and "yowzah," that was like the richest vein of profanity.

In the year before our 1965 visit, an event had occurred that would change Don Sheldon for good: the lifelong loner had been married. Don's bride, seventeen years his junior, was Roberta Reeve, the daughter of Bob Reeve, Alaska's premier pilot of the 1930s. We met Roberta that summer. She was strikingly pretty, a slender woman with dark black hair. Somewhat shy, she had a sharp intelligence that she had put to work acting as Don's radio operator and bookkeeper. She also devised a chart to keep track of pick-up dates and parties; no longer would Sheldon file the whereabouts and needs of his myriad clients only in his head.

Don didn't talk about Roberta, but I got an inkling of the impact of marriage on him in a comment relayed by a genial older woman, Mildred Campbell, who taught school in Talkeetna. "One day a few months back," she recounted, "Don came out where I was working in the garden, and he just stood there looking at me, grinning from ear to ear. 'What's got into you, Don?' I asked him. 'Campbell,' he said, 'I didn't know a man could be so happy.' "

Finally the weather cleared and Don could fly us in. We wanted him to land in a narrow basin at the head of the Tokositna Glacier; all our expedition plans hinged on that approach. But no pilot had ever landed anywhere on the Tokositna, let alone at its head, under cliffs rotten with avalanches. Aware of the problem, we had sent Don some excellent Washburn photographs of our proposed landing site months before. But photographs meant as little to Sheldon as radar. Just before take-off he cut a bunch of green boughs from a bush in his front yard, then piled them on the lap of my friend Matt Hale, sitting in the back seat of the Cessna 180.

As we flew over the upper Tokositna, I was scared out of my pants. The rock wall on my right seemed a couple of jumps beyond the wing tip. It didn't help matters when Sheldon turned the plane straight toward it. I let out an involuntary yell. Of course I had misjudged the scale; Sheldon calmly circled within the wall to lose altitude. The light on the snow in the basin below us was flat. Sheldon peered, wordless, out his window. At last he straightened out; opening the rear window, he ordered Matt, with a series of "Now!"s, to fling the green boughs out of the plane. They fluttered down to the glacier. By the time Sheldon turned around, he had a series of dark objects laid out in a line to help him read the slope.

He took the plane in for the landing. As I tried to swallow my fear, I realized that the airdrop on McKinley had been, for Don, routine fun; this was serious business. Everything seemed to go all right. Then, suddenly, Don jerked back on the stick; the stall warning shrieked. I saw, several seconds after Don had seen it, a huge lump of glacier into which we might have plowed head on; the flat light had hidden it completely. Don crested the glacier and landed in one motion, light as a feather.

In 1970 I flew with Don again, on an expedition to the Cathedral

Spires. By now the demands on Sheldon's summer time were incredible, for mountaineering in Alaska had become a popular craze—thanks in large part to Sheldon himself. He was working himself to a frazzle, it seemed, but he hated to turn down any customer. Once we got into the air, Don asked me, "How'd you like to try your hand?" I said, "Sure, why not?" He demonstrated the controls, then let me, in the copilot's seat, experiment. "Not so tough, is it?" he asked. I grinned agreement. "Okay," he said, "wake me up when we get over near the Spires." In one minute he was asleep.

By 1970 Don and Roberta had two daughters, Kate and Holly who were given to building mud castles on the edge of the airstrip. A son, Robert, followed the next year. For the family man, however, there was less rest than ever. Roberta, who still lives with her children in Talkeetna, estimates that in the 1970s Don *averaged* four to five hours' sleep a night between April and the end of September. "He was so short of sleep from the summer," she recalls, "that he would literally sleep most of the winter." During the eleven years of their marriage, Don went "Outside" only twice—once to Bellingham, Washington, for parts for a plane, and then to Wyoming for five days near the end of his life—in effect, a farewell trip to the cousins he had not seen in decades. To take a vacation would never have occurred to Sheldon. According to Roberta, "Don was fond of saying, 'I'm on a permanent vacation.' "

As glamorous as the bush pilot business might seem, it was always a desperate proposition financially. In 1964, the year of their wedding, Don charged $55 an hour for flights in his Cessna 180, a mere $20 an hour for the Super Cub. By flying the back-breaking total of almost 900 hours, the pilot grossed some $40,000 for the year. Out of that sum came aircraft maintenance and repairs, fuel, insurance, payments to the bank for recently-purchased airplanes, overhead—and, of course, Don's and Roberta's living expenses. In 1964 a new Cessna, without any accessories, cost $25,000; typically it took Sheldon five or six years to pay it off. "The minute we got one airplane paid off," says Roberta, "it was worn out and we needed another one. We were out of debt twenty-four hours one time. I said, 'Oh, boy, we're out of debt.' The next day Don took out a new loan for thousands of dollars on a new airplane."

Passenger liability insurance, which was mandatory, cost Don $1500 in 1964. (By 1970 it cost $7000 for the year.) No client ever made a claim against Sheldon. Hull insurance, which would pay for damaged craft, cost roughly a third of the price of a new plane, so Don could never afford it. "In January 1971," Roberta remembers, "We went to the bank and borrowed $40,000 to buy this airplane. Two months later Don totaled it on Mount Hayes. It was the weirdest feeling. You have no airplane, but you still owe the bank forty thousand dollars."

Despite the precarious finances, Don was generous. "He would come back from a flight," recalls Roberta, "and say, 'I'm not going to charge for that trip.' I'd be worried, because I knew how much debt he was in. He'd say, 'Well, they've given me quite a bit of traffic,' or 'Those guys are down and out, they really can't afford it.' " Sheldon, however, refused to haggle over his rates. At least one climber, a Wall Street stock analyst, found this out the hard way. After an expedition the analyst approached the pilot and suggested a pow-wow over prices. Don fixed his eyes on a distant mountain and said, "Yessiree, there's some fine bear huntin' up in the Dutch Hills." The analyst missed the point. Sheldon never flew him again.

Despite his marriage, Don remained a private person. Roberta guesses that he counted only four or five people in the world as truly close friends. She confesses today that she knows little about the Sheldon of the years before their marriage. So absorbed was he in flying, he had few hobbies. In his early years, he seems to have been an inveterate card player; later he spent many winter hours turning huge cross-cut sections of trees into exquisitely worked tables and chairs. "I never saw him read a book, even *Wager With the Wind* [James Greiner's biography of Sheldon]," says Roberta. "One night he took it and opened it up in the middle and read a couple of pages. And maybe the next night he'd open it again at random and read a couple more pages. . . . "

Don had a bad knee that caused him to limp most of his life. "I got it packing moose meat, where you twist and grind," he told Tony Smythe, the British climber. Nevertheless, savs Roberta, he was a graceful dancer; the two would cross Talkeetna's muddy main street of an evening to enter the Fairview Inn, where they played the juke box and danced the waltz, the polka, and the schottische. Don played old cowboy songs on an accordion. "He was really in essence a cowboy," says Roberta with a smile. "A cowboy with class."

Don had at least one genuine enemy, his Talkeetna rival pilot Cliff Hudson. For years the two men fought bitterly over customers; the stories are legion of each stealing the other's passengers. After an incident in which Hudson alleged that Sheldon had buzzed his plane in mid-air, the two pilots ended up in court on the opposite sides of a nasty lawsuit. And once, when "the Rat," as Sheldon called him, refused to move his truck, which was blocking Sheldon's plane, the antipathy escalated into a fistfight in the local grocery store. Neither man "won" the fight, say witnesses, but the store lost its candy case.

Mike Fisher, who flew back-up for Don for a decade and probably knew his flying abilities better than anyone, offers a fascinating appraisal of Sheldon's strengths and weaknesses. "He had excellent eyesight, and a finely tuned kinesthetic sense. He was aware of nuances in an airplane's motion that were indiscernible to the average pilot. He had a nice, gentle touch, especially on landings. He used to be a cowboy, back in Wyoming—maybe he learned that touch with horses. On glaciers he had an uncanny sense of alignment. Every glacier has a thing called a fall line, and if you're not aligned with that, you can make a tilted landing that could be very dangerous. Don was never able to articulate what he did but he could analyze the fall line intuitively.

"He was a classic seat-of-the-pants flyer. But he was an atrocious theoretician. He had these outrageous theories about how an airplane worked. I often said, 'If Don actually flew the way he talked about flying, he wouldn't be able to talk about flying, because he wouldn't be here.' He thought, for instance, that an airplane had a higher stalling speed downwind than upwind, which is pure nonsense.

"Still, he was an intuitive expert at extracting the last available ounce of performance out of a plane. He knew from experience what wouldn't work. He had a tremendous memory for landscape—he was like an Indian who knew every wrinkle of his own territory. But he wasn't a great navigator. Outside his home valley he really had to watch himself. He spent a lot of time lost. We were flying separate planes back from the Coleen country once. I got him on the radio and said, 'Hey, Don, how come we're crossing the Yukon River fifty miles west of where we're supposed to be?' He answered, 'Must be a pretty stiff cross wind.' "

At making difficult landings where planes had never been, says Fisher, Don was without a rival. Once Fisher was very nervous about taking an airplane into a high glacier where only Sheldon had previously landed. "Don said, 'Don't worry about it. It's nothing but a big old cow pasture up high.' It worked. He was right."

And, says Fisher laconically, "Don took his rescue work pretty seriously." On Christmas Day 1958 Sheldon came close to losing his Super Cub on the volcano Mount Iliamna, but he found the wreckage of an Air Force transport plane that had crashed there, killing all hands. In 1962 he plucked Tony Smythe and his companion off a sand bar in the raging Chulitna River in the middle of the night. The two climbers' makeshift raft had disintegrated, stranding them on the island, soaked and foodless; only hours before they had watched the rising river reduce their spot of land to a tabletop. When seven men froze to death high on McKinley in 1967, Sheldon fought hurricane winds to direct would-be rescuers on the ground to the bodies.

His most famous rescue took place on McKinley in 1960. The West Buttress route had by then become the most popular approach, and in May of that year there were several parties on it simultaneously. On the same day at the 17,000 foot level, one climber descending from the summit suffered a long fall, damaging the ligaments in his leg so severely he could not walk; another climber, a woman, fell seriously ill with cerebral edema. A radio message alerted Sheldon, and climbers from Seattle and Anchorage rushed to Talkeetna to set in motion a rescue.

For a while Sheldon ferried the rescuers to the base of the West Buttress, from which they hoped to climb up to the victims and evacuate them by stretcher. But the woman's condition was deteriorating so rapidly, it was clear she would die before the reinforcements could reach her. The only cure for cerebral edema is to get the victim to low altitude immediately. The woman's teammates thought they could drag her with ropes down to a basin at 14,300 feet. Could Sheldon, they wanted to know, possibly land there and fly her off?

No one had landed at anything like 14,000 feet on McKinley. Worse, there was not even a stretch of flat snow for a runway: the only conceivable site was a narrow shelf that angled up at a considerable pitch. Probably no other pilot in Alaska would have attempted to land there; Sheldon, however, thought he could make it. He chose the Super Cub, his lightest plane, and carefully calculated just how low he could leave the fuel in the tanks and still get to the mountain and back.

It turned out to be an incredibly dicey landing. There was a series of huge crevasses just below the 2000-foot "runway," and the pilot faced the real possibility that if his skis did not bite and hold, he might slide, helpless, back down the slope and into a crevasse. Because of the thin air and the angle of the slope, Sheldon had to come in at full power, something no pilot relishes. At the last moment he pulled the nose up sharply so the plane's glide matched the slope. He hit the snow, sped upwards, bounced several times, then, at the end of the landing, turned the craft abruptly sideways. The skis held. Several hours later he was in the air with the woman, who was so ill that her skin had begun to turn blue and green. She later recovered totally. The same day, Sheldon returned to McKinley to guide a nervy helicopter pilot who landed to rescue the climber with the bad leg.

In 1974 I wrote Don to ask if he would fly our three-man expedition to Mount Dickey. The climbing grapevine had circulated the word that Sheldon had been sick the year before; cancer was rumored. In my letter I expressed my concern. Don wrote back telling me to get on up to Talkeetna; his only allusion to his illness was the claim that he had "escaped the hospital" to fly his heaviest traffic yet in the summer of 1973.

Almost no one knew then that in December 1972, Don had undergone an operation for cancer of the colon. He was bedridden through January and February, but forced himself back to work. By the end of the year he had amassed 818 hours in the air. The grueling pace must have required incredible courage, for Don was on chemotherapy the whole time.

Don let Roberta, but no one else, know that the treatment made him constantly nauseous. A man who had all his life refused to take aspirin, he was forced now to rely on hateful pain-killing drugs. The nausea kept him from eating, and he lost weight. But, says Roberta, "He was so determined to regain his old self. We never discussed the illness. I think he had the attitude, if I refuse to acknowledge it, that's one way I can fight it."

When I saw Don in July 1974, he looked gaunt, but the boyish facial expressions were as lively as ever, as were the wit and banter. Despite my efforts to lend a sympathetic ear, we never talked about whether he was sick or well. He flew, I thought, if anything a little more carefully than he had before. There was the same impetuous take-off, the same feather touch on landing.

As always, Don looked after us while we were on Dickey. After the climb, so that I could retrieve our base camp, Don showed his best stuff once more, landing on an extremely narrow branch of the Ruth Gorge in dark shadow on a couple of inches of slush. It was one more site in the Alaska Range where no one had previously landed.

In 1974 Don again flew more than 800 hours. By October, says Roberta, he knew he was badly sick once more. He went into the hospital on Christmas Day. He had made the last flight of his life only ten days before. On January 26, 1975 he died.

Bush flying in Alaska will never again be what it was in Sheldon's heyday. He was the last of his breed—the maverick freelancer holding together a one-man operation, his pluck and courage worth all the radio equipment in the state. Rescues today are carried out with the coordinated technology of a military exercise.

During the years I knew Don, he went from being my hero to

becoming my friend, yet he never entirely shed that quality of having stepped out of the pages of some latter-day *Odyssey*. Today, seven years after his death, wherever you go in Alaska, Sheldon's name seems to have that legendary ring.

I suppose each of us has toyed with fantasies of how he would conduct himself in the last months if he knew he had contracted a fatal disease. The temptations are numerous—to drive a sports car at the limit, to attempt a great symphony, to run riot in Tahiti. Perhaps Don never believed that cancer would claim him. No matter what the truth, those who knew him cannot imagine him behaving in any other way than he did. In that last summer of flying, it was not the daredevil rescuer who came to the fore, but the day-in day-out competence of the seasoned aviator, the man whose proudest boast was, "I've never hurt a passenger." Surely there is no higher integrity in life than that—to perform to the very end, without fuss or fanfare, what one has always done best.

The Maze and Aura
by Jack Turner

Jack Turner (born 1942) is a philosopher who writes about wilderness. A plane crash led him to an authentically wild place when he was very young, and the experience marked him forever.

Just before dawn sometime in April 1964, I shoved my Kelty behind the seat of a small Piper Cub, climbed into the passenger seat, and fastened my safety belt as we motored onto the airport runway at Moab, Utah. Since it was empty, we kept going into the take-off without stopping and then climbed slowly, the little plane grinding for altitude. Soon we banked west, and as we cleared the cliffs bordering the Spanish Valley, a vast array of mesas spread before us, glowing faintly in the morning light.

We turned again, southwest, and set a course for Junction Butte, a landmark tower at the confluence of the Green and Colorado Rivers. Beyond the confluence was the Maze, a terra incognita some people wanted preserved as part of the newly proposed Canyonlands National Park. *National Geographic* magazine believed the Maze might harbor something to persuade Congress to include it in the new park. My friend Huntley Ingalls and I were to explore the area for three days and photograph what we found. The plane would drop us as close to the Maze as possible. In the darkness of the runway we had flipped a coin to see who would go in first, and I won.

The pilot—Bud—was silent. Since he knew the country below from landing at remote sites for uranium and oil companies, I tried to question him about features in the landscape. But the noise of the motor made conversation difficult so we lapsed into silence and flew on, bouncing like a boat in rapids off the thermals coming up from the canyons. Below, the Colorado River meandered through swells of slickrock muted by purple shadow, while to the north, miles of fluted red walls led to Grand View Point. By the time we crossed the Green River, the first light had illuminated the grass covering the sandbars, and pools of water in the slickrock gleamed like tiny silver mirrors. There was not a cloud in the sky—a perfect day.

At Junction Butte we had turned west toward Ekker Butte. Beneath it, to the south, was Horse Canyon, an open valley that receded into a labyrinth of slots—the Maze. On a bench between Ekker Butte and the canyon was an airfield that looked like a matchstick. Bud dropped the nose of the Piper Cub and we made a pass several hundred feet above the dirt strip. It had not been used in years, Bud said, and I believed him. It was covered with small plants and netted with arroyos. Worse, the south fork of Horse Canyon was far away, and since it led into the heart of the Maze, I feared that if we landed here, we'd never reach our main objective. So I began to search for options.

Beyond the nearest fork of Horse Canyon—the north fork—a twotrack struck south to the edge of the south fork, a point now called the Maze Overlook. It was a perfect place to start from and I wanted to land there. Bud turned south. The road turned out to be old Caterpillar scrape, one blade wide—probably cut by a seismographic survey crew when oil companies explored this basin in the fifties. I asked Bud if he could land on the scrape. He wasn't sure. I wanted him to try. He was silent.

We dropped down for a closer look and banked slightly left above the narrow dirt path, Bud's face pressed against the window. Then we gained altitude and headed back, still in silence. Bud flipped switches and studied the instrument panel. Soon we were sinking toward the road, then slowly we settled in.

Several feet above the ground, a gust of wind blew us to the right and we landed hard in the blackbush flats. The right wheel hit first, and when the wheel strut punctured the floor between my feet, I pitched forward, striking my head against the instrument panel and spewing blood over the cockpit. The plane bounced gracefully into the air and Bud worked the stick, murmuring softly, "Whoa Baby, Whoa Baby." We lost control in slow motion, but we were without panic, a space I've encountered many times. Then the plane hit again, the wheels snagged a shallow arroyo, and we flipped upside down, sliding across the desert with a sickening screech.

When we stopped, we were hanging upside down from our seat belts. The pressure of our body weight made it difficult to release them so we hung there kicking, trying to brace ourselves against the windshield. I smelled my own blood—that strange metallic tang. I tried to smell gas, and all the while I'm thinking, "We're gonna get roasted." Finally Bud released his buckle and crashed into the windshield. He helped me release mine, and we sat together on the roof of the cockpit, trying to open the doors. Unfortunately, the wings were bent up just enough to prevent the doors from opening, so we both kicked hard on one door until something gave. Then we crawled out into the warm silence of a desert morning.

We were ecstatic—laughing, shaking hands, kicking our heels, and praising each other as though we had by sheer intelligence and talent achieved a magnificent goal. I licked the blood off my hands and congratulated myself for surviving my first airplane wreck. I was twenty-two years old.

While Bud searched for the first-aid kit, I got some water from the Kelty. I had six quarts, the standard rock climber's ration: two quarts per person per day, anywhere, under any conditions. We patched the gash in my head. Then, the adrenaline wearing off, we considered our plight. Bud felt he should walk to Anderson Bottom, a grassy stretch along the Green River with a line shack occupied by one of the local ranchers. I thought we should stay put. We had warm clothes, one sleeping bag, gas from the plane, matches for a brush fire, food, and water. Furthermore, we were highly visible—a light green airplane on a red desert. Within hours, Huntley would organize a rescue flight and easily spot us from above the airfield across the north fork. Bud would not stay, however, and after a few minutes he left, walking north with neither water nor supplies. The next day he was picked up near the Green River.

I examined my Kelty for what, typically, was not there: no compass, no maps, no tent, no stove, no binoculars, no flares, no signal mirror. This probably had something to do with being kicked out of Boy Scouts. There were just two climbing ropes, some rock-climbing gear, a bivouac tarp, a sleeping bag, a Leica M2, the usual climber's food— summer sausage, cheese, gorp—and water.

I walked to the rim of the south fork. It was perhaps five hundred feet to the bottom of Horse Canyon. Across the canyon were spires of shale topped by dollops of White Rim sandstone, a formation now called "the Chocolate Drops." The canyon walls were more eroded than the Navajo and Kayenta sandstone I was familiar with from Glen Canyon, but everywhere were braids of a real labyrinth. The so-called south fork divided into at least three more canyons and everything kept forking. To my delight I saw marshes and a pool of water. It was utterly still. I sat on the rim and asked a question that came up often during the next thirty years: Why, exactly, am I here?

I was there because of Huntley. During the fifties he worked in southern Utah for the Coast and Geodetic Survey, traveling by jeep and foot throughout the canyonlands conducting magnetic surveys. During those years he photographed spires he thought would make interesting rock climbs and showed his slides to other climbers living in Boulder, Colorado. He had photographs of the Fisher Towers, Totem Pole, Spider Rock, Standing Rock, Castleton Tower, and the Six-Shooter Peaks. By 1964 these spires had been climbed, some by

Yosemite climbers, but many by Huntley and Layton Kor. Huntley had published articles on the first ascents of the Fisher Tower and Standing Rock in *National Geographic*, and now they thought he might use his climbing expertise to explore the Maze. Since I had climbed a lot with Kor and Huntley, was interested in wild places and was Huntley's friend, here I was staring at the labyrinth.

The Utah desert was relatively unknown in the early sixties. In 1960 the road south of Blanding was dirt most of the way to Tuba City; the bridges were often one lane and made of wood. Eliot Porter's *Glen Canyon: The Place No One Knew* was not published until 1963, and Edward Abbey's *Desert Solitaire* did not come out until 1968. There were no guidebooks to these wild lands. Many of the parks and monuments and wilderness areas that now cover the area did not exist, and the country was vast and wild and easy to get lost in; there were no restrictions, and little management. We wandered the desert as we wished, lounged in the pools at Havasu, waded the Zion Narrows, climbed the desert towers, drifted down Glen Canyon, and explored the Escalante enjoying virtually no contact with other people. The Maze was simply another place on Huntley's long list of wild places to see.

Although the Maze was de facto wilderness, I did not then think of wilderness as a separate place needing preservation. The Wilderness Act was not passed until 1964. To the degree I even thought about preservation, I presumed it was conducted by nice old ladies in big cities. It certainly had nothing to do with me. I simply liked climbing big walls and spires and exploring remote places, preferably before anyone else did. Like most rock climbers, I didn't even like to hike. I didn't know the name of a single wildflower, and Huntley had to tell me, "These are cottonwoods" or "These are Utah juniper." My knowledge of animals derived mainly from hunting and killing them. (Years later, when I read Schopenhauer, I recognized myself in those days: "in the mind of a man who is filled with his own aims, the world appears as a beautiful landscape appears on the plan of a battlefield.")

I walked back to the plane and wrote a message on the road with the heel of my boot: "All OK," "Bud"—then an arrow—and "Anderson

Bottom." I drank a quart of water, pulled out my foam pad, and settled into the shade beside the fuselage. I had no books, no paints or nature guides. I wasn't worried, I was bored.

Around eleven in the morning I heard a plane and soon Huntley flew over in a Cessna 180 piloted by George Hubler, the owner of the Moab airport. After several passes to make sure I was ambulatory, they dropped a message saying they would land Huntley on the old airstrip. He would then cross the north fork and meet me at the wreck.

I settled back into the shade, even more bored. I could not get over the silence; it ate at me and I couldn't sit still. I wandered around looking for something interesting to do and found nothing. So I sat in the shade, oblivious to the glory that engulfed my every moment.

The day passed slowly with no sign of Huntley. In the evening I walked to the rim of the north fork of Horse Canyon and searched for him, but to no avail. That night I consumed more of my water supply. I slept fitfully.

The next morning, when there was still no sign of Huntley, I went back and walked the rim searching for him. Finally, in the late afternoon, I found him placing an expansion bolt several feet below the White Rim sandstone cap. He had already done some wild unroped climbing, but the cap was featureless, and that meant bolting. Soon he was up. We shook hands and greeted each other formally by last name, in the best British mountaineering tradition.

Huntley had left most of his gear at the bottom of the canyon while searching for a way through the cliffs. Since Hubler would return to the airfield the following day at noon, we had less than twenty-four hours to explore the Maze. We decided to leave Huntley's gear where it was and go on into the south fork. The plan was simple: we would walk into the Maze until dark, hike back through the night to the north fork, collect Huntley's things, and climb to the airfield to meet Hubler in the morning.

We returned to the wreck, gathered my gear, and after some scrambling and several rappels, reached the bottom of the canyon. After filling the water bottles at the algae-filled pool (we never treated water in those days), we hiked to the main canyon and up the middle of the three forks.

Soon Huntley began moving slowly and muttering about new boots. (Eventually he would lose all his toenails, which for years he kept in a small jar as a reminder.) After awhile he urged me to go on so I could cover as much ground as possible before dark. We dropped our packs in an obvious spot and I hurried up the canyon in fading light, moving rapidly, my eyes sweeping the landscape like radar. I missed the soaring walls and alcoves of the Escalante, the water, the seeps. I was still bored. But mostly from a sense of obligation, I walked on doggedly through the extraordinary silence.

Then, in the last light of day, I was startled by a line of dark torsos and a strange hand on a wall just above the canyon floor. I froze, rigid with fear. My usual mental categories of alive and not-alive became permeable. The painted figures stared at me, transmuted from mere stone as if by magic, and I stared back in terror.

After a few seconds, my body intervened with my mind, pulling it away from a gaze that engulfed me. The torsos became *just* pictures. My mind discovered a comfortable category for the original perception and the confusion passed. But strangely, seeing them as representations did not reduce the emotion I felt. I was chilled, shivering, though the air was warm. I could not override the feeling that the figures were looking at me, and that I was seeing what I wasn't supposed to see.

I can say now this fear resulted from confusion: perhaps from the exhaustion of the past two days, perhaps because of my anxiety for Huntley's situation and the increasing extremity of our position. But in retrospect, I believe it was the inherent power of the figures.

They were pictographs, but not the usual stick figures and crude animals I'd seen before. There were fifteen of them, painted a dark, almost indigo blue. Some were life-size, some smaller. Some were abstract, like mummies with big buggy eyes and horns. Others had feet and hands. One particularly beautiful figure I assumed was female. Among the figures were small animals, insects, snakes, and birds, all painted in remarkable detail. The most unusual figure displayed an enlarged hand with clearly articulated fingers; springing from the end of the middle finger was a fountain of what looked like blood—a spurting wound. Farther left along the wall were more figures. One did not appear abstract at all. It was dressed and masked, had feet, perhaps even moccasins, and held what looked like a spear.

I yelled for Huntley, hoping he would hear me and be able to see the figures before dark. In a few minutes he came hobbling up the canyon. Although he'd seen many examples of rock art throughout the canyon country, he had never seen anything like these figures, and he too was captured by their powerful presence. While photographing them with long time-exposures, we stared in silence. Although spooky and unsettling, they absorbed us, and we did not want to leave.

Reluctantly, we walked down canyon and collected my gear. By the time we headed for the north fork, it was dark, and Huntley kept walking into things and stubbing his painful toes. After a mile or so, we bivouacked, dividing up my clothes and sleeping bag and adopting fetal positions on a sandstone slab in the middle of the wash. Such nights pass slowly, like time in a hospital, where disturbed sleep confuses what is dream and what is real. I dreamed of traps and spears. Huntley talked in his sleep and screamed at nightmares.

At first light we were up and moving, eating gorp and summer sausage as we walked. By now Huntley was beyond cursing. We walked slowly, reaching his equipment by mid-morning. Then we climbed to the rim by way of a chimney that pierced the White Rim sandstone just below the airfield. Hubler arrived on time, hopping his Cessna over the arroyos, and soon we were back at Moab. We tried to drive home to Boulder, but after several hours we stopped to sleep on the bare ground under a cottonwood, my head resting on my folded hands. Then we drove on into the night, talking about the figures and making plans to return. I did not know then that when I returned—and I knew I would—it would be in another context, with expectations and knowledge that would erode their power.

The contrast between that long weekend and my job appalled me. I knew I wanted to have more experiences like that, even if I couldn't explain what "like that" meant. There was the adventure and the wilderness, of course, but what interested me was something more. Two months later we went back.

By May it was clear that the Maze would be left out of the new park, so *National Geographic* was no longer interested in our photographs. We were on our own.

Huntley and I had been talking up the Maze, showing pictures, and researching rock art, so numerous people were now interested in seeing the pictographs. There would be five of us on this trip. Besides Huntley and me, there was my wife Anne and our friends Judith and David. Since we wanted to stay for a week, the main problem was getting supplies into the Maze. None of us had four-wheel drive, so we decided on an airdrop.

By June we were back at the Moab airport. Hubler was piloting the Cessna. We removed the passenger door and seat, and I sat on the floor tied in with a climbing sling. It was going to be an airy ride. Huntley was in the back with a pile of Army duffel bags stuffed with camping supplies and canned food packed in crushed newspapers—there was not much freeze-dried food in those days.

The idea, again, was simple. We would drop into the south fork and sort of stall the plane while Huntley handed me duffels, and I would toss them out. Hubler said we would be close to the ground and moving so slowly they'd survive the fall. Having been a fighter pilot in Korea, he had the right spirit for such an enterprise.

An hour later we were above the Maze Overlook. The Piper Cub was gone, disassembled and hauled out to the old Colorado River crossing at Hite—no mean feat. As we dropped into the south fork, Hubler cut the engine back and we soared between the canyon walls, carving turns with the streambed as we lost altitude. When we were about forty feet above the ground, I shoved a duffel out the doorway and Hubler gunned the plane into what seemed like a ninety-degree turn, straight up the rock walls. From my choice view at the door I could almost pick plants as we cleared the cliffs. Hubler was smiling and allowed that this was better than working for the oil companies. We came around and dropped in again, and this time I got several bags out. A third pass finished the task, and after dropping Huntley and me at the Ekker Butte landing strip, Hubler returned to Moab for the others. By midafternoon, we were all hiking into the south fork.

Most periods of bliss in life are forgotten, but our week in that wild canyon is an exception. The weather was flawless, with days of blue skies following one another like waves out of the sea. We explored all the south fork canyons, and David and Huntley descended the steep and isolated Jasper Canyon, which led directly to the Colorado River. Huntley found a perfect arrowhead. We sat in the sun, bathed in slickrock pools, dreamed of other explorations— and studied the pictographs.

The pictographs were still wonderful, but now they were just things we were visiting. I had become a tourist to my own experience. I tried unsuccessfully to recapture the magic of those first moments. I took notes, but they exceeded my power of description. I kept photographing, first in 35 mm, then with my 2¼ X 3¼ Zeiss. But what I sought could not be captured with photography or language. Indeed, the more we talked, described, and photographed, the more common they seemed. Everyone was appreciative, impressed, but the unmediated, the raw, and the unique was history.

I tried sitting with them alone in the dark, but they neither gazed at nor engulfed me now. The pictographs remained as they had for centuries, preserved by their isolation and the dry desert air, but what I would later learn to call their "aura" seemed to be gone.

When we returned to Boulder, Anne wrote a paper on the pictographs for an anthropology class and used my photographs as illustrations. That fall, Huntley returned with other friends for still another exploration, but then the Maze passed from our lives. I did not return for thirty-one years.

• • •

In the years that followed, my life diverged along an axis I came to understand as central to my life. Those early visits to the Maze, Glen Canyon, and the Escalante led me to the margins of the modern world, areas wild in the sense Thoreau meant when he said that in wildness is the preservation of the world: places where the land, the flora and fauna, the people, their culture, their language and arts were still ordered by energies and interests fundamentally their own, not by the homogenization and normalization of modern life.

After divorces and attempts at ordinary jobs, Judith, Huntley, and I drifted into Asia, not so much for adventure as for what existed only at the limits of our world: the archaic, wildness, a faintly criminal madness, drugs, passion, art, Eastern religion—the Other.

Huntley was the first to go. In 1965 he cashed in his retirement and with four thousand dollars headed east. He was gone two and a half years. His first letter came from Herat, Afghanistan, where he had spent most of a winter. The next was from India and concerned blue monkeys and a yogi with a master's degree in physics from Oxford who had taken a vow of silence and who spent his time playing classical Indian instruments. A year later an aerogram arrived from a hill town in northern India. Huntley had been traveling in Sri Lanka, India, and Nepal and was now living among a Gurdjieff group in a small bungalow overlooking the Himalayas.

By the time Huntley returned, I was in graduate school studying philosophy. We talked endlessly of his travels, of gurus, temples, Indian music, drugs, neurophysiology, Cantor sets, and Tibetans. I was envious. My life seemed small and I could not imagine how to make it larger.

Years passed. In 1974, Judith left for Asia. I was living on the southern coast of Crete for the summer, so we met in Istanbul and traveled down the western coast of Turkey and around to Side on the southern shore. Then we hugged good-bye. I rode the Orient Express back to Europe and flew home to Chicago to be a professor; she went overland, alone, to Nepal. Except for short periods, she has lived there ever since. She has a guru, she and her second husband were married in a Hindu ceremony, she studies with teachers of Tibetan Buddhism. Her photographs of Nepali craftsmen are in the Smithsonian Institution, and she has written a book on the indigenous crafts of Nepal. Several years ago, to celebrate her fiftieth birthday, she trekked for five weeks across northwestern Nepal with a porter. Then, worrying about his safety, she crossed the border alone and continued into western Tibet. She bathed naked in the sacred lake of Manasarowar and bowed to sacred Mount Kailas, believed by Hindus, Buddhists, and Jains to be the center of the universe. Judith's letters that first year further underlined my misery in Chicago and with academia, and I determined to go myself.

I spent the following summer wandering the Karakoram Himalaya and the Hindu Kush. By autumn I knew I would leave academia to see as much of the old world as I could before it was gone. Like the bear that went over the mountain, all I wanted to see was the other side, again and again. And I saw a lot. For the next eighteen years I traveled part of each year in the mountains of Pakistan, India, Nepal, Bhutan, China, Tibet, and Peru, scouting or guiding treks and easy mountaineering expeditions.

In retrospect, Judith and Huntley and I were part of a modern exodus of hundreds of thousands of Western people who left home and went to Asia. Some were hippies; some were pilgrims who ended up with Rajneesh in Poona, with Vipassana monks in the forests of Thailand, with Tibetan masters in Kathmandu, with Zen teachers in Kamakura; some were the first wave of what would become the adventure travel and ecotourism industries; some went to war in Vietnam; some went into the Peace Corps; some were merely ambassadors of capitalism and consumerism.

This great exodus and its consequences, especially the transformations of subjective experience that were both the end and means of many journeys to the East, remain unstudied and unknown. Some say, cynically, this is because everyone fried their brains with drugs. I think we still lack the language to describe why people went or what we found. This much, however, is clear: we dragged the modern world with us. We left home with a love of difference, but carried within us the seeds of homogeny. By the eighties it was over, and the cultures we loved were forever altered by modernity. We traveled a modern Asia that was no longer very Other.

My understanding of these events, and my own journey, is anchored in that early experience of those strange figures in the Maze—and in Walter Benjamin's justly famous essay, "The Work of Art in the Age of Mechanical Reproduction." It began with a specific event.

I was standing in a meditation room at Hemis Monastery in Ladakh watching a German professor of Tibetology lecture his tour group. German-speaking members of other groups were attempting, with varying degrees of success, to translate his comments to their comrades. Behind him, two Tibetan monks faced a crowd of perhaps eighty Germans, Americans, French, and Japanese armed with cameras, flash units, camcorders, and tape players. The older monk wore a large white Pan Am button on the lapel of his maroon robe. The younger monk looked scared.

After a while it became clear that the high point of the professor's presentation would be the first public viewing of a particularly sacred *thangka*, a scroll painting on linen depicting a powerful Tibetan deity. Until that moment, it had been viewed just once a year in a religious ceremony attended only by the monks at Hemis. With a flourish the professor asked the senior monk to unveil the *thangka*. The senior monk turned to the young monk, and he froze. Then the professor yelled, the senior monk yelled, and the young monk finally removed a soiled silk veil. As the room exploded with flashes, motor drives, and camcorders, the young monk stood paralyzed, waiting for his blasphemy to be justly punished. But, of course, objectively, nothing happened. The professor smiled, everyone (including me) stretched their necks to see, and the earth continued to spin on its axis.

Later I thought of a passage in Benjamin's essay:

> The elk portrayed by the man of the Stone Age on the walls
> of his cave was an instrument of magic. He did expose it to

his fellow men, but in the main it was meant for the spirits. Today the cult value would seem to demand that the work of art remain hidden. Certain statues of gods are accessible only to the priest in the cella; certain Madonnas remain covered nearly all year round; certain sculptures on medieval cathedrals are invisible to the spectator on ground level. With the emancipation of the various art practices from ritual go increasing opportunities for the exhibition of their products.

What I observed that day in the Hemis Monastery was the passage of an object from ritual to exhibition. The object remained; I am sure it is still there today. But something changed that is reflected only in human experience, in, for example, the experience of that young monk. Similarly, the Maze and those wonderful pictographs remain, but for me something is lost, a quality of my experience of them, something Benjamin calls the "aura" of art and landscape: "its presence in time and space, its unique existence at the place where it happens to be."

Benjamin's essay examines two of the processes that diminish aura, both "related to the increasing significance of the masses in contemporary life. Namely, the desire of contemporary masses to bring things 'closer' spatially and humanly, which is just as ardent as their bent toward overcoming the uniqueness of every reality by accepting its reproduction." The primary mode of reproduction is photography; the primary means of bringing the natural and cultural worlds closer is mass tourism. The pictographs and the Maze started down this path when I yelled for Huntley, took photographs, researched rock art, and gave slide shows, and when I brought others there. Had we remained silent, others could have, for a while, shared that powerful experience. And what if everyone remained silent?

Benjamin also discusses the many ways that loss of aura affects an art object: it undermines authenticity, jeopardizes the object's authority, shatters tradition, diminishes the importance of ritual, and perhaps most important, "the quality of its presence is always depreciated." This last point is for me the heart of the matter. If I have an interest in preservation, it is in preserving the power of presence—of landscape, art, flora, and fauna. It is more complicated than merely preserving habitat and species, and one might suppose it is something that could be added on later, after we successfully preserve biodiversity, say. But no, it's the other way around: the loss of aura and presence is the main reason we are losing so much of the natural world.

Photographic reproduction and mass tourism are now commonplace and diminish a family of qualities broader than, though including, our experience of art: aura is affected, but so is wildness, spirit, enchantment, the sacred, holiness, magic, and soul. We understand these terms intuitively, but they evade definition, analysis, and measurement because they refer to our experience of the material world rather than the material world itself. Hence they are excluded from the rationalized discourse of preservation, and we are hard pressed to figure out how to keep them in the world of our experience. You will not read much about them in *Art Forum*, *Sierra*, or *Conservation Biology*.

Unfortunately, these qualities deserve as much, if not more, attention as the decline of wilderness and biodiversity, because the decline of the latter has its root cause in the decline of the former. We treat the natural world according to our experience of it. Without aura, wildness, magic, spirit, holiness, the sacred, and soul, we treat flora, fauna, art, and landscape as resources and amusement. Fun. Their importance is merely a function of current fashions in hobbies. Virtually all of southern Utah is now photographed and exhibited to the public, so much so that looking at photographs of arches or pictographs, reading a guide book, examining maps, receiving instructions on where to go, where to camp, what to expect, how to act—and being watched over the entire time by a cadre of rangers—is now the normal mode of experience. Most people know no other.

• • •

In May of 1995 I returned to the Maze. Things had changed. The Maze is now part of Canyonlands National Park, and the pictographs that so moved me are no longer unknown. They have a name—the Harvest Site (or Bird Site)—and they are marked on topographic maps. A small library of books and articles describes, displays, compares, and analyzes each mark and figure, and various theories pigeonhole the paintings into categories created by these theories themselves. This doesn't mean we know much about them, however. Castleton, in the second volume of his encyclopedic *Petroglyphs and Pictographs of Utah*, concludes his discussion of the Barrier Canyon style, which includes the Harvest Site, with admirable candor: "The dearth of extensive archeological study of them makes it impossible to suggest the cultural affiliation or chronology of the style with any certainty." Nonetheless, it is widely assumed that the paintings are the work of an archaic desert people, hunters and gatherers who occupied the Colorado Plateau from approximately 5500 B.C. until the time of Christ. It was their home in a sense we can no longer imagine.

The Maze itself is laced with trails all clearly marked on maps available at the ranger station, and the roads in and around it are described in detail by a series of books. Indeed, there is a hiking guide to virtually every canyon on the Colorado Plateau, a guide to every dirt road, another for every stretch of the Green and Colorado Rivers, and yet another to every river, creek, and stream in the state of Utah. Not to mention, of course, the rock-climbing guides or mountain-biking guides, or slot-canyon guides, or . . . And this is why southern Utah is no longer wild. Maps and guides destroy the wildness of a place just as surely as photography and mass tourism destroy the aura of art and nature. Indeed, the three together—knowledge (speaking generally), photography, and mass tourism—are the unholy trinity that destroys the mysteries of both art and nature.

The Maze is, however, by modern standards, still remote and difficult to reach—the standard approach is an eighty-mile excursion from the nearest paved road. The park describes it as "a rugged and wild area with remoteness and self-reliance the principal elements of the visitor experience." A visit requires a four-wheel-drive vehicle or a mountain bike, and a hard walk. The scrape where we crashed the plane is now the road to the Maze Overlook. At the end are two designated camp-sites and a parking lot. There's also a trail now, a difficult one that drops into the canyon and requires a bit of climbing.

To the degree that can be expected, the Maze is preserved and pro-tected. In 1995 the park passed a tough backcountry management plan that limits both four-wheel-drive camping and hiking, and the rangers stationed there clearly love the place and guard it with a fierce devo-tion all too rare in the National Park Service. The pictographs remain unmarred.

I am thankful for all these things.

Enough history of the Maze is now known to place our little adventure in a historical context. We were not the first modern people to see the pictographs. Dean Brimhall, a journalist from Salt Lake City, photographed the Harvest Site in 1954 and later explored the intricacies of the south fork for other pictographs and petroglyphs. Local ranchers also knew about the site. Fortunately, I did not know any of this. Had I known the location of the paintings and seen Brimhall's photographs, there would have been less adventure, no exploration, and no aura—the "quality of its presence" would have been diminished if not erased. I can only wonder how many other gifts from the gods have been obscured by knowledge.

The man who visited the Maze in the spring of 1995 had also changed. I drove a 4x4 and played old Dylan and Emmylou tapes until I reached the infamous drop named the Flint Trail—a lovely so-called road requiring four-wheel drive, compound low, first gear, and lots of attention. For that I switched to Bach and Yo-Yo Ma. Spring had brought unusually heavy rains, and the desert was alive with lupine, globemallow, evening primrose, and little ruby clusters of Indian paintbrush. When I stopped and turned off the tape player, the silence was still there, but I was no longer bored.

I parked my truck and hiked into the south fork. From my pack hung a tag—my camping permit. I had reserved a spot by phone, paying for it with my Visa card and verifying my existence with lots of numbers. When I arrived at the Harvest Site, a couple was sitting in the shade of a cottonwood across from the pictographs. After we talked a few minutes, they asked if the paintings were the same as they were thirty-one years ago. When I said they were, the woman said she was glad to hear that. And I was glad to say so. To explain otherwise would have been too dark and sad.

After they left, I painted a small watercolor of the wall and figures, ate summer sausage, cheese, and gorp, and waited for dusk. Then I meditated with the figures for an hour, occasionally raising my eyes to study their mysterious visages. In the silence of the evening light, some of their presence returned. I saw the figures as a work of art, a group portrait—the shaman, the goddess, the hunter, the gatherers, an extended family including the birds and snakes and rabbits and insects. Perhaps the little band returned each year to this place and, as animals do, marked their territory. Whoever they were, they knew how to express and present something we have lost. At the end of my meditation I thanked them and bowed to them.

I am pleased the Harvest Site is preserved in the Maze District of Canyonlands National Park. I am happier still that the pictographs remain difficult to visit. I am delighted they remain in such good condition. I support the tough new backcountry management plan. I praise the rangers for their courage, their vision, and their devotion to a place I love.

But I wish we were wise enough to preserve something more. I wish that children seven generations from now could wander into an unknown canyon and receive at dusk the energy captured by a now-forgotten but empowered people. I wish these children could endure their gaze and, if only for a moment, bask in the aura of their gift.

from The First Men in the Moon
by H. G. Wells

English writer Herbert George Wells (1866-1946) wrote more than a hundred books, many of them science fiction stories. The First Men in the Moon *features a man named Cavor, who invents an anti-gravitational compound he calls Cavorite. His friend Bedford (the narrator) helps him to build a space ship out of this new material.*

I remember the occasion very distinctly when Cavor told me of his idea of the sphere. He had had intimations of it before, but at the time it seemed to come to him in a rush. We were returning to the bungalow for tea, and on the way he fell to humming. Suddenly he shouted, "That's it! That finishes it! A sort of roller blind!"

"Finishes what?" I asked.

"Space—anywhere! The moon."

"What do you mean?"

"Mean? Why—it must be a sphere! That's what I mean!"

I saw I was out of it, and for a time I let him talk in his own fashion. I hadn't the ghost of an idea then of his drift. But after he had taken tea he made it clear to me.

"It's like this," he said. "Last time I ran this stuff that cuts things off from gravitation into a flat tank with an overlap that held it down. And directly it had cooled and the manufacture was completed all that uproar happened, nothing above it weighed anything, the air went squirting up, the house squirted up, and if the stuff itself hadn't squirted up too, I don't know what would have happened! But suppose the substance is loose, and quite free to go up?"

"It will go up at once!"

"Exactly. With no more disturbance than firing a big gun."

"But what good will that do?"

"I'm going up with it!"

I put down my teacup and stared at him.

"Imagine a sphere," he explained, "large enough to hold two people and their luggage. It will be made of steel lined with thick glass; it will contain a proper store of solidified air, concentrated food, water distilling apparatus, and so forth. And enameled, as it were, on the outer steel—"

"Cavorite?"

"Yes."

"But how will you get inside?"

"There was a similar problem about a dumpling."

"Yes, I know. But how?"

"That's perfectly easy. An air-tight manhole is all that is needed. That, of course, will have to be a little complicated; there will have to be a valve, so that things may be thrown out, if necessary, without much loss of air."

"Like Jules Verne's thing in *A Trip to the Moon*?"

But Cavor was not a reader of fiction.

"I begin to see," I said slowly. "And you could get in and screw yourself up while the Cavorite was warm, and as soon as it cooled it would become impervious to gravitation, and off you would fly—"

"At a tangent."

"You would go off in a straight line—" I stopped abruptly. "What is to prevent the thing traveling in a straight line into space forever?" I asked. "You're not sure to get anywhere, and if you do—how will you get back?"

"I've just thought of that," said Cavor. "That's what I meant when I said the thing is finished. The inner glass sphere can be air-tight, and, except for the manhole, continuous, and the steel sphere can be made in sections, each section capable of rolling up after the fashion of a roller blind. These can easily be worked by springs, and released and checked by electricity conveyed by platinum wires fused through the glass. All that is merely a question of detail. So you see, that except for the thickness of the blind rollers, the Cavorite exterior of the sphere will consist of windows or blinds, whichever you like to call them. Well, when all these windows or blinds are shut, no light, no heat, no gravitation, no radiant energy of any sort will get at the inside of the sphere, it will fly on through space in a straight line, as you say. But open a window, imagine one of the windows open. Then at once any heavy body that chances to be in that direction will attract us—"

I sat taking it in.

"You see?" he said.

"Oh, I see."

"Practically we shall be able to tack about in space just as we wish. Get attracted by this and that."

"Oh, yes. That's clear enough. Only—"

"Well?"

"I don't quite see what we shall do it for! It's really only jumping off the world and back again."

"Surely! For example, one might go to the moon."

"And when one got there? What would you find?"

"We should see—!Oh! consider the new knowledge."

"Is there air there?"

"There may be."

"It's a fine idea," I said, "but it strikes me as a large order all the same. The moon! I'd much rather try some smaller things first."

"They're out of the question—because of the air difficulty."

"Why not apply that idea of spring blinds—Cavorite blinds in strong steel cases—to lifting weights?"

"It wouldn't work," he insisted. "After all, to go into outer space is not so much worse, if at all, than a polar expedition. Men go on polar expeditions."

"Not business men. And besides, they get paid for polar expeditions. And if anything goes wrong there are relief parties. But this—it's just firing ourselves off the world for nothing."

"Call it prospecting."

"You'll have to call it that. . . . One might make a book of it perhaps," I said.

"I have no doubt there will be minerals," said Cavor.

"For example?"

"Oh! sulphur, ores, gold perhaps, possibly new elements."

"Cost of carriage," I said. "You know you're not a practical man. The moon's a quarter of a million miles away."

"It seems to me it wouldn't cost much to cart any weight anywhere if you packed it in a Cavorite case."

I had not thought of that. "Delivered free on head of purchaser, eh?"

"It isn't as though we were confined to the moon."

"You mean—?"

"There's Mars—clear atmosphere, novel surroundings, exhilarating sense of lightness. It might be pleasant to go there."

"Is there air on Mars?"

"Oh, yes!"

"Seems as though you might run it as a sanatorium. By the way, how far is Mars?"

"Two hundred million miles at present," said Cavor airily; "and you go close by the sun."

My imagination was picking itself up again. "After all," I said, there's something in these things. There's travel—"

An extraordinary possibility came rushing into my mind. Suddenly I saw, as in a vision, the whole solar system threaded with Cavorite liners and spheres de luxe. "Rights of pre-emption," came floating into my head—planetary rights of pre-emption. I recalled the old Spanish monopoly in American gold. It wasn't as though it was just this planet or that—it was all of them. I stared at Cavor's rubicund face, and suddenly my imagination was leaping and dancing. I stood up, I walked up and down; my tongue was unloosened.

"I'm beginning to take it in," I said; "I'm beginning to take it in." The transition from doubt to enthusiasm seemed to take scarcely any time at all. "But this is tremendous!" I cried. "This is imperial! I haven't been dreaming of this sort of thing."

Once the chill of my opposition was removed, his own pent-up excitement had play. He too got up and paced. He too gesticulated and shouted. We behaved like men inspired. We *were* men inspired.

"We'll settle all that!" he said in answer to some incidental difficulty that had pulled me up. "We'll soon settle that! We'll start the drawings for mouldings this very night."

"We'll start them now," I responded, and we hurried off to the laboratory to begin upon this work forthwith.

I was like a child in Wonderland all that night. The dawn found us both still at work—we kept our electric light going heedless of the day. I remember now exactly how these drawings looked. I shaded and tinted while Cavor drew—smudged and haste-marked they were in every line, but wonderfully correct. We got out the orders for the steel blinds and frames we needed from that night's work, and the glass sphere was designed within a week. We gave up our afternoon conversations and our old routine altogether. We worked, and we slept and ate when we could work no longer for hunger and fatigue. Our enthusiasm infected even our three men, though they had no idea what the sphere was for. Through those days the man Gibbs gave up walking, and went everywhere, even across the room, at a sort of fussy run.

And it grew—the sphere. December passed, January—I spent a day with a broom sweeping a path through the snow from bungalow to laboratory—February, March. By the end of March the completion was in sight. In January had come a team of horses, a huge packing-case; we had our thick glass sphere now ready, and in position under the crane we had rigged to sling it into the steel shell. All the bars and blinds of the steel shell—it was not really a spherical shell, but polyhedral, with a roller blind to each facet—had arrived by February, and the lower half was bolted together. The Cavorite was half made by March, the metallic paste had gone through two of the stages in its manufacture, and we had plastered quite half of it on to the steel bars and blinds. It was astonishing how closely we kept to the lines of Cavor's first inspiration in working out the scheme. When the bolting together of the sphere was finished, he proposed to remove the rough roof of the temporary laboratory in which the work was done, and build a furnace about it. So the last stage of Cavorite making, in which the paste is heated to a dull red glow in a stream of helium, would be accomplished then it was already on the sphere.

And then we had to discuss and decide what provisions we were to take—compressed foods, concentrated essences, steel cylinders containing reserve oxygen, an arrangement for removing carbonic acid and waste from the air and restoring oxygen by means of sodium peroxide, water condensers, and so forth. I remember the little heap they made in the corner—tins, and rolls, and boxes—convincingly matter-of-fact.

It was a strenuous time, with little chance of thinking. But one day, when we were drawing near the end, an odd mood came over me. I had been bricking up the furnace all the morning, and I sat down by these possessions dead beat. Everything seemed dull and incredible.

"But look here, Cavor," I said. "After all! What's it all for?"

He smiled. "The thing now is to go."

"The moon," I reflected. "But what do you expect? I thought the moon was a dead world."

He shrugged his shoulders.

"We're going to see."

"Are we?" I said, and stared before me.

"You are tired," he remarked. "You'd better take a walk this afternoon."

"No," I said obstinately; "I'm going to finish this brickwork."

And I did, and insured myself a night of insomnia. I don't think I have ever had such a night. I had some bad times before my business collapse, but the very worst of those was sweet slumber compared to this infinity of aching wakefulness. I was suddenly in the most enormous funk at the thing we were going to do.

I do not remember before that night thinking at all of the risks we were running. Now they came like that array of spectres that once beleaguered Prague, and camped around me. The strangeness of what we were about to do, the unearthliness of it, overwhelmed me. I was like a man awakened out of pleasant dreams to the most horrible surroundings. I lay, eyes wide open, and the sphere seemed to get more flimsy and feeble, and Cavor more unreal and fantastic, and the whole enterprise madder and madder every moment.

I got out of bed and wandered about. I sat at the window and stared at the immensity of space. Between the stars was the void, the unfathomable darkness—! I tried to recall the fragmentary knowledge of astronomy I had gained in my irregular reading, but it was all too vague to furnish any idea of the things we might expect. At last I got back to bed and snatched some moments of sleep—moments of nightmare rather—in which I fell and fell and fell for evermore into the abyss of the sky.

I astonished Cavor at breakfast. I told him shortly, "I'm not coming with you in the sphere."

I met all his protests with a sullen persistence. "The thing's too mad," I said, "and I won't come. The thing's too mad."

I would not go with him to the laboratory. I fretted about my bungalow for a time, and then took hat and stick and set out alone, I knew not whither. It chanced to be a glorious morning: a warm wind and deep blue sky, the first green of spring abroad, and multitudes of birds singing. I lunched on beef and beer in a little public-house near Elham, and startled the landlord by remarking, *à propos* of the weather, "A man who leaves the world when days of this sort are about is a fool!"

"That's what I says when I heerd on it!" said the landlord, and I found that for one poor soul at least this world had proved excessive, and there had been a throat-cutting. I went on with a new twist to my thoughts.

In the afternoon I had a pleasant sleep in a sunny place, and went on my way refreshed.

I came to a comfortable-looking inn near Canterbury. It was bright with creepers, and the landlady was a clean old woman and took my eye. I found I had just enough money to pay for my lodging with her. I decided to stop the night there. She was a talkative body, and among many other particulars learnt she had never been to London. "Canterbury's as far as ever I been," she said. "I'm not one of your gadabout sort."

"How would you like a trip to the moon?" I cried.

"I never did hold with them ballooneys," she said evidently under the impression that this was a common excursion enough. "I wouldn't go up in one—not for ever so."

This struck me as being funny. After I had supped I sat on a bench by the door of the inn and gossiped with two labourers about brick-making, and motor cars, and the cricket of last year. And in the sky a faint new crescent, blue and vague as a distant Alp, sank westward over the sun.

The next day I returned to Cavor. "I am coming," I said. "I've been a little out of order, that's all."

That was the only time I felt any serious doubt about our enterprise. Nerves purely! Alter that I worked a little more carefully, and took a trudge for an hour every day. And at last, save for the heating in the furnace, our labours were at an end.

"Go on," said Cavor, as I sat across the edge of the manhole, and looked down into the black interior of the sphere. We two were alone. It was evening, the sun had set, and the stillness of the twilight was upon everything.

I drew my other leg inside and slid down the smooth glass to the bottom of the sphere, then turned to take the cans of food and other impedimenta from Cavor. The interior was warm, the thermometer stood at eighty, and as we should lose little or none of this by radiation, we were dressed in shoes and thin flannels. We had, however, a bundle of thick woolen clothing and several thick blankets to guard against mischance. By Cavor's direction I placed the packages, the cylinders of oxygen, and so forth, loosely about my feet; and soon we had everything in. He walked about the roofless shed for a time seeking anything we had overlooked, and then crawled in after me. I noted something in his hand.

"What have you got there?" I asked.

"Haven't you brought anything to read?"

"Good Lord! No."

"I forgot to tell you. There are uncertainties—The voyage may last— We may be weeks!"

"But—"

"We shall be floating in this sphere with absolutely no occupation."

"I wish I'd known—"

He peered out of the manhole. "Look!" he said. "There's something there!"

"Is there time?"

"We shall be an hour."

I looked out. It was an old number of *Tit-Bits*, that one of the men must have brought. Farther away in the corner I saw a torn *Lloyd's News*. I scrambled back into the sphere with these things. "What have you got?" I said.

I took the book from his hand and read, *The Works of William Shakespeare*.

He coloured slightly. "My education has been so purely scientific—" he said apologetically.

"Never read him?"

"Never."

"He knew a little, you know—in an irregular sort of way."

"Precisely what I am told," said Cavor.

I assisted him to screw in the glass cover of the manhole, and then he pressed a stud to close the corresponding blind in the outer case. The little oblong of twilight vanished. We were in darkness. For a time neither of us spoke. Although our case would not be impervious to sound, everything was very still. I perceived there was nothing to grip when the shock of our start should come, and I realized that I should be uncomfortable for want of a chair.

"Why have we no chairs?" I asked.

"I've settled all that," said Cavor. "We won't need them."

"Why not?"

"You will see," he said, in the tone of a man who refuses to talk.

I became silent. Suddenly it had come to me clear and vivid that I was a fool to be inside that sphere. Even now, I asked myself, is it too late to withdraw? The world outside the sphere, I knew, would be cold and inhospitable enough for me—for weeks I had been living on subsidies from Cavor—but after all, would it be as cold as the infinite zero, as inhospitable as empty space? If it had not been for the appearance of cowardice, I believe that even then I should have made him let me out. But I hesitated on that score, and hesitated, and grew fretful and angry, and the time passed.

There came a little jerk, a noise like champagne being uncorked in another room, and a faint whistling sound. For just one instant I had a sense of enormous tension, a transient conviction that my feet were pressing downward with a force of countless tons. It lasted for an infinitesimal time.

But it stirred me to action. "Cavor!" I said into the darkness, "my nerve's in rags. I don't think—"

I stopped. He made no answer.

"Confound it!" I cried; "I'm a fool! What business have I here? I'm not coming, Cavor. The thing's too risky. I'm getting out."

"You can't," he said.

"Can't! We'll soon see about that!"

He made no answer for ten seconds. "It's too late for us to quarrel now, Bedford," he said. "That little jerk was the start. Already we are flying as swiftly as a bullet up into the gulf of space."

"I—" I said, and then it didn't seem to matter what happened. For a time I was, as it were, stunned; I had nothing to say. It was just as if I had never heard of this idea of leaving the world before. Then I perceived an

unaccountable change in my bodily sensations. It was a feeling of lightness, of unreality. Coupled with that was a queer sensation in the head,
an apoplectic effect almost, and a thumping of blood vessels at the ears.
Neither of these feelings diminished as time went on, but at last I got so
used to them that I experienced no inconvenience.

I heard a click, and a little glow lamp came into being.

I saw Cavor's face, as white as I felt my own to be. We regarded one
another in silence. The transparent blackness of the glass behind him
made him seem as though he floated in a void.

"Well, we're committed," I said at last.

"Yes," he said, "we're committed."

"Don't move," he exclaimed, at some suggestion of a gesture. "Let
your muscles keep quite lax—as if you were in bed. We are in a little
universe of our own. Look at those things!"

He pointed to the loose cases and bundles that had been lying on
the blankets in the bottom of the sphere. I was astonished to see that
they were floating now nearly a foot from the spherical wall. Then I
saw from his shadow that Cavor was no longer leaning against the
glass. I thrust out my hand behind me, and found that I too was suspended in space, clear of the glass.

I did not cry out nor gesticulate, but fear came upon me. It was like
being held and lilted by something—you know not what. The mere
touch of my hand against the glass moved me rapidly. I understood
what had happened, but that did not prevent my being afraid. We were
cut off from all exterior gravitation, only the attraction of objects
within our sphere had effect. Consequently everything that was not
fixed to the glass was falling—slowly because of the slightness of our
masses—towards the centre of gravity of our little world, which
seemed to be somewhere about the middle of the sphere, but rather
nearer to myself than Cavor, on account of my greater weight.

"We must turn round," said Cavor, "and float back to back, with the
things between us."

It was the strangest sensation conceivable, floating thus loosely in
space, at first indeed horribly strange, and when the horror passed, not

disagreeable at all, exceeding restful; indeed, the nearest thing in earthly experience to it that I know is lying on a very thick, soft feather bed. But the quality of utter detachment and independence! I had not reckoned on things like this. I had expected a violent jerk at starting, a giddy sense of speed. Instead I felt—as if I were disembodied. It was not like the beginning of a journey; it was like the beginning of a dream.

Presently Cavor extinguished the light. He said we had not overmuch energy stored, and that what we had we must economise for reading. For a time, whether it was long or short I do not know, there was nothing but blank darkness.

A question floated up out of the void. "How are we pointing?" I said. "What is our direction?"

"We are flying away from the earth at a tangent, and as the moon is near her third quarter we are going somewhere towards her. I will open a blind—"

Came a click, and then a window in the outer case yawned open. The sky outside was as black as the darkness within the sphere, but the shape of the open window was marked by an infinite number of stars.

Those who have only seen the starry sky from the earth cannot imagine its appearance when the vague, half luminous veil of our air has been withdrawn. The stars we see on earth are the mere scattered survivors that penetrate our misty atmosphere. But now at last I could realise the meaning of the hosts of heaven! Stranger things we were presently to see, but that airless, star-dusted sky! Of all things, I think that will be one of the last I shall forget.

The little window vanished with a click, another beside it snapped open and instantly closed, and then a third, and for a moment I had to close my eyes because of the blinding splendour of the waning moon.

For a space I had to stare at Cavor and the white-lit things about me to season my eyes to light again, before I could turn them towards that pallid glare.

Four windows were open in order that the gravitation of the moon might act upon all the substances in our sphere. I found I was no longer floating freely in space, but that my feet were resting on the glass in the direction of the moon. The blankets and cases of provisions were also creeping slowly down the glass, and presently came to rest so as to block out a portion of the view. It seemed to me, of course, that I looked "down" when I looked at the moon. On earth "down" means earthward, the way things fall, and "up" the reverse direction. Now the pull of gravitation was towards the moon, and for all I knew to the contrary our earth was overhead. And, of course, when all the Cavorite blinds were closed, "down" was towards the centre of our sphere, and "up" towards its outer wall.

It was curiously unlike earthly experience, too, to have the light coming up to one. On earth light falls from above, or comes slanting down sideways, but here it came from beneath our feet, and to see our shadows we had to look up.

At first it gave me a sort of vertigo to stand only on thick glass and look down upon the moon through hundreds of thousands of miles of vacant space; but this sickness passed very speedily. And then—the splendour of the sight!

The reader may imagine it best if he will lie on the ground some warm summer's night and look between his upraised feet at the moon, but for some reason, probably because the absence of air made it so much more luminous, the moon seemed already considerably larger than it does from earth. The minutest details of its surface were acutely clear. And since we did not see it through air, its outline was bright and sharp, there was no glow or halo about it, and the star-dust that covered the sky came right to its very margin, and marked the outline of its unilluminated part. And as I stood and stared at the moon between my feet, that perception of the impossible that had been with me off and on ever since our start, returned again with tenfold conviction.

"Cavor," I said, "this takes me queerly. Those companies we were going to run, and all that about minerals?"

"Well?"

"I don't see 'em here."

"No," said Cavor; "but you'll get over all that."

"I suppose I'm made to turn right side up again. Still, this—for a moment I could half believe there never was a world."

"That copy of *Lloyd's News* might help you."

I stared at the paper for a moment, then held it above the level of my face, and found I could read it quite easily. I struck a column of mean little advertisements. "A gentleman of private means is willing to lend money," I read. I knew that gentleman. Then somebody eccentric wanted to sell a Cutaway bicycle, "quite new and cost £15," for £5; and a lady in distress wished to dispose of some fish knives and forks, "a wedding present," at a great sacrifice. No doubt some simple soul was sagely examining these knives and forks, and another triumphantly riding off on that bicycle, and a third trustfully consulting that benevolent gentleman of means even as I read. I laughed, and let the paper drift from my hand.

"Are we visible from the earth?" I asked.

"Why?"

"I knew someone—who was rather interested in astronomy. It occurred to me that it would be rather odd if—my friend—chanced to be looking through come telescope."

"It would need the most powerful telescope on earth even now to see us as the minutest speck."

For a time I stared in silence at the moon.

"It's a world," I said; "one feels that infinitely more than one ever did on earth. People perhaps—"

"People!" he exclaimed. "No! Banish all that! Think yourself a sort of ultra Arctic voyager exploring the desolate places of space. Look at it!"

He waved his hand at the shining whiteness below. "It's dead—dead! Vast extinct volcanoes, lava wildernesses, tumbled wastes of snow, or frozen carbonic acid, or frozen air, and everywhere landslip seams and cracks and gulfs. Nothing happens. Men have watched this planet systematically with telescopes for over two hundred years. How much change do you think they have seen?"

"None."

"They have traced two indisputable landslips, a doubtful crack, and one slight periodic change of colour, and that's all."

"I didn't know they'd traced even that."

"Oh, yes. But as for people—!"

"By the way," I asked, how small a thing will the biggest telescopes show upon the moon?"

"One could see a fair-sized church. One could certainly see any towns or buildings, or anything like the handiwork of men. There might perhaps be insects, something in the way of ants, for example, so that they could hide in deep burrows from the lunar light, or some new sort of creatures having no earthly parallel. That is the most probable thing, if we are to find life there at all. Think of the difference in conditions! Life must fit itself to a day as long as fourteen earthly days, a cloudless sun-blaze of fourteen days, and then a night of equal length, growing ever colder and colder under these, cold, sharp stars. In that night there must be cold, the ultimate cold, absolute zero, 273 C. below the earthly freezing point. Whatever life there is must hibernate through that—and rise again each day."

He mused. "One can imagine something worm-like," he said, "taking its air solid as an earthworm swallows earth, or thick-skinned monsters—"

"By the bye," I said, "why didn't we bring a gun?"

He did not answer that question. "No," he concluded, "we just have to go. We shall see when we get there."

I remembered something. "Of course, there's my minerals, anyhow," I said; "whatever the conditions may be."

Presently he told me he wished to alter our course a little by letting the earth tug at us for a moment. He was going to open one earthward blind for thirty seconds. He warned me that it would make my head swim, and advised me to extend my hands against the glass to break my fall. I did as he directed, and thrust my feet against the bales of food cases and air cylinders to prevent their falling upon me. Then with a click the window flew open. I fell clumsily upon hands and face, and saw for a moment between my black extended fingers our mother earth—a planet in a downward sky.

We were still very near—Cavor told me the distance was perhaps eight hundred miles—and the huge terrestrial disc filled all heaven. But already it was plain to see that the world was a globe. The land below us was in twilight and vague, but westward the vast gray stretches of the Atlantic shone like molten silver under the receding day. I think I recognised the cloud-dimmed coast-lines of France and Spain and the south of England, and then, with a click, the shutter closed again, and I found myself in a state of extraordinary confusion sliding slowly over the smooth glass.

When at last things settled themselves in my mind again, it seemed quite beyond question that the moon was "down" and under my feet, and that the earth was somewhere away on the level of the horizon, the earth that had been "down" to me and my kindred since the beginning of things.

So slight were the exertions required of us, so easy did the practical annihilation of our weight make all we had to do, that the necessity for taking refreshment did not occur to us for nearly six hours (by Cavor's chronometer) after our start. I was amazed at that lapse of time. Even then I was satisfied with very little. Cavor examined the apparatus for absorbing carbonic acid and water, and pronounced it to be in satisfactory order, our consumption of oxygen having been extraordinarily slight. And our talk being exhausted for the time, and there being nothing further for us to do, we gave way to a curious drowsiness that had come upon us, and spreading our blankets on the bottom of the sphere in such a manner as to shut out most of the moonlight, wished each other good-night, and almost immediately fell asleep.

And so, sleeping, and sometimes talking and reading a little, and at times eating, although without any keenness of appetite,[*] but for the

---

[*] It is a curious thing, that while we were in the sphere we felt not the slightest desire for food, nor did we feel the want of it when we abstained. At first we forced our appetite, but afterwards we fasted completely. Altogether we did not consume one-twentieth part of the compressed provisions we had brought with us. The amount of carbonic acid we breathed was also unnaturally low, but why this was, I am quite unable to explain.

most part in a sort of quiescence that was neither waking nor slumber, we fell through a space of time that had neither night nor day in it, silently, softly, and swiftly down towards the moon.

I remember how one day Cavor suddenly opened six of our shutters and blinded me so that I cried aloud at him. The whole area was moon, a stupendous scimitar of white dawn with its edge hacked out by notches of darkness, the crescent shore of an ebbing tide of darkness, out of which peaks and pinnacles came glittering into the blaze of the sun. I take it the reader has seen pictures or photographs of the moon and that I need not describe the broader features of that landscape, those spacious ringlike ranges vaster than any terrestrial mountains, their summits shining in the day, their shadows harsh and deep; the gray disordered plains, the ridges, hills, and craterlets, all passing at last from a blazing illumination into a common mystery of black. Athwart this world we were flying scarcely a hundred miles above its crests and pinnacles. And now we could see, what no human eye had ever seen before, that under the blaze of the day the harsh outlines of the rocks and ravines of the plains and crater floor grew gray and indistinct under a thickening haze, that the white of their lit surfaces broke into lumps and patches and broke again and shrank and vanished, and that here and there strange tints of brown and olive grew and spread.

But little time we had for watching then. For now we had come to the real danger of our journey. We had to drop ever closer to the moon as we spun about it, to slacken our pace and watch our chance, until at last we could dare to drop upon its surface.

For Cavor that was a time of intense exertion; for me it was an anxious inactivity. I seemed perpetually to be getting out of his way. He leapt about the sphere from point to point with an agility that would have been impossible on earth. He was perpetually opening and closing the Cavorite windows, making calculations, consulting his chronometer by means of the glow lamp during those last eventful hours. For a long time we had all our windows closed and hung silently in darkness hurling through space.

Then he was feeling for the shutter studs, and suddenly four windows were open. I staggered and covered my eyes, drenched and scorched and blinded by the unaccustomed splendour of the sun beneath my feet. Then again the shutters snapped, leaving my brain spinning in a darkness that pressed against the eyes. And after that I floated in another vast, black silence.

Then Cavor switched on the electric light, and told me he proposed to bind all our luggage together with the blankets about it, against the concussion of our descent. We did this with our windows closed, because in that way our goods arranged themselves naturally at the centre of the sphere. That too was a strange business; we two men floating loose in that spherical space, and packing and pulling ropes. Imagine it if you can! No up nor down, and every effort resulting in unexpected movements. Now I would be pressed against the glass with the full force of Cavor's thrust, now I would be kicking helplessly in a void. Now the star of the electric light would be overhead, now under foot. Now Cavor's feet would float up before my eyes, and now we would be crossways to each other. But at last our goods were safely bound together in a big soft bale, all except two blankets with head holes that we were to wrap about ourselves.

Then for a flash Cavor opened a window moonward, and we saw that we were dropping towards a huge central crater with a number of minor craters grouped in a sort of cross about it. And then again Cavor flung our little sphere open to the scorching, blinding sun. I think he was using the sun's attraction as a brake. "Cover yourself with a blanket," he cried, thrusting himself from me, and for a moment I did not understand.

Then I hauled the blanket from beneath my feet and got it about me and over my head and eyes. Abruptly he closed the shutters again, snapped one open again and closed it, then suddenly began snapping them all open, each safely into its steel roller. There came a jar, and then we were rolling over and over, bumping against the glass and against the big bale of our luggage, and clutching at each other, and outside some white substance splashed as if we were rolling down a slope of snow. . .

Over, clutch, bump, clutch, bump, over. . .

Came a thud, and I was half buried under the bale of our possessions, and for a space everything was still. Then I could hear Cavor puffing and grunting, and the snapping of a shutter in its sash. I made an effort, thrust back our blanket-wrapped luggage, and emerged from beneath it. Our open windows were just visible as a deeper black set with stars.

We were still alive, and we were lying in the darkness of the shadow of the wall of the great crater into which we had fallen.

We sat getting our breath again, and feeling the bruises on our limbs. I don't think either of us had had a very clear expectation of such rough handling as we had received. I struggled painfully to my feet. "And now," said I, "to look at the landscape of the moon! But—! it's tremendously dark, Cavor!"

The glass was dewy, and as I spoke I wiped at it with my blanket. "We're half an hour or so beyond the day," he said. "We must wait."

It was impossible to distinguish anything. We might have been in a sphere of steel for all that we could see. My rubbing with the blanket simply smeared the glass, and as fast as I wiped it, it became opaque again with freshly condensed moisture mixed with an increasing quantity of blanket hairs. Of course I ought not to have used the blanket. In my efforts to clear the glass I slipped upon the damp surface, and hurt my shin against one of the oxygen cylinders that protruded from our bale.

The thing was exasperating—it was absurd. Here we were just arrived upon the moon, amidst we knew not what wonders, and all we could see was the gray and streaming wall of the bubble in which we had come.

"Confound it!" I said, "but at this rate we might have stopped at home!" and I squatted on the bale and shivered, and drew my blanket closer about me.

Abruptly the moisture turned to spangles and fronds of frost. "Can you reach the electric heater," said Cavor. "Yes—that black knob. Or we shall freeze."

I did not wait to be told twice. "And now," said I, "what are we to do?"

"Wait," he said.

"Wait?"

"Of course. We shall have to wait until our air gets warm again, and then this glass will clear. We can't do anything till then. It's night here yet; we must wait for the day to overtake us. Meanwhile, don't you feel hungry?"

For a space I did not answer him, but sat fretting. I turned reluctantly from the smeared puzzle of the glass and stared at his face. "Yes," I said, "I am hungry. I feel somehow enormously disappointed. I had expected—I don't know what I had expected, but not this."

I summoned my philosophy, and rearranging my blanket about me sat down on the bale again and began my first meal on the moon. I don't think I finished it—I forget. Presently, first in patches, then running rapidly together into wider spaces, came the clearing of the glass, came the drawing of the misty veil that hid the moon world from our eyes.

We peered out upon the landscape of the moon.

As we saw it first it was the wildest and most desolate of scenes. We were in an enormous amphitheatre, a vast circular plain, the floor of the giant crater. Its cliff-like walls closed us in on every side. From the westward the light of the unseen sun fell upon them, reaching to the very foot of the cliff, and showed a disordered escarpment of drab and grayish rock, lined here and there with banks and crevices of snow. This was perhaps a dozen miles away, but at first no intervening atmosphere diminished in the slightest the minutely detailed brilliancy with which these things glared at us. They stood out clear and dazzling against a background of starry blackness that seemed to our earthly eyes rather a gloriously spangled velvet curtain than the spaciousness of the sky.

The eastward cliff was at first merely a starless selvedge to the starry dome. No rosy flush, no creeping pallor, announced the commencing day. Only the Corona, the Zodiacal light, a huge cone-shaped, luminous haze, pointing up towards the splendour of the morning star, warned us of the imminent nearness of the sun.

Whatever light was about us was reflected by the westward cliffs. It showed a huge undulating plain, cold and gray, a gray that deepened eastward into the absolute raven darkness of the cliff shadow. Innumerable rounded gray summits, ghostly hummocks, billows of snowy substance, stretching crest beyond crest into the remote obscurity, gave us our first inkling of the distance of the crater wall. These hummocks looked like snow. At the time I thought they were snow. But they were not—they were mounds and masses of frozen air?

So it was at first, and then, sudden, swift, and amazing, came the lunar day.

The sunlight had crept down the cliff, it touched the drifted masses at its base and incontinently came striding with seven-leagued boots towards us. The distant cliff seemed to shift and quiver, and at the touch of the dawn a reek of gray vapour poured upward from the crater floor, whirls and puffs and drifting wraiths of gray, thicker and broader and denser, until at last the whole westward plain was steaming like a wet handkerchief held before the fire, and the westward cliffs were no more than refracted glare beyond.

"It is air," said Cavor. "It must be air—or it would not rise like this— at the mere touch of a sunbeam. And at this pace. . . ."

He peered upwards. "Look!" he said.

"What?" I asked.

"In the sky. Already. On the blackness—a little touch of blue. See! The stars seem larger. And the little ones and all those dim nebulosities we saw in empty space—they are hidden!"

Swiftly, steadily, the day approached us. Gray summit after gray summit was overtaken by the blaze, and turned to a smoking white intensity. At last there was nothing to the west of us but a bank of surging fog, the tumultuous advance and ascent of cloudy haze. The distant cliff had receded farther and farther, had loomed and changed through the whirl, and foundered and vanished at last in its confusion.

Nearer came that steaming advance, nearer and nearer, coming as fast as the shadow of a cloud before the south-west wind. About us rose a thin anticipatory haze.

Cavor gripped my arm. "What?" I said.

"Look! The sunrise! The sun!"

He turned me about and pointed to the brow of the eastward cliff, looming above the haze about us, scarce lighter than the darkness of the sky. But now its line was marked by strange reddish shapes, tongues of vermilion flame that writhed and danced. I fancied it must be spirals of vapour that had caught the light and made this crest of fiery tongues against the sky, but indeed it was the solar prominences I saw, a crown of fire about the sun that is forever hidden from earthly eyes by our atmospheric veil.

And then—the sun!

Steadily, inevitably came a brilliant line, came a thin edge of intolerable effulgence that took a circular shape, became a bow, became a blazing sceptre, and hurled a shaft of heat at us as though it was a spear.

It seemed verily to stab my eyes! I cried aloud and turned about blinded, groping for my blanket beneath the bale.

And with that incandescence came a sound, the first sound that had reached us from without since we left the earth, a hissing and rustling, the stormy trailing of the aerial garment of the advancing day. And with the coming of the sound and the light the sphere lurched, and blinded and dazzled we staggered helplessly against each other. It lurched again, and the hissing grew louder. I had shut my eyes perforce, I was making clumsy efforts to cover my head with my blanket, and this second lurch sent me helplessly off my feet. I fell against the bale, and opening my eyes had a momentary glimpse of the air just outside our glass. It was running—it was boiling—like snow into which a white-hot rod is thrust. What had been solid air had suddenly at the touch of the sun become a paste, a mud, a slushy liquefaction, that hissed and bubbled into gas.

There came a still more violent whirl of the sphere and we clutched one another. In another moment we were spun about again. Pound we went and over, and then I was on all fours. The lunar dawn had hold of us. It meant to show us little men what the moon could do with us.

I caught a second glimpse of things without, puffs of vapour, half liquid slush, excavated, sliding, falling, sliding. We dropped into darkness. I went down with Cavor's knees in my chest. Then he seemed to fly away from me, and for a moment I lay with all the breath out of my body staring upward. A toppling crag of the melting stuff had splashed over us, buried us, and now it thinned and boiled off us. I saw the bubbles dancing on the glass above. I heard Cavor exclaiming feebly.

Then some huge landslip in the thawing air had caught us, and spluttering expostulation, we began to roll down a slope, rolling faster and faster, leaping crevasses and rebounding from banks, faster and faster, westward into the white-hot boiling tumult of the lunar day.

Clutching at one another we spun about, pitched this way and that, our bale of packages leaping at us, pounding at us. We collided, we gripped, we were torn asunder—our heads met, and the whole universe burst into fiery darts and stars! On the earth we should have smashed one another a dozen times, but on the moon, luckily for us, our weight was only one-sixth of what it is terrestrially, and we fell very mercifully. I recall a sensation of utter sickness, a feeling as if my brain were upside down within my skull, and then—

Something was at work upon my face, some thin feelers worried my ears. Then I discovered the brilliance of the landscape around was mitigated by blue spectacles. Cavor bent over me, and I saw his face upside down, his eyes also protected by tinted goggles. His breath came irregularly, and his lip was bleeding from a bruise. "Better?" he said, wiping the blood with the back of his hand.

Everything seemed swaying for a space, but that was simply my giddiness. I perceived that he had closed some of the shutters in the outer sphere to save me from the direct blaze of the sun. I was aware that everything about us was very brilliant.

"Lord!" I gasped. "But this—"

I craned my neck to see. I perceived there was a blinding glare outside, an utter change from the gloomy darkness of our first impressions. "Have I been insensible long?" I asked.

"I don't know—the chronometer is broken. Some little time. . . . My dear chap! I have been afraid. . ."

I lay for a space taking this in. I saw his face still bore evidences of emotion. For a while I said nothing. I passed an inquisitive hand over my contusions, and surveyed his face for similar damages. The back of my right hand had suffered most, and was skinless and raw. My forehead was bruised and had bled. He handed me a little measure with some of the restorative—I forget the name of it—he had brought with us. After a time I felt a little better. I began to stretch my limbs carefully. Soon I could talk.

"It wouldn't have done," I said, as though there had been no interval.

"No, it *wouldn't!*"

He thought, his hands hanging over his knees. He peered through the glass and then stared at me. "Good Lord!" he said. "No!"

"What has happened?" I asked after a pause; "have we jumped to the tropics?"

"It was as I expected. This air has evaporated. If it is air. At any rate, it has evaporated, and the surface of the moon is showing. We are lying on a bank of earthy rock. Here and there bare soil is exposed; a queer sort of soil!"

It occurred to him that it was unnecessary to explain. He assisted me into a sitting position, and I could see with my own eyes.

The harsh emphasis, the pitiless black and white of the scenery had altogether disappeared. The glare of the sun had taken upon itself a faint tinge of amber; the shadows upon the cliff of the crater wall were deeply purple. To the eastward a dark bank of fog still crouched and sheltered from the sunrise, but to the westward the sky was blue and clear. I began to realize the length of my insensibility.

We were no longer in a void. An atmosphere had arisen about us. The outline of things had gained in character, had grown acute and varied; save for a shadowed space of white substance here and there, white substance that was no longer air but snow, the Arctic appearance had gone altogether. Everywhere broad, rusty-brown spaces of bare and tumbled earth spread to the blaze of the sun. Here and there at the edge of the snowdrifts were transient little pools and eddies of water, the only things stirring in that expanse of barrenness. The sunlight inundated the upper two blinds of our sphere and turned our climate to high summer, but our feet were still in shadow and the sphere was lying upon a drift of snow.

And scattered here and there upon the slope, and emphasized by little white threads of unthawed snow upon their shady sides, were shapes like sticks—dry twisted sticks of the same rusty hue as the rock upon which they lay. That caught one's thoughts sharply. Sticks! On a lifeless world? Then as my eye grew more accustomed to the texture of their substance, I perceived that almost all this surface had a fibrous texture, like the carpet of brown needles one finds beneath the shade of pine trees.

"Cavor!" I said.

"Yes."

"It may be a dead world now—but once—"

Something arrested my attention. I had discovered among these needles a number of little round objects. And it seemed to me that one of these had moved.

"Cavor," I whispered.

"What?"

But I did not answer at once. I stared incredulous. For an instant I could not believe my eyes. I gave an inarticulate cry. I gripped his arm. I pointed. "Look!" I cried, finding my tongue. "There! Yes! And there!"

His eyes followed my pointing finger. "Eh?" he said.

How can I describe the thing I saw? It is so petty a thing to state, and yet it seemed so wonderful, so pregnant with emotion. I have said that amidst the stick-like litter were these rounded bodies, these little oval bodies that might have passed as very small pebbles. And now first one and then another had stirred, had rolled over and cracked, and down the crack of each of them showed a minute line of yellowish green, thrusting outward to meet the hot encouragement of the newly-risen sun. For a moment that was all, and then there stirred, and burst a third!

"It is a seed," said Cavor. And then I heard him whisper very softly, "*Life!*"

"Life!" And immediately it poured upon us that our vast journey had not been made in vain, that we had come to no arid waste of minerals, but to a world that lived and moved! We watched intensely. I remember I kept rubbing the glass before me with my sleeve, jealous of the faintest suspicion of mist.

The picture was clear and vivid only in the middle of the field. All about that centre the dead fibres and seeds were magnified and distorted by the curvature of the glass. But we could see enough! One after another all down the sunlit slope these miraculous little brown bodies burst and gaped apart, like seed-pods, like the husks of fruits; opened eager mouths that drank in the heat and light pouring in a cascade from the newly risen sun.

Every moment more of these seed coats ruptured, and even as they did so the swelling pioneers overflowed their rent distended seed-cases and passed into the second stage of growth. With a steady assurance, a swift deliberation, these amazing seeds thrust a rootlet downward to the earth and a queer little bundle-like bud into the air. In a little while the whole slope was dotted with minute plantlets standing at attention in the blaze of the sun.

They did not stand for long. The bundle-like buds swelled and strained and opened with a jerk, thrusting out a coronet of little sharp tips, spreading a whorl of tiny, spiky, brownish leaves, that lengthened rapidly, lengthened visibly even as we watched. The movement was slower than any animal's, swifter than any plant's I have ever seen before. How can I suggest it to you—the way that growth went on? The leaf tips grew so that they moved onward even while we looked at them. The brown seed-case shriveled and was absorbed with an equal rapidity. Have you ever on a cold day taken a thermometer into your warm hand and watched the little thread of mercury creep up the tube? These moon plants grew like that.

In a few minutes, as it seemed, the buds of the more forward of these plants had lengthened into a stem and were even putting forth a second whorl of leaves, and all the slope that had seemed so recently a lifeless stretch of litter was now dark with the stunted olive-green herbage of bristling spikes that swayed with the vigour of their growing.

I turned about, and behold! along the upper edge of a rock to the eastward a similar fringe, in a scarcely less forward condition, swayed and bent, dark against the blinding glare of the sun. And beyond this fringe was the silhouette of a plant mass, branching clumsily like a cactus, and swelling visibly, swelling like a bladder that fills with air.

Then to the westward also I discovered that another such distended form was rising over the scrub. But here the light fell upon its sleek sides, and I could see that its colour was a vivid orange. It rose as one watched it; if one looked away from it for a minute and then back, its outline had changed: it thrust out blunt congested branches until in a little time it rose a coralline shape of many feet in height. Compared with such a growth the terrestrial puff-ball which will sometimes swell a foot in diameter in a single night, would be a hopeless laggard. But then the puff-ball grows against a gravitational pull six times that of the moon. Beyond, out of gullies and flats that had been hidden from us, but not from the quickening sun, over reefs and banks of shining rock, a bristling beard of spiky and fleshy vegetation was straining into view, hurrying tumultuously to take advantage of the brief day in which it must flower and fruit and seed again and die. It was like a mir-acle, that growth. So, one must imagine, the trees and plants arose at the Creation and covered the desolation of the new-made earth.

Imagine it! Imagine that dawn! The resurrection of the frozen air, the stirring and quickening of the soil, and then this silent uprising of vegetation, this unearthly ascent of fleshiness and spikes. Conceive it all lit by a blaze that would make the most intense sunlight of earth seem watery and weak. And still around this stirring jungle wherever there was shadow lingered banks of bluish snow. And to have the picture of our impression complete, you must bear in mind that we saw it all through a thick bent glass, distorting it as things are distorted by a lens, acute only in the centre of the picture, and very bright there, and towards the edges magnified and unreal.

We ceased to gaze. We turned to each other, the same thought, the same question in our eyes. For these plants to grow, there must be some air, however attenuated—air that we also should be able to breathe.

"The manhole?" I said.

"Yes," said Cavor, "if it is air we see!"

"In a little while," I said, "these plants will be as high as we are. Suppose—suppose after all—Is it certain? How do you know that stuff *is* air? It may be nitrogen; it may be carbonic acid even!"

"That's easy," he said, and set about proving it. He produced a big piece of crumpled paper from the bale, lit it, and thrust it hastily through the man-hole valve. I bent forward and peered down through the thick glass for its appearance outside, that little flame on whose evidence depended so much!

I saw the paper drop out and lie lightly upon the snow. The pink flame of its burning vanished. For an instant it seemed to be extinguished. . . . And then I saw a little blue tongue upon the edge of it that trembled and crept and spread!

Quietly the whole sheet, save where it lay in immediate contact with the snow, charred and shrivelled and sent up a quivering thread of smoke. There was no doubt left to me; the atmosphere of the moon was either pure oxygen or air, and capable therefore—unless its tenuity was excessive—of supporting our alien life. We might emerge—and live!

I sat down with my legs on either side of the manhole and prepared to unscrew it, but Cavor stopped me. "There is first a little precaution," he said. He pointed out that although it was certainly an oxygenated atmosphere outside, it might still be so rarefied as to cause us grave injury. He reminded me of mountain sickness, and of the bleeding that often afflicts aeronauts who have ascended too swiftly, and he spent some time in the preparation of a sickly tasting drink which he insisted on my sharing. It made me feel a little numb, but otherwise had no effect on me. Then he permitted me to begin unscrewing.

Presently the glass stopper of the manhole was so far undone that the denser air within our sphere began to escape along the thread of the screw, singing as a kettle sings before it boils. Thereupon he made me desist. It speedily became evident that the pressure outside was very much less than it was within. How much less it was we had no means of telling.

I sat grasping the stopper with both hands, ready to close it again if, in spite of our intense hope, the lunar atmosphere should after all prove too rarefied for us, and Cavor sat with a cylinder of compressed oxygen at hand to restore our pressure. We looked at one another in silence, and then at the fantastic vegetation that swayed and grew visibly and noiselessly without. And ever that shrill piping continued.

My blood-vessels began to throb in my ears, and the sound of Cavor's movements diminished. I noted how still everything had become, because of the thinning of the air.

As our air sizzled out from the screw the moisture of it condensed in little puffs.

Presently I experienced a peculiar shortness of breath—that lasted indeed during the whole of the time of our exposure to the moon's exterior atmosphere, and a rather unpleasant sensation about the ears and finger-nails and the back of the throat grew upon my attention, and presently passed off again.

But then came vertigo and nausea that abruptly changed the quality of my courage. I gave the lid of the manhole half a turn and made a hasty explanation to Cavor; but now he was the more sanguine. He answered me in a voice that seemed extraordinarily small and remote, because of the thinness of the air that carried the sound. He recommended a nip of brandy, and set me the example, and presently I felt better. I turned the manhole stopper back again. The throbbing in my ears grew louder, and then I remarked that the piping note of the outrush had ceased. For a time I could not be sure that it had ceased.

"Well?" said Cavor, in the ghost of a voice.

"Well?" said I.

"Shall we go on?"

I thought, "Is this all?"

"If you can stand it."

By way of answer I went on unscrewing. I lifted the circular operculum from its place and laid it carefully on the bale. A flake or so of snow whirled and vanished as that thin and unfamiliar air took possession of our sphere. I knelt, and then seated myself at the edge of the manhole; peering over it. Beneath, within a yard of my face, lay the untrodden snow of the moon.

There came a little pause. Our eyes met.

"It doesn't distress your lungs too much?" said Cavor.

"No," I said. "I can stand this."

He stretched out his hand for his blanket, thrust his head through its central hole, and wrapped it about him. He sat down on the edge of the manhole, he let his feet drop until they were within six inches of the lunar ground. He hesitated for a moment, then thrust himself forward, dropped these intervening inches, and stood upon the untrodden soil of the moon.

As he stepped forward he was refracted grotesquely by the edge of the glass. He stood for a moment looking this way and that. Then he drew himself together and leapt.

The glass distorted everything, but it seemed to me even then to be an extremely big leap. He had at one bound become remote. He seemed twenty or thirty feet off. He was standing high upon a rocky mass and gesticulating back to me. Perhaps he was shouting—but the sound did not reach me. But how the deuce had he done this? I felt like a man who has just seen a new conjuring trick.

In a puzzled state of mind I too dropped through the manhole. I stood up. Just in front of me the snowdrift had fallen away and made a sort of ditch. I made a step and jumped.

I found myself flying through the air, saw the rock on which he stood coming to meet me, clutched it and clung in a state of infinite amazement. I gasped a painful laugh. I was tremendously confused. Cavor bent down and shouted in piping tones for me to be careful. I had forgotten that on the moon, with only an eighth part of the earth's mass and a quarter of its diameter, my weight was barely a sixth what it was on earth. But now that fact insisted on being remembered.

"We are out of Mother Earth's leading-strings now," he said.

With a guarded effort I raised myself to the top and moving as cautiously as a rheumatic patient, stood up beside him under the blaze of the sun. The sphere lay behind us on its dwindling snow-drift thirty feet away.

As far as the eye could see over the enormous disorder of rocks that formed the crater floor the same bristling scrub that surrounded us was starting into life, diversified here and there by bulging masses of a cactus form, and scarlet and purple lichens that grew so fast they seemed to crawl over the rocks. The whole area of the crater seemed to me then to be one similar wilderness up to the very foot of the surrounding cliff.

This cliff was apparently bare of vegetation save at its base, and with buttresses and terraces and platforms that did not very greatly attract our attention at the time. It was many miles away from us in every direction; we seemed to be almost at the centre of the crater, and we saw it through a certain haziness that drove before the wind. For there was even a wind now in the thin air—a swift yet weak wind that chilled exceedingly but exerted little pressure. It was blowing round the crater, as it seemed, to the hot illuminated side from the foggy darkness under the sunward wall. It was difficult to look into this eastward fog; we had to peer with half-closed eyes beneath the shade of our hands, because of the fierce intensity of the motionless sun.

"It seems to be deserted," said Cavor, "absolutely desolate."

I looked about me again. I retained even then a clinging hope of some quasi-human evidence, some pinnacle of building, some house or engine; but everywhere one looked spread the tumbled rocks in peaks and crests, and the darting scrub and those bulging cacti that swelled and swelled, a flat negation as it seemed of all such hope.

"It looks as though these plants had it to themselves," I said. "I see no trace of any other creature."

"No insects—no birds, no! Not a trace, not a scrap nor particle of animal life. If there was—what would they do in the night? . . . No; there's just these plants alone."

I shaded my eyes with my hand. "It's like the landscape of a dream. These things are less like earthly land plants than the things one imagines among the rocks at the bottom of the sea. Look at that yonder! One might imagine it a lizard changed into a plant. And the glare!"

"This is only the fresh morning," said Cavor.

He sighed and looked about him. "This is no world for men," he said. "And yet in a way—it appeals."

He became silent for a time, then commenced his meditative humming. I started at a gentle touch, and found a thin sheet of livid lichen lapping over my shoe. I kicked at it and it fell to powder, and each speck began to grow. I heard Cavor exclaim sharply, and perceived that one of the fixed bayonets of the scrub had pricked him.

He hesitated, his eyes sought among the rocks about us. A sudden blaze of pink had crept up a ragged pillar of crag. It was a most extraordinary pink, a livid magenta.

"Look!" said I, turning, and behold Cavor had vanished.

For an instant I stood transfixed. Then I made a hasty step to look over the verge of the rock. But in my surprise at his disappearance I forgot once more that we were on the moon. The thrust of my foot that I made in striding would have carried me a yard on earth; on the moon it carried me six—a good five yards over the edge. For the moment the thing had something of the effect of those nightmares when one falls and falls. For while one falls sixteen feet in the first second of a fall on earth, on the moon one falls two, and with only a sixth of one's weight. I fell, or rather I jumped down, about ten yards I suppose. It seemed to take quite a long time—five or six seconds, I should think. I floated through the air and fell like a feather, knee-deep in a snow-drift in the bottom of a gully of blue-gray, white-veined rock.

I looked about me. "Cavor!" I cried, but no Cavor was visible.

"Cavor!" I cried louder, and the rocks echoed me.

I turned fiercely to the rocks and clambered to the summit of them. "Cavor," I cried. My voice sounded like the voice of a lost lamb.

The sphere, too, was not in sight, and for a moment a horrible feeling of desolation pinched my heart.

Then I saw him. He was laughing and gesticulating to attract my attention. He was on a bare patch of rock twenty or thirty yards away. I could not hear his voice, but "Jump!" said his gestures. I hesitated, the distance seemed enormous. Yet I reflected that surely I must be able to clear a greater distance than Cavor.

I made a step back, gathered myself together, and leapt with all my might. I seemed to shoot up in the air as though I should never come down.

It was horrible and delightful, and as wild as a nightmare, to go flying off in this fashion. I realised my leap had been altogether too violent. I flew clean over Cavor's head and beheld a spiky confusion in a gully spreading to meet my fall. I gave a yelp of alarm. I put out my hands and straightened my legs.

I hit a huge fungoid bulk that burst all about me, scattering a mass of orange spores in every direction, and covering me with orange powder. I rolled over spluttering, and came to rest convulsed with breathless laughter.

I became aware of Cavor's little round face peering over a bristling hedge. He shouted some faded inquiry. "Eh?" I tried to shout, but could not do so for want of breath. He made his way towards me, coming gingerly among the bushes. "We've got to be careful!" he said. "This moon has no discipline. She'll let us smash ourselves."

He helped me to my feet. "You exerted yourself too much," he said, dabbing at the yellow stuff with his hand to remove it from my garments.

I stood passive and panting, allowing him to beat off the jelly from my knees and elbows and lecture me upon my misfortunes. "We don't quite allow for the gravitation. Our muscles are scarcely educated yet. We must practice a little, when you have got your breath."

I pulled two or three little thorns out of my hand, and sat for a time on a boulder of rock. My muscles were quivering, and I had that feeling of personal disillusionment that comes at the first fall to the learner of cycling on earth.

It suddenly occurred to Cavor that the cold air in the gully after the brightness of the sun, might give me a fever. So we clambered back into the sunlight. We found that beyond a few abrasions I had received no serious injuries from my tumble, and at Cavor's suggestion we were presently looking round for some safe and easy landing-place for my next leap. We chose a rocky slab some ten yards off, separated from us by a little thicket of olive-green spikes.

"Imagine it there!" said Cavor, who was assuming the airs of a trainer, and he pointed to a spot about four feet from my toes. This leap I managed without difficulty, and I must confess I found a certain satisfaction in Cavor's falling short by a foot or so and tasting the spikes of the scrub. "One has to be careful, you see," he said, pulling out his thorns, and with that he ceased to be my mentor and became my fellow-learner in the art of lunar locomotion.

We chose a still easier jump and did it without difficulty, and then leapt back again, and to and fro several times, accustoming our muscles to the new standard. I could never have believed, had I not experienced it, how rapid that adaptation would be. In a very little time indeed, certainly after fewer than thirty leaps, we could judge the effort necessary for a distance with almost terrestrial assurance.

And all this time the lunar plants were growing around us, higher and denser and more entangled, every moment thicker and taller, spiked plants, green cactus masses, fungi, fleshy and lichenous things, strangest radiate and sinuous shapes. But we were so intent upon our leaping, that for a time we gave no heed to their unfaltering expansion.

An extraordinary elation had taken possession of us. Partly, I think, it was our sense of release from the confinement of the sphere. Mainly, however, the thin sweetness of the air, which I am certain contained a much larger proportion of oxygen than our terrestrial atmosphere. In spite of the strange quality of all about us, I felt as adventurous and experimental as a Cockney would do placed for the first time among mountains and I do not think it occurred to either of us, face to face though we were with the unknown, to be very greatly afraid.

We were bitten by a spirit of enterprise. We selected a lichenous kopje perhaps fifteen yards away, and landed neatly on its summit one after the other. "Good!" we cried to each other, "good;" and Cavor made three steps and went off to a tempting slope of snow a good twenty yards and more beyond. I stood for a moment struck by the grotesque effect of his soaring figure, his dirty cricket cap and spiky hair, his little round body, his arms and his knickerbockered legs tucked up tightly against the weird spaciousness of the lunar scene. A gust of laughter seized me, and then I stepped off to follow. Plump! I dropped beside him.

We made a few Gargantuan strides, leapt three or four times more, and sat down at last in a lichenous hollow. Our lungs were painful. We sat holding our sides and recovering our breath, looking appreciatively at one another.

acknowledgments

Many people made this anthology.

At Thunder's Mouth Press and Avalon Publishing Group:
Thanks to Ghadah Alrawi, Will Balliett, Sue Canavan, Kristen Couse, Maria Fernandez, Linda Kosarin, Shona McCarthy, Dan O'Connor, Neil Ortenberg, Paul Paddock, Susan Reich, David Riedy, Simon Sullivan, and Mike Walters for their support, dedication and hard work.

At The Writing Company:
Kate Fletcher, Nate Hardcastle and Nathaniel May did most of the research. Nathaniel May also oversaw rights research and negotiations. Mark Klimek, Taylor Smith and March Truedsson took up slack on other projects.

At the Portland Public Library in Portland, Maine:
The librarians helped collect books from around the country.

Among friends and family:
Eric Schurenberg kindly helped us to identify some of the best writing about aerial warfare during World War I.

Finally, I am grateful to the writers whose work appears in this book.

p e r m i s s i o n s

We gratefully acknowledge everyone who gave permission for written material to appear in this book. We have made every effort to trace and contact copyright holders. If an error or omission is brought to our notice we will be pleased to correct the situation in future editions of this book. For further information, please contact the publisher.

Excerpt from *To Fly and Fight* by Col. Clarence E. Anderson and Joseph P. Hamelin. Copyright © 1990 by Col. Clarence E. Anderson. Reprinted by permission of St. Martin's Press, LLC. ✤ Excerpt from *Yeager* by Chuck Yeager and Leo Janos. Copyright © 1985 by Yeager, Inc. Used by permission of Bantam Books, a division of Random House, Inc. ✤ Excerpt from *Kamikaze* by Yasuo Kuwahara and Gordon T. Allred. Copyright © 1957 by Gordon T. Allred. Used by permission of Ballantine Books, a division of Random House, Inc. ✤ "The Pilot's Tale" by Matthew Klam. Copyright © 1999 by Matthew Klam. Reprinted by permission of International Creative Management, Inc. ✤ Excerpt from *The Right Stuff* by Tom Wolfe. Copyright © 1979 by Tom Wolfe. Reprinted by permission of Farrar, Straus and Giroux, LLC. ✤ Excerpt from *Last Man on the Moon* by Eugene Cernan with Don Davis. Copyright © 1999 by Eugene Cernan and Don Davis. Reprinted by permission of St. Martin's Press, LLC. ✤ Excerpt from *A Man on the Moon* by Andrew Chaikin. Copyright © 1994 by Andrew Chaikin. Used by permission of Viking Penguin, a division of Penguin Putnam, Inc. ✤ "Heart of the Delta" by Donovan Webster. Copyright © 1991 by Donovan Webster. Used by permission of the author. ✤ "Remembering Don Sheldon" from *Moments of Doubt* by David Roberts. Copyright © 1986 by David Roberts. Reprinted with permission of the publisher,

The Mountaineers, Seattle, WA. ✤ "The Maze and Aura" from *The Abstract Wild* by Jack Turner. Copyright © 1996 by John S. Turner. Reprinted by permission of the University of Arizona Press.

b i b l i o g r a p h y

The selections used in this anthology were taken from the editions listed below. In some cases, other editions may be easier to find. Hard-to-find or out-of-print titles often are available through inter-library loan services or through Internet booksellers.

Anderson, Col. Clarence E. with Joseph P. Hamelin. *To Fly and Fight: Memoirs of Triple Ace.* New York: St. Martin's Press, 1990.

Cernan, Eugene with Don Davis. *Last Man on the Moon: Astronaut Eugene Cernan and America's Race in Space.* New York: St. Martin's Press, 1999.

Chaikin, Andrew. *A Man on the Moon: The Voyages of the Apollo Astronauts.* New York: Penguin, 1998.

Hall, James Norman. *High Adventure: A Narrative of Air Fighting in France.* New York: Houghton Mifflin Company, 1918.

Klam, Matthew. "The Pilot's Tale." Originally appeared in *Harper's Magazine,* February 1999.

Kuwahara, Yasuo and Gordon T. Allred. *Kamikaze.* New York: Ballantine, 1957.

Rickenbacker, Eddie. *Fighting the Flying Circus.* http://richthofen.com/rickenbacker/

Roberts, David. *Moments of Doubt and Other Mountain Writings.* Seattle, WA: The Mountaineers, 1986. (For "Remembering Don Sheldon")

Turner, Jack. *The Abstract Wild.* Tucson, AZ: The University of Arizona Press, 1996. (For "The Maze and Aura")

Webster, Donovan. "Heart of the Delta." Originally appeared in *The New Yorker,* July 8, 1991.

Wells. H.G. *The First Men in the Moon.* New York: Avenel Books, 1978.

Wolfe, Tom. *The Right Stuff.* New York: Farrar, Straus and Giroux, 1979.

Yeager, Chuck and Leo Janos. *Yeager: An Autobiography.* New York: Bantam Books, 1985.

adrenaline®

Exciting titles from Adrenaline Books

WILD BLUE: Stories of Survival from Air and Space

Edited by David Fisher and William Garvey
Series Editor, Clint Willis

Wild Blue collects the most gripping accounts of what may be the greatest achievement of the century: manned flight. From flying a Piper Cub over the Rockies at the age of 16 to a nigh-time carrier approach, *Wild Blue* puts you right in the cockpit.
$16.95 ($26 Canada), 352 pages

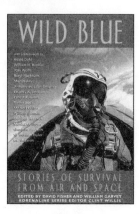

THE WAR: Stories of Life and Death from World War II

Edited by Clint Willis

The greatest writing about the War, from Okinawa to Normandy. This entry in the Adrenaline Books series is about courage, conscience, and loss. It features work by Stephen E. Ambrose, A. J. Liebling, William Manchester, Paul Fussell, and 13 others.
$16.95 ($26 Canada), 384 pages

BLOOD: Stories of Life and Death from the Civil War

Edited by Peter Kadzis; Series Editor, Clint Willis

The most dramatic moment in this nation's history, also produced some of our greatest literature. From tragic charges to prison escapes to the desolation wrought on those who stayed behind, *Blood* is composed mainly of the vivid stories of those who were there. Includes accounts by General George Pickett, Walt Whitman, Ulysses S. Grant, Michael Shaara and Shelby Foote among others.
$16.95 ($26 Canada); 320 pages

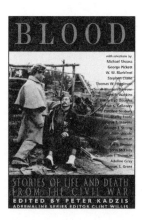

adrenaline ®

Exciting titles from Adrenaline Books

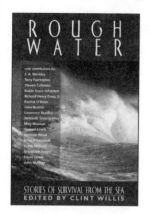

ROUGH WATER: Stories of Survival from the Sea

Edited by Clint Willis

A unique collection of 16 pieces of great writing about storms, shipwrecks and human resourcefulness. Includes work by Patrick O'Brian, John McPhee and Herman Wouk, as well as a Sebastian Junger story previously unpublished in book form.
$16.95 ($26 Canada), 368 pages

DEEP BLUE: Stories of Shipwreck, Sunken Treasure and Survival

Edited by Nate Hardcastle
Series Editor, Clint Willis

Deep Blue brings together some of the best stories about survival on and under the sea, from Nathaniel Philbrick's account of the sinking of the whaleship *Essex* to Farley Mowat's misadventures in a rotting schooner.
$17.95 ($29.95 Canada), 336 pages

STORM: Stories of Survival from Land and Sea

Edited by Clint Willis

Storm offers 18 gripping stories of people facing nature in all of its fury: blizzards, typhoons, windstorms, gales and hurricanes. These accounts come from all over the globe: from the South Pacific to Saskatchewan; from Everest's summit to Antarctica's wastes. Includes works by Sebastian Junger, Annie Proulx, Rick Bass, Barry Lopez, Richard E. Byrd, and Jack London.
$16.95 ($26.00 Canada) 384 pages

adrenaline®

Exciting titles from Adrenaline Books

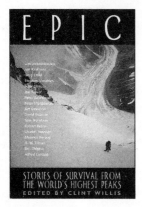

EPIC: Stories of Survival from the World's Highest Peaks

Edited by Clint Willis
A collection of 15 gripping accounts of legend-making expeditions to the world's most challenging mountains, including selections by Greg Child, David Roberts and Maurice Herzog.
$16.95 ($26 Canada), 352 pages

HIGH: Stories of Survival from Everest and K2

Edited by Clint Willis
The first anthology ever to focus exclusively on the two highest, most formidable mountains in the world. Includes accounts by Chris Bonington, Robert Bates, Charles Houston and Matt Dickinson.
$16.95 ($26 Canada), 336 pages

CLIMB: Stories of Survival from Rock, Snow and Ice

Edited by Clint Willis
This collection focuses on the most exciting descriptions of the hardest climbing in the world. From the cliffs of Yosemite to the windswept towers of Patagonia to the high peaks of Alaska and the Himalaya, *Climb* offers more than a dozen classic accounts.
$16.95 ($26 Canada), 272 pages